# Lecture Notes in Computer Science     1127

Edited by G. Goos, J. Hartmanis and J. van Leeuwen

Advisory Board: W. Brauer   D. Gries   J. Stoer

# Springer

*Berlin*
*Heidelberg*
*New York*
*Barcelona*
*Budapest*
*Hong Kong*
*London*
*Milan*
*Paris*
*Santa Clara*
*Singapore*
*Tokyo*

László Böszörményi   (Ed.)

# Parallel Computation

Third International ACPC Conference
with Special Emphasis on Parallel Databases
and Parallel I/O
Klagenfurt, Austria, September 23-25, 1996
Proceedings

 Springer

Series Editors

Gerhard Goos, Karlsruhe University, Germany

Juris Hartmanis, Cornell University, NY, USA

Jan van Leeuwen, Utrecht University, The Netherlands

Volume Editor

László Böszörményi
Universität Klagenfurt, Institut für Informatik
Universitätsstraße 65-67, A-9020 Klagenfurt, Austria
E-mail:laszlo@ifi.uni-klu.ac.at

Cataloging-in-Publication data applied for

Die Deutsche Bibliothek - CIP-Einheitsaufnahme

**Prallel computation** : proceedings / Third International ACPC
Conference with Special Emphasis on Parallel Databases and
Parallel I/O, Klagenfurt, Austria, September 1996. László
Böszörményi (ed.). - Berlin ; Heidelberg ; New York ;
Barcelona ; Budapest ; Hong Kong ; London ; Milan ; Paris ;
Santa Clara ; Singapore ; Tokyo : Springer, 1996
(Lecture notes in computer science ; Vol. 1127)

ISBN 3-540-61695-0
NE: Böszörményi, László [Hrsg.]; International Conference with Special
Emphasis on Parallel Databases and Parallel I/O <3, 1996,
Klagenfurt>; Austrian Center for Parallel Computation; GT

CR Subject Classification (1991): D.1.3, D.2.6, F.2.1-2, D.3.2, C.1.2, B.2.1,
B.4, H.2

ISSN 0302-9743
ISBN 3-540-61695-0 Springer-Verlag Berlin Heidelberg New York

© Springer-Verlag Berlin Heidelberg 1996
Printed in Germany

Typesetting: Camera-ready by author
SPIN 10513568    06/3142 – 5 4 3 2 1 0    Printed on acid-free paper

# Preface

The Austrian Center for Parallel Computation (ACPC) is a co-operative research organization founded in 1989 to promote research and education in the field of software for parallel computer systems. The areas in which the ACPC is active include algorithms, languages, compilers, programming environments, parallel databases, parallel I/O, and applications for parallel and high-performance computing systems.

The partner institutions of the ACPC are the University of Vienna, the Technical University of Vienna, and the Universities of Linz, Salzburg, and Klagenfurt. They carry out joint research projects, share a pool of hardware resources, and offer a curriculum in parallel computation for graduate and postgraduate students. In addition, an international conference is organized every other year.

The *Third International Conference of the ACPC* took place in Klagenfurt, Austria, from September 23 to September 25, 1996. The conference attracted many participants from around the world. Authors from 13 countries submitted 31 papers, from which 15 were selected and presented at the conference. Six contributions were accepted for a poster session. In addition, two distinguished researchers presented invited papers. The papers from these presentations are contained in this proceedings volume.

The organization of the conference was the result of the dedicated work of a large number of individuals, not all of whom can be mentioned here. I would like, in paricular, to acknowledge the efforts made by the members of the program committee and the referees. The organizational and administrative support from Mag. Karl-Heinz Eder and Silvia Nedizavec was exceptionally valuable.

Finally, we gratefully acknowledge the support of the following organizations:

The Austrian Federal Ministry of Science, Transport and the Arts
Stadt Klagenfurt
Land Kärnten
University of Klagenfurt
Creditanstalt-Bankverein
Digital Equipment Corporation
International Business Machines

Klagenfurt, July 1996                                             László Böszörményi

# Conference Committee

## Programm Committee

**Chairman:**

L. Böszörményi                     University of Klagenfurt, Austria

**Programm Committee Members:**

| | |
|---|---|
| P. Apers | University of Twente, The Netherlands |
| B. Brezany | University of Vienna, Austria |
| B. Buchberger | University of Linz, Austria |
| H. Burkhart | University of Basel, Switzerland |
| J. Eder | University of Klagenfurt, Austria |
| A. Ferscha | University of Vienna, Austria |
| A. Hameurlain | IRIT, France |
| G. Haring | University of Vienna, Austria |
| H. Hong | University of Linz, Austria |
| W. Kleinert | Technical University of Vienna, Austria |
| D. Kotz | Dartmouth College, USA |
| O. Steinhauser | University of Vienna, Austria |
| P. Valduriez | INRIA, France |
| J. Volkert | University of Linz, Austria |
| P. Wang | Kent State University, USA |
| G. Weikum | University of Saarbrücken, Germany |
| H. Zima | University of Vienna, Austria |
| P. Zinterhof | University of Salzburg, Austria |

## Organizing Committee

**Chairman:**

L. Böszörmenyi                     University of Klagenfurt, Austria

**Local Organizing**

K.-H. Eder                         University of Klagenfurt, Austria

# List of Referees

Each paper was carefully reviewed by 3 reviewers. We thank all referees listed below.

Apers, Peter M.G.
Bouganim, Luc
Böszörmenyi, Laszlo
Brezany, Peter
Burkhart, Helmar
Eder, Johann
Eder, Karl-Heinz
Ferscha, Alois
Grabner, Siegfried R.A.
Hameurlain, A.
Haring, Günter
Hellekalek, Peter
Hinterberger, Hans
Hong, Hoon
Howell, Jon
Jebelean, Tudor
Kotsis, Gabriele
Kotz, David
Larcher, Gerhard
Liebhart, Walter
Luethi, Johannes
Purgathofer, Werner
Robinson, Guy
Russo, Stefano
Schikuta, Erich
Spalt, Alfred
Stopper, Andreas
Strohmer, Thomas
Toledo, Sivan
Valduriez, Patrick
Van Gemund, Arjan J.C.
Volkert, Jens
Weich, Carsten
Weikum, Gerhard
Würtz, Diethelm
Ziane, Mikal
Zima, Hans-Peter
Zinterhof, Peter

# Contents

# Parallel Databases

# Tools & Languages

# Parallel Algorithms

# Industrial Session

# Posters

# Flexibility and Performance
# of Parallel File Systems

David Kotz and Nils Nieuwejaar

Department of Computer Science
Dartmouth College
Hanover, NH 03755 USA
{dfk,nils}@cs.dartmouth.edu

**Abstract.** As we gain experience with parallel file systems, it becomes increasingly clear that a single solution does not suit all applications. For example, it appears to be impossible to find a single appropriate interface, caching policy, file structure, or disk-management strategy. Furthermore, the proliferation of file-system interfaces and abstractions make applications difficult to port.

We propose that the traditional functionality of parallel file systems be separated into two components: a fixed core that is standard on all platforms, encapsulating only primitive abstractions and interfaces, and a set of high-level libraries to provide a variety of abstractions and application-programmer interfaces (APIs).

We present our current and next-generation file systems as examples of this structure. Their features, such as a three-dimensional file structure, strided read and write interfaces, and I/O-node programs, are specifically designed with the flexibility and performance necessary to support a wide range of applications.

## 1 Introduction

Scientific applications are increasingly dependent on multiprocessor computers to satisfy their computational needs. Many scientific applications, however, also use tremendous amounts of data [11]: input data collected from satellites or seismic experiments, checkpointing output, and visualization output. Worse, some applications manipulate data sets too large to fit in main memory, requiring either explicit or implicit virtual memory support. The I/O system becomes the bottleneck in all of these applications, a bottleneck that is worsening as processor speeds continue to improve more rapidly than disk speeds.

Fortunately, it is now possible to configure most parallel systems with sufficient I/O hardware [22]. Most of today's parallel computers interconnect tens

This research was funded by NSF under grant number CCR-9404919 and by NASA Ames under agreement numbers NCC 2-849 and NAG 2-936.

This paper appeared previously in *ACM Operating Systems Review* 30(2), April 1996, pp. 63–73. The only changes are the format, a shorter abstract, and updates to Section 7 and the references.

or hundreds of processor *nodes*, each of which has a processor and memory, with a high-speed network. Nodes with attached disks are usually reserved as *I/O nodes*, while applications run on some cluster of the remaining *compute nodes*.

In the past few years, many parallel file systems have been described in the literature, including Bridge/PFS [12], CFS [35], nCUBE [9], OSF/PFS [38], sfs [27], Vesta/PIOFS [6], HFS [25], PIOUS [30], RAMA [29], PPFS [19], Scotch [15], and Galley [31, 32]. Many more techniques for improving the performance of parallel file systems have been described, including caching and prefetching [24, 23, 34], two-phase I/O [10], disk-directed I/O [20], compute-node caching [37], chunking [40], compression [41], filtering [21, 2], and so forth.

The diversity of current systems and techniques indicates that there is clearly no consensus about the structure of, interface to, or even functionality of parallel file systems. Indeed, it seems that no one interface or structure will be appropriate for all parallel applications; for maximum performance, flexibility of the underlying system is critical [25]. It is important that applications be able to choose the interface and policies that work best for them, and for application programmers to have control over I/O [46, 8].

This diversity of current systems, particularly of the application-programmer's interface (API), also makes it difficult to write portable applications. Nearly every file system mentioned above has its own API. A standard interface is being developed, MPI-IO [5], but even that interface is appropriate only for a certain class of applications.

## 2   Solution

We believe that flexibility is needed for performance. An application programmer should be able to choose the interfaces and abstractions that work best for that application. To be practical, however, these interfaces and abstractions should be available on all platforms, so the application is portable, and each platform should support multiple interfaces and abstractions, so the platform is usable by many applications.

Consider Figure 1. Most traditional parallel file-system solutions attempt to provide a common file system that hopes to fit all applications. This common "core" file system is fixed, in that it must be used by all applications accessing parallel files.[1] To increase flexibility, we propose to move much of the functionality out of the core and into application libraries. Our new Galley Parallel File System takes this "RISC"-like approach.

The new core file system provides only a minimal set of services, leaving higher-level interfaces, semantics, and functionality to application-selectable libraries. While the implementation of the core is platform dependent, and provided by the platform vendor, its interface is standard across all platforms. This approach has proven successful with the MPI message-passing standard [28].

---

[1] We avoid the term "kernel," as the core may be comprised of user-level libraries, server daemons, and kernel code.

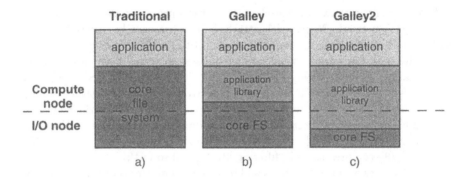

**Fig. 1.** Our proposed evolution of parallel file-system structure. Traditional systems depend on a fixed "core" file system that attempts to serve all applications. In our Galley File System, we shrink the core to leave the API and many of the parallel features to an application-selectable library. In our next-generation Galley2 File System, we shrink the core further to allow user-selected code to run on the I/O nodes.

Application programmers may then choose from a variety of different languages and libraries, to select one that best fits the application's needs. Some languages or libraries would provide a traditional read-write abstraction; others (probably with compiler support) would provide transparent out-of-core data structures; still others may provide persistent objects. Some libraries may be designed for particular application classes like computational chemistry [13] or to support a particular language [7, 4]. Finally, some compilers and programmers may choose to generate application-specific code using the core interface directly.

The concept of I/O libraries is not new; the C `stdio` library and the C++ `iostreams` library are common examples, both layered above the "core" kernel interface. Yet few parallel file systems have been designed specifically to support a variety of high-level libraries. The difficulty is in deciding how to divide features between the core and the application libraries, and then in designing an appropriate core interface. In our research to explore this issue, we are building two generations of file systems. In the first, Galley, we investigate the underlying file abstraction, a low-level read/write interface, and resource-scheduling alternatives. In the second, with the tentative name Galley2, we go a step further and allow user code to run on the I/O nodes. The next two sections discuss each file system in more detail.

## 3 The Galley Parallel File System

Our current parallel file system, Galley [31, 32], looks like Figure 1b. A more detailed picture is shown in Figure 2. The core file system includes servers that run on the I/O nodes and a tiny interface library that runs on the compute nodes. The I/O-node servers manage file-system metadata, I/O-node caching, and disk scheduling. The interface library translates library calls into messages to servers on the I/O nodes and arranges the movement of data between compute and I/O nodes. The higher-level application library, if any, is responsible for providing a convenient API, data declustering, file-access semantics, and any compute-node caching.

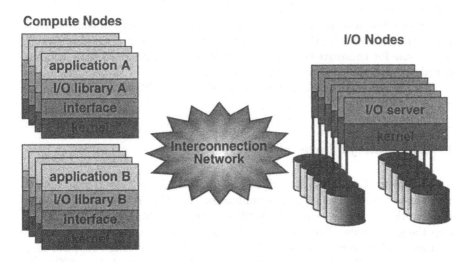

**Fig. 2.** The structure of the Galley parallel file system includes a tiny interface library on the compute node, which coordinates communication between application I/O libraries on the compute nodes and servers on the I/O nodes.

Galley's servers provide a unified global file-name space. Each file is actually a collection of *subfiles*, each of which resides entirely on one I/O node. Each subfile is itself a collection of one or more named *forks*. Each fork is a sequence of bytes, the traditional file abstraction. Galley's core file system provides no automatic data declustering; a library may choose to stripe data across subfiles, for example.

Galley's forks are specifically designed to support libraries. In particular, some libraries may wish to store metadata in one or more forks of the subfile, with data in other forks. The traditional approach is to place the metadata in an auxiliary file or in a "header" at the beginning of the data. The former approach makes file management awkward, as there is more than one file name involved in a single data set. The latter approach makes it difficult to access the file through multiple libraries, each of which expects its own header, and can complicate declustering calculations. In Galley each library can add its own fork to the subfiles, containing its own metadata.

The structure of parallel files, beyond the fact that they are collections of local files, is completely determined by library code. Multiple applications wishing to use the same parallel files must maintain a mutually agreed structure, by convention.

In an extensive characterization of parallel scientific applications [33], we found that many applications access files in small pieces, typically in a regular "strided" pattern. To allow application libraries to support these patterns efficiently, the Galley interface supports both structured (e.g., strided and nested strided) and unstructured read and write requests. This interface leads to dramatically better performance [32].

Galley's features, including the global name space, three-dimensional file structure, and structured read and write requests, make it a suitable and efficient base for constructing parallel file systems, much more so than building directly on distributed Unix systems.

More information about Galley is available on the WWW[2] and in forthcoming papers [31, 32].

## 4    The Galley2 Parallel File System

Our next-generation file system, which we so far call "Galley2" for lack of a better name, goes beyond Galley to allow application control over I/O-node activities. We keep the same three-dimensional file structure of subfiles and forks, and we keep the global name space, but we otherwise reduce the core file system to a minimal local file system on each I/O node, and allow application-supplied code to run on the I/O nodes (see Figure 1c). Indeed, we expect that an I/O node would have an active process (or thread) for each application with files on that I/O node. Figure 3 gives a more detailed picture of this structure.

This structure breaks away from the traditional client-server structure to allow for "programmable" servers. A fixed, common server always forces designers to choose between specific high-level services that may not fit the needs of all applications, and primitive low-level operations that permit flexibility in the clients but at the cost of extensive client-server communications. Galley makes a reasonable choice here, but (for example) uses a fixed caching policy.

In Galley2 the core file system is extremely simple: there is no caching, prefetching, or remote access. It provides a (local) interface to open, close, read and write forks through a block-level interface, and it arbitrates among I/O-node programs competing for processor time, memory, disk access, and network access. In short, it focuses on the shared aspects of the file system.

Thus, Galley2 applications can choose nearly all features of the parallel file system, including the API, caching, prefetching, declustering, inter-node communication protocols, synchronization and consistency, and so forth. Again, we expect most applications to choose from pre-defined libraries, but we also encourage use of application-specific code written by application programmers, generated automatically by compilers, or generated at run time [36]. We refer to all of these choices as "application-selected code."

---

[2] http://www.cs.dartmouth.edu/~nils/galley.html

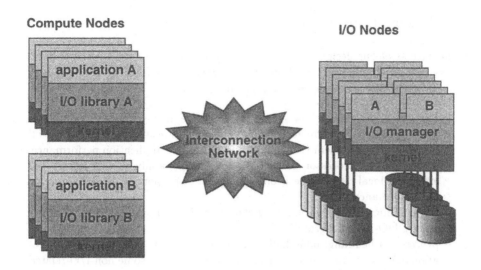

**Fig. 3.** The structure of the Galley2 parallel file system depends on application I/O libraries that have components on both the compute and I/O nodes. The I/O-node servers shrink down to simple I/O managers that arbitrate resources among the local user-selected library modules.

There are many reasons to allow application-selected code on the I/O node. Application-specific optimizations can be applied to I/O-node caching and prefetching. Mechanisms like disk-directed I/O [20] can be implemented, using application-specific data-distribution information. File data can be distributed among memories according to a data-dependent mapping function, for example, in applications with a data-dependent decomposition of unstructured data [21]. Incoming data can be filtered in a data-dependent way, passing only the necessary data on to the compute node, saving network bandwidth and compute-node memory [21, 2]. Blocks can be moved directly between I/O nodes, for example, to rearrange blocks between disks during a copy or permutation operation, without passing through compute nodes. Format conversion, compression, and decompression are also possible. In short, there are many ways that we can optimize memory and disk activity at the I/O node, and reduce disk and network traffic, by moving what is essentially application code to run at the I/O node in addition to the compute nodes.

Although it would be feasible to use a Unix file system as the local file system, the semantics and interface are not appropriate for the highest performance. In particular, the Unix file-system interface does not give the applications enough control, would have no global name space, and has an inefficient copy-based interface.

# 5 Research directions

The success of our design clearly depends on the ability of the I/O-node operating system to efficiently manage its resources while providing the necessary
functionality. We are exploring the following issues:

- resource management: how should the I/O node manage its shared resources
  in the presence of competing applications? The result must be a tradeoff
  between overall system throughput and individual application performance.
  Traditional uniprocessor policies do not directly apply to this distributed
  situation; local resource decisions can have a disproportionate global impact
  on performance.
- physical memory allocation: how should we best allocate physical memory
  among I/O-node programs?
- processor scheduling: how shall we schedule the CPU among I/O-node programs? What about applications that choose to move some non-I/O-related
  computation to the I/O node?
- disk transfers: what is an appropriate interface for requesting I/O to and
  from buffers?
- message-passing: what is the best interface for I/O-node programs to communicate with the compute nodes, and with each other?
- What is the appropriate mechanism to support I/O-node programs? We are
  considering three alternatives: processes, threads within a safe language like
  Java [16] or Python[3], and threads running sandboxed code [45]. There are
  three primary issues in this consideration:
  1. how is the I/O-node manager protected from I/O-node programs? With
     normal hardware protection, in the case of processes; with type-safe lan-
     guages like Java; or with sandboxing.
  2. how is the code loaded onto the I/O node? Presumably they can be
     loaded from disk in the same way as the compute-node code. The tricky
     part might be dynamic linking of sandboxed code.
  3. what is the overhead?

# 6 Related work

The Hurricane File System (HFS) [25], a parallel file system for the Hector multiprocessor, is also designed with the philosophy that flexibility is critical for
performance. Indeed, their results clearly demonstrate the tremendous performance impact of choosing the right file structure and management policies for
the application's access pattern. HFS is actually a collection of building-block
objects that can be plugged together differently according to application needs.
For example, some building blocks distribute data across multiple disks, others
provide prefetching policies, and others define an API. HFS allows the programmer to replace or extend application-level building blocks, but these do not

---

[3] http://www.python.org/

include the objects that control declustering, replication, parity, or other server-side attributes. Galley permits, but does not enforce, a building-block approach to library design; other approaches are possible. Finally, the Hurricane operating system does not dedicate nodes to I/O, so it is not unusual for application code to run on "I/O" nodes.

The Portable Parallel File System (PPFS) [19] is a testbed for experimenting with parallel file-system issues. It includes many alternative policies for declustering, caching, prefetching, and consistency control, and allows application programmers to select appropriate policies for their needs. It also supports user-defined declustering patterns through an upcall function. Unlike Galley, however, there is no clearly defined lower-level interface to which programmers may write new high-level libraries. Unlike Galley2, it does not allow application-selected code (beyond that already included in PPFS) to execute on the I/O nodes.

In the Transparent Informed Prefetching (TIP) system [34] an application provides a set of *hints* about its future accesses to the file system. The file system uses these hints to make intelligent caching and prefetching decisions. While this technique can lead to better performance through better prefetching, it only affects prefetching and caching behavior. It is possible to provide "hints that disclose," in their words, for other aspects of the system, but it is unclear that these hints can provide the same amount of flexibility offered by Galley and Galley2.

All three of these systems provide the application programmer some control over the parallel file system, primarily by selecting existing policies from the built-in alternatives.

Galley2 promotes the use of application-selected code on the I/O nodes. Several operating systems can download user code into the kernel [14, 26, 1]. Other researchers have noted that it is useful to move the function to the data rather than to move the data to the function [3, 42, 17]. Some distributed database systems execute part of the SQL query in the server rather than the client, to reduce client-server traffic [2]. Hatcher and Quinn hint that allowing user code to run on nCUBE I/O nodes would be a good idea [18].

# 7   Status

Galley runs on the IBM SP-2 and on workstation clusters [31], and has so far been extremely successful [32]. We have ported several application libraries on top of Galley, including a traditional striped-file library, Panda [39, 43], Vesta [6], and SOLAR [44]. We are also using Galley to investigate policies for managing multi-application workloads.

We are building a simulator for Galley2, to evaluate some of the key ideas, and a full implementation, to experiment with real applications. There is no question that it will be a much more flexible system than Galley and its predecessors. We will declare success if that flexibility provides better performance on a wider range of applications. That will occur if the benefits of application-specific

I/O-node programs outweigh the cost of the extension mechanism (sandboxing, context switching, or interpretation). We are optimistic!

More information about our research can be found at

`http://www.cs.dartmouth.edu/research/pario.html`

# References

1. B. Bershad, S. Savage, P. Pardyak, E. Gün Sirer, M. E. Fiuczynski, D. Becker, C. Chambers, and S. Eggers. Extensibility, safety and performance in the SPIN operating system. In *Proc. of the 15th ACM SOSP*, pages 267–284, Dec. 1995.
2. A. J. Borr and F. Putzolu. High performance SQL through low-level system integration. In *Proc. of the ACM SIGMOD Conf.*, pages 342–349, 1988.
3. J. B. Carter, J. K. Bennett, and W. Zwaenepoel. Techniques for reducing consistency-related communication in distributed shared-memory systems. *ACM TOCS*, 13(3):205–243, Aug. 1995.
4. A. Choudhary, R. Bordawekar, M. Harry, R. Krishnaiyer, R. Ponnusamy, T. Singh, and R. Thakur. PASSION: parallel and scalable software for input-output. Technical Report SCCS-636, ECE Dept., NPAC and CASE Center, Syracuse University, Sept. 1994.
5. P. Corbett, D. Feitelson, Y. Hsu, J.-P. Prost, M. Snir, S. Fineberg, B. Nitzberg, B. Traversat, and P. Wong. MPI-IO: a parallel file I/O interface for MPI. Technical Report NAS-95-002, NASA Ames Research Center, Jan. 1995. Version 0.3.
6. P. F. Corbett, D. G. Feitelson, J.-P. Prost, G. S. Almasi, S. J. Baylor, A. S. Bolmarcich, Y. Hsu, J. Satran, M. Snir, R. Colao, B. Herr, J. Kavaky, T. R. Morgan, and A. Zlotek. Parallel file systems for the IBM SP computers. *IBM Sys. Journal*, 34(2):222–248, Jan. 1995.
7. T. H. Cormen and A. Colvin. ViC*: A preprocessor for virtual-memory C*. Technical Report PCS-TR94-243, Dept. of Computer Science, Dartmouth College, Nov. 1994.
8. T. H. Cormen and D. Kotz. Integrating theory and practice in parallel file systems. In *Proc. of the 1993 DAGS/PC Symposium*, pages 64–74, Hanover, NH, June 1993. Dartmouth Inst. for Adv. Graduate Studies. Revised as Dartmouth PCS-TR93-188 on 9/20/94.
9. E. DeBenedictis and J. M. del Rosario. nCUBE parallel I/O software. In *Proc. of the 11th IPCCC*, pages 0117–0124, Apr. 1992.
10. J. M. del Rosario, R. Bordawekar, and A. Choudhary. Improved parallel I/O via a two-phase run-time access strategy. In *IPPS '93 Workshop on I/O in Par. Comp. Sys.*, pages 56–70, 1993. Also published in Computer Architecture News 21(5), December 1993, pages 31–38.
11. J. M. del Rosario and A. Choudhary. High performance I/O for parallel computers: Problems and prospects. *IEEE Computer*, 27(3):59–68, Mar. 1994.
12. P. C. Dibble. *A Parallel Interleaved File System*. PhD thesis, University of Rochester, Mar. 1990.
13. I. Foster and J. Nieplocha. ChemIO: High-performance I/O for computational chemistry applications. WWW http://www.mcs.anl.gov/chemio/, Feb. 1996.
14. R. S. Gaines. An operating system based on the concept of a supervisory computer. *Comm. of the ACM*, 15(3):150–156, Mar. 1972.

15. G. A. Gibson, D. Stodolsky, P. W. Chang, W. V. Courtright II, C. G. Demetriou, E. Ginting, M. Holland, Q. Ma, L. Neal, R. H. Patterson, J. Su, R. Youssef, and J. Zelenka. The Scotch parallel storage systems. In *Proc. of 40th IEEE Computer Society International Conference (COMPCON 95)*, pages 403–410, San Francisco, Spring 1995.

16. J. Gosling and H. McGilton. The Java language: A white paper. Sun Microsystems, 1994.

17. R. S. Gray. Agent Tcl: A transportable agent system. In *Proceedings of the CIKM Workshop on Intelligent Information Agents, Fourth International Conference on Information and Knowledge Management (CIKM 95)*, Baltimore, Maryland, Dec. 1995.

18. P. J. Hatcher and M. J. Quinn. C*-Linda: A programming environment with multiple data-parallel modules and parallel I/O. In *Proc. of the 24th HICSS*, pages 382–389, 1991.

19. J. Huber, C. L. Elford, D. A. Reed, A. A. Chien, and D. S. Blumenthal. PPFS: A high performance portable parallel file system. In *Proc. of the 9th ACM Int'l Conf. on Supercomp.*, pages 385–394, Barcelona, July 1995.

20. D. Kotz. Disk-directed I/O for MIMD multiprocessors. In *Proc. of the 1994 Symp. on OS Design and Impl.*, pages 61–74, Nov. 1994. Updated as Dartmouth TR PCS-TR94-226 on November 8, 1994.

21. D. Kotz. Expanding the potential for disk-directed I/O. In *Proc. of the 1995 IEEE SPDP*, pages 490–495, Oct. 1995.

22. D. Kotz. Introduction to multiprocessor I/O architecture. In R. Jain, J. Werth, and J. C. Browne, editors, *Input/Output in Parallel and Distributed Computer Systems*, chapter 4, pages 97–123. Kluwer Academic Publishers, 1996.

23. D. Kotz and C. S. Ellis. Caching and writeback policies in parallel file systems. *J. of Par. and Dist. Comp.*, 17(1–2):140–145, January and February 1993.

24. D. Kotz and C. S. Ellis. Practical prefetching techniques for multiprocessor file systems. *J. of Dist. and Par. Databases*, 1(1):33–51, Jan. 1993.

25. O. Krieger and M. Stumm. HFS: A performance-oriented flexible file system based on building-block compositions. In *4th Workshop on I/O in Par. and Dist. Sys.*, pages 95–108, Philadelphia, May 1996.

26. C. H. Lee, M. C. Chen, and R. C. Chang. HiPEC: High performance external virtual memory caching. In *Proc. of the 1994 Symp. on OS Design and Impl.*, pages 153–164, 1994.

27. S. J. LoVerso, M. Isman, A. Nanopoulos, W. Nesheim, E. D. Milne, and R. Wheeler. sfs: A parallel file system for the CM-5. In *Proc. of the 1993 Summer USENIX Conf.*, pages 291–305, 1993.

28. Message Passing Interface Forum. *MPI: A Message-Passing Interface Standard*, 1.0 edition, May 5 1994. http://www.mcs.anl.gov/Projects/mpi/standard.html.

29. E. L. Miller and R. H. Katz. RAMA: Easy access to a high-bandwidth massively parallel file system. In *Proc. of the 1995 Winter USENIX Conf.*, pages 59–70, Jan. 1995.

30. S. A. Moyer and V. S. Sunderam. PIOUS: a scalable parallel I/O system for distributed computing environments. In *Proc. of the Scalable High-Perf. Comp. Conf.*, pages 71–78, 1994.

31. N. Nieuwejaar and D. Kotz. The Galley parallel file system. In *Proc. of the 10th ACM Int'l Conf. on Supercomp.*, pages 374–381, May 1996.

32. N. Nieuwejaar and D. Kotz. Performance of the Galley parallel file system. In *4th Workshop on I/O in Par. and Dist. Sys.*, pages 83–94, May 1996.

33. N. Nieuwejaar, D. Kotz, A. Purakayastha, C. S. Ellis, and M. Best. File-access characteristics of parallel scientific workloads. Technical Report PCS-TR95-263, Dept. of Computer Science, Dartmouth College, Aug. 1995. To appear in IEEE TPDS.

34. R. H. Patterson, G. A. Gibson, E. Ginting, D. Stodolsky, and J. Zelenka. Informed prefetching and caching. In *Proc. of the 15th ACM SOSP*, pages 79–95, Dec. 1995.

35. P. Pierce. A concurrent file system for a highly parallel mass storage system. In *Proc. of the Fourth Conf. on Hypercube Concurrent Comp. and Appl.*, pages 155–160. Golden Gate Enterprises, Los Altos, CA, Mar. 1989.

36. C. Pu, T. Autrey, A. Black, C. Consel, C. Cowan, J. Inouye, L. Kethana, J. Walpole, and K. Zhang. Optimistic incremental specialization: Streamlining a commercial operating system. In *Proc. of the 15th ACM SOSP*, pages 314–324, Dec. 1995.

37. A. Purakayastha, C. S. Ellis, and D. Kotz. ENWRICH: a compute-processor write caching scheme for parallel file systems. In *4th Workshop on I/O in Par. and Dist. Sys.*, pages 55–68, May 1996.

38. P. J. Roy. Unix file access and caching in a multicomputer environment. In *Proc. of the Usenix Mach III Symposium*, pages 21–37, 1993.

39. K. E. Seamons, Y. Chen, P. Jones, J. Jozwiak, and M. Winslett. Server-directed collective I/O in Panda. In *Proc. of Supercomp. '95*, Dec. 1995.

40. K. E. Seamons and M. Winslett. An efficient abstract interface for multidimensional array I/O. In *Proc. of Supercomp. '94*, pages 650–659, Nov. 1994.

41. K. E. Seamons and M. Winslett. A data management approach for handling large compressed arrays in high performance computing. In *Proc. of the 5th Symp. on the Frontiers of Massively Par. Comp.*, pages 119–128, Feb. 1995.

42. J. W. Stamos and D. K. Gifford. Remote execution. *ACM TOPLAS*, 12(4):537–565, Oct. 1990.

43. J. T. Thomas. The Panda array I/O library on the Galley parallel file system. Technical Report PCS-TR96-288, Dept. of Computer Science, Dartmouth College, June 1996. Senior Honors Thesis.

44. S. Toledo and F. G. Gustavson. The design and implementation of SOLAR, a portable library for scalable out-of-core linear algebra computations. In *4th Workshop on I/O in Par. and Dist. Sys.*, pages 28–40, Philadelphia, May 1996.

45. R. Wahbe, S. Lucco, T. E. Anderson, and S. L. Graham. Efficient software-based fault isolation. In *Proc. of 14th ACM SOSP*, pages 203–216, 1993.

46. D. Womble, D. Greenberg, R. Riesen, and S. Wheat. Out of core, out of mind: Practical parallel I/O. In *Proc. of the Scalable Par. Libraries Conf.*, pages 10–16, Mississippi State University, Oct. 1993.

# Study of Data Distribution Strategies for Parallel I/O Management

Peter Kwong[1], Shikharesh Majumdar
Department of Systems and Computer Engineering,
Carleton University, Ottawa, Canada.
email: majumdar@sce.carleton.ca

## Abstract

Recent studies have demonstrated that significant I/O operations are performed by a number of different classes of parallel applications. Appropriate I/O management strategies are required however for harnessing the power of parallel I/O. This paper focuses on two I/O management issues that affect system performance in multiprogrammed parallel environments. Characterization of the I/O behavior of parallel applications in terms of four different models is discussed first, followed by an investigation of the performance of a number of different data distribution strategies. Using computer simulations, this research shows I/O characteristics of applications and data distribution have an important effect on system performance. Applications which can simultaneously do computation and I/O, plus strategies that can incorporate centralized I/O management are found to be beneficial for a multiprogrammed parallel environment.

## 1.0 Introduction

Processing power as well as memory speed for computing systems have been increasing regularly and continuously. The improvements in hard disk technology, however, have mainly achieved increases in storage density and size. Because of their electro-mechanical construction, the access time for disks has improved only minimally over the past twenty years [Patt94]. In addition to the increase in CPU speed, the past decade has experienced a large improvement in computation speedup achieved through parallelizing applications and running these on a multiprocessor system. As a result, the CPU processing times of programs have improved considerably, thereby pushing the performance bottleneck towards the I/O subsystem.

Studies show that significant I/O is done by a variety of classes of parallel applications that include the grand challenge programs and scientific applications [Patt94] as well as graphics software [Cyph93] [Kotz 94]. To alleviate the problems inherent in the slow electro-mechanical technology used to build I/O devices, disk caches and arrays of disks have been introduced [Patt88]. Although multiple I/O devices can potentially improve system performance, effective methods of using I/O in an application as well as appropriate management of the I/O devices are required to harness the power of the parallel I/O subsystem. This research is motivated by such requirements on the effective management of parallel I/O.

A large number of commercial shared memory as well as distributed memory multiple processor systems are currently in use. Examples include shared memory systems produced by Sequent and Encore; processes or threads in an application exchange information through shared variables stored in the global memory provided on such a system. Distributed memory systems on which processes communicate through message passing include the Intel's Hypercube and the NCube systems. A hybrid between these two classes is the class of non-uniform-memory-access (NUMA) systems such as the Teracomputer and the KSR-1. The availability of parallel hardware along with tools such as restructuring compilers for developing parallel application software are increasing the popularity of parallel systems. Many multiprocessor systems are dedi-

---

1. Author is currently with Nortel Ltd., Ottawa, Canada.

cated to running a single computationally intensive application in isolation. The usage of multiprocessor systems is becoming more and more widespread, however, so general purpose systems that run a variety of applications are becoming popular. Environments running such a variety of different applications need to *multiprogram* the system to provide user satisfaction and enhance resource utilization. Multiple parallel applications are active simultaneously on such an environment.

Work on resource management on multiprogrammed parallel systems has concentrated on how to schedule the processing resources among competing applications to achieve good system performance [Maju88][Leut90][Maju91][Sevc94]. In comparison to processor scheduling, much less work has been done in the area of management of parallel I/O on multiprogrammed systems. Existing work on parallel I/O has focused primarily on environments that run a single application in isolation. A number of different I/O subsystem architectures that are of importance in the context of shared memory and distributed memory systems are discussed by [Delr94]. A comparison of different disk configurations that include disk striping, disk synchronization, for a transaction system workload as well as for a scientific application workload, is presented in [Redd89]. A comparison between two multiple disk management approaches, clustered and declustered, is presented in [Livn87]. User defined file partitioning and dynamic decomposition of files in a parallel file system is considered in [Corb93]. A two-phase data access strategy in which the data distribution on computational nodes is decoupled from storage distribution is proposed in [Delr 93]. Scheduling I/O requests for reducing the total completion time for the schedule is discussed in [Jain93]. Characterization of file access patterns exhibited by parallel scientific workload is discussed in [Kotz95].

Current studies on parallel I/O have not addressed adequately basic issues underlying the effective overall management of parallel I/O on a *multiprogrammed* parallel systems. The way applications perform I/O, and the strategies for the management of parallel I/O such as scheduling of I/O requests and data distribution can have a significant impact on the performance of a multiprogrammed system. Research on scheduling of I/O requests is underway at a number of institutions (see [Kwon96] for example). Some work on characterization of I/O and data distribution has been reported in [Maju95] which characterized three application models (NO, O1, O2) and three data distribution strategies (Replicated-C, Replicated-D and FixedRW(Rand)). A number of additional distribution policies (eg. FixedR, FixedRW(RR)) and another application model (NOP) are presented and characterized in this short paper to address the following high level questions. The research provides insights into system behaviour and are important for operating systems for multiprogrammed parallel environments.

- Applications perform I/O in many ways. Do the I/O characteristics of applications have a strong relationship with I/O management and performance? Is there a clear winner among the different I/O models? These questions are investigated for systems running a single job in isolation as well as for multiprogrammed systems.
- Replicating input data for an application on a number of I/O devices may improve performance in a multiprogrammed system. The I/O requests for an application, for example, may be sent to any free I/O device on the system. What is the impact of data replication on performance?

- Management of I/O may be performed in a number of different ways. A centralized management of I/O requests may be appropriate for small to medium scale parallel systems where the status of each I/O device (idle/busy) may be stored easily in a centralized database on such a system. A decentralized approach is necessary for larger systems. How do the distributed and centralized approaches to I/O management affect system performance?
- Does the performance of a given I/O model depend on the way data is distributed on the different devices? How does the performance of data distribution strategies vary when the I/O management approach is changed from centralized to decentralized?

A discrete event simulator was used to build an abstract model of a multiprogrammed parallel system, the data distribution policies and the I/O applications. Such a model is appropriate for the high level questions addressed in this paper. The simulation results are calculated to a 95% confidence level and values obtained generally are within 5% of the mean value. A representative subset of the data is presented in this paper. More data are available in [Kwon96]. The remainder of the paper is organized as follows. The system model is presented in Section 2.0 and the performance comparison of different I/O models is presented in Section 3.0. The data distribution strategies are presented in Section 4.0 and their performance is described in Section 5.0. Section 6.0 presents our conclusions.

## 2.0 The Multiprogrammed System Model

This study uses an abstract model of a multiprogrammed system consisting of multiple processors and I/O devices. The system model consists of two components: a model of the processor & I/O subsystem and the workload model. Each is briefly described.

### 2.1 The Processor & I/O Subsystem Model

The processor and I/O subsystems are characterized by the number of processors, P, and the number of I/O devices, I, respectively (see Table 1). Statistically identical (ie. of a single class or type) jobs enter and run in this open system. During its execution, a job performs computations in the processor subsystem and requests I/O from the I/O subsystem. When all the I/O and computations performed by a job are completed, the job exits the system.

The P identical CPUs in the processor subsystem are grouped into M processor sets (job nodes). Each set has $N_p$ CPUs, but if P is not a multiple of $N_p$, then one of the sets will have only $P-N_p*(M-1)$ CPUs. Each job that enters the system is sent to the first free job node. If no job node is idle, then the newly arrived job waits in a FIFO queue for the first idle job node. Static scheduling of processors is used so once a job acquires a job node, all the processors in the node are held by the job until the job has terminated.

TABLE 1. Parameters characterizing the processor & I/O subsystem model

| Parameter | Description |
|---|---|
| P | Number of CPUs in processor subsystem |
| $N_p$ | Number of CPUs allocated to a job |
| $M=ceiling(P/N_p)$ | Multiprogramming level |
| I | Number of I/O devices in I/O subsystem |
| $d_s$ | Mean seek time of an I/O device |

**TABLE 1. Parameters characterizing the processor & I/O subsystem model**

| Parameter | Description |
|-----------|-------------|
| $CV_s$ | Coefficient of variation of the device seek time |
| R | Mean job response time (queueing + execution times) |

Such a CPU scheduling strategy has been investigated by a number of researchers (see [Sevc94]), [Maju91] for example) and is effective in environments which have a large cost associated with switching processors among different applications. Examples of such environments are large scale NUMA shared memory systems and distributed memory systems. Processors allocated to the same job are shareable by the threads in the job that share the same address space. After a thread issues an I/O request, the thread is blocked waiting for the I/O request to finish. During this period, the CPU on which the thread was running becomes available for use by other threads in the same job. Processors may be shared by threads in an application in different ways; in this research, a ready thread is set to run on the first available processor.

An I/O request from a job is sent to one of the I/O devices in the I/O subsystem. Every I/O device is identical and each is characterized by a mean seek time, $d_s$, and a coefficient of variation of seek time, $CV_s$. For a disk drive, the value of $d_s$ would include the mean rotational latency and the mean track seek time. Each I/O request is characterized by a data transfer time (I/O demand) to represent the time needed to transfer a chunk of data. This I/O demand is a random variable characterized by a mean value. Each I/O device operates independently (as opposed to synchronously [Kim86]) and more than one device may be concurrently active servicing multiple requests from a job. I/O devices in the I/O subsystem are shared by all jobs.

The performance measure of interest is the mean job response time, R. The response time of a job is defined as the difference between the time at which the last thread in the job completes and the arrival time of the job into the system.

Because the experiments conducted for this research focus on systems characterized by large computational workloads and I/O transfer times, the mean and coefficient of variation of seek time are set to relatively small values. In the experiments, $d_s$ is held at 1% of the mean CPU demand, d (which is described in the following subsection), and $CV_s$ is set to 1.0. To maintain focus on the higher level issues of I/O management, overheads associated with scheduling and context switching are not considered. Costs associated with communicating with and controlling of the I/O subsystem also have been excluded from the experiments. This is appropriate for small and medium scale systems where the cost of maintaining a central database of device status and the communications costs are low. Where communication costs are significant, a non-centralized strategy may be more appropriate.

## 2.2 Models of Applications with Parallel I/O

Existing work on resource management on parallel systems has used jobs with a fork and join architecture (see [Leut90] for example). An adaptation of this fork and join architecture to represent I/O performed by jobs is used in this research. The workload that is applied to the system uses one of four types of fork and join jobs with parallel I/O. Three of these job models (shown in Figure 1), called the NO (No Overlap), O1 (Overlap #1), and O2 (Overlap #2), have been used in previous studies [Maju94] of I/O management. The fourth type, called NOP (No Overlap-Parallel), is introduced in this paper. Although all these models are fork and join jobs, they differ in when and where I/O is performed within the job. These models are appropriate for the high level questions investigated in this research and they also reflect the behaviour of certain classes of programs executing on real systems. For example, both jobs characterized by no CPU-I/O overlap as well as jobs characterized by CPU-I/O overlap, have been observed in real parallel systems that include scientific code and graphics software [Cyph93]. Similar observations for parallel scientific workload are reported in [Kotz94]. Each of these application models is described in detail below.

The NO Model (see Figure 1a): A NO job begins by first reading in some data using a single read operation from a single I/O device. When the read is done, the job forks into several children threads, each of which performs only computations. When all these threads complete, the job performs a single write operation to a single I/O device. This write operation can correspond to the writing of the results of the computation. The job terminates when its I/O completes. This job model does not have CPU-I/O overlap because the job can only be either doing I/O or computation, but not both simultaneously.

**FIGURE 1. Fork and Join job models**

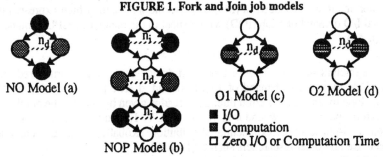

NO Model (a)

NOP Model (b)

O1 Model (c)

O2 Model (d)

■ I/O
▧ Computation
□ Zero I/O or Computation Time

The NOP Model (see Figure 1b): A NOP job begins like a NO job by first reading in some data. The read, however, is done using parallel I/O operations. When all these read operations have completed, the job forks several children threads, each of which only performs computations. When all these threads complete their computations, the job performs a parallel write operation. After all the writes are completed, the job terminates. No CPU-I/O overlap is present in this job model.

The O1 Model (see Figure 1c): This represents jobs which overlap I/O with computations. A job starts by forking a number of children threads, each of which reads its input data from an I/O device and then performs some computation. After completing its computation, each thread writes the results onto an I/O device. When all the children threads have completed their writes, the job terminates. This job model has CPU-I/O overlap because the I/O performed by a thread can overlap with the computation performed by another thread of the same job.

The O2 Model (see Figure 1d): This is similar to the O1 model but has more overlap between I/O and computations. A thread alternates between doing computations and doing I/O (either reads or writes). The last operation a child thread does is to write some data onto a device. When all the threads have completed their last write, the job terminates.

The NOP is similar to the O1 job model in that both can do parallel I/O. A NOP job, however, must complete all its read I/O operations before it can start its computations, and all its computations must complete before the job can start its write operations. An O1 job does not have this restriction because a child thread can do its I/O and computation independently of the job's other child threads so an O1 job can be simultaneously doing I/O and computation. Additionally, a NOP job can have more parallel I/O operations, $n_i$, than children threads, $n_d$, whereas an O1 job is constrained to have $n_i = n_d$.

The workload the system is subjected to consists of applications characterized by any one of the job models. The four job models can be characterized using a common set of parameters (Table 2) plus the mean CPU demand per burst and mean I/O demand per burst. Jobs arrive as a Poisson process characterized by an arrival rate $\lambda$ into the processor subsystem. The number of children threads and the number of parallel I/O operations are represented by $n_d$ and $n_i$ respectively. The mean CPU demand of a child thread is d, and the coefficient of variation of a CPU burst is $CV_d$. The mean size of a CPU burst for NO, NOP, O1 and O2 is: d, d, d and $d/(k-1)$, respectively. The mean size of an I/O burst for NO, NOP, O1 and O2 is: $IOD/2$, $IOD/(2*n_i)$, $IOD/(2*n_d)$ and $IOD/(k*n_d)$, respectively, where IOD is the mean total I/O demand for a job. The coefficient of variation of an I/O burst is $CV_i$. An important characteristic of parallel applications introduced in [Maju94] was the I/O factor which expresses the mean total I/O demand of a job (IOD) with respect to the mean total CPU demand of the job ($n_d*d$):

$$IOD = n_d * d * F_i.$$

All the parameters such as response times and device demand are normalized with respect to the mean CPU demand of a child thread, d. The probability that an I/O operation done by an O2 job's child thread is a read is given by p while the number of I/O operations per O2 child thread is k. When any CV>1, random value generation is based on a bi-phase hyper-exponential distribution [Koba81]. Similar techniques have been used by other researchers such as [Leut90].

**TABLE 2. Common Set of Workload Model Parameters**

| Parameter | Description |
|---|---|
| $\lambda$ | Mean arrival rate of jobs |
| $n_d$ | Number of children threads in a job. |
| d | Mean CPU demand of a child thread. |
| $CV_d$ | Coefficient of variation of CPU demand for CPU burst. |
| $F_i$ | I/O factor. |
| $CV_i$ | Coefficient of variation of I/O demand for an I/O burst. |
| $n_i$ | Number of NOP parallel read/write I/O operations. |
| k | Number of I/O operations per O2 child thread (k >= 2). |
| p | Probability an O2 job's I/O request is a read. |

## 3.0 Performance Comparison of the I/O Models

The performances of the four job models are first analyzed by studying the effect of increasing the number of I/O devices on the mean job response time, R, when only one job runs in the system (M=1) and all the available processors are used by that job. The results for $F_i$=2.0 is shown in Figure 2a for the four job models.

The experiment for Figure 2a demonstrates the large improvement possible by parallelizing the I/O performed by an application and using multiple I/O devices. A read-anywhere-write-anywhere I/O management strategy where all I/O requests are routed to idle devices using a central router is used in this experiment (see Replicated-C policy in Section 4.0). Because a NO job only has one I/O operation active at any one time, the mean job response time is invariant with respect to the number of I/O devices in a uniprogrammed environment. For the NOP, O1 and O2 jobs, the mean job response time drops dramatically when the first few devices are added to the system. The performance gain then decreases and soon R becomes insensitive to the addition of any more devices. Note that the values of I at which R becomes somewhat insensitive to the addition of more I/O devices are less than either $n_i$ or $n_d$. Because each I/O request's demand is variable (some big, some small), the devices servicing the small requests become idle sooner than the devices servicing big requests. Those idle devices are then reused to service any waiting requests so fewer I/O devices than $n_i$ or $n_d$ may be adequate to service a job's parallel I/O operations. Decreasing $F_i$ is observed to produce a lower value for I at which R becomes invariant [Kwon96]. Figure 2 also reveals the superior performance obtainable by using CPU-I/O overlap (O1 and O2 models).

**FIGURE 2. Uniprogrammed & multiprogrammed job model performance**

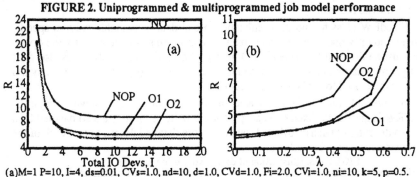

(a)M=1 P=10, I=4, ds=0.01, CVs=1.0, nd=10, d=1.0, CVd=1.0, Fi=2.0, CVi=1.0, ni=10, k=5, p=0.5.

(b) M=4, P=20, I=4, ds=0.01, CVs=1.0, Fi=0.5, nd=10, d=1.0, CVd=1.0, CVi=1.0, ni=10, k=5, p=0.5

In a multiprogrammed environment, more than one job can be running concurrently. Figure 2b shows the mean job response times obtained with the NOP, O1 and O2 job models as $\lambda$ is increased. The results show that the O1 jobs complete quicker than the NOP and O2 jobs over a wide range of $\lambda$. NO model was found to perform poorly in [Maju95] and is omitted from this experiment. In a uniprogrammed environment, although O2 jobs can be marginally superior to O1 jobs when $F_i$ is high (see Figure 2a), in a multiprogrammed environment, O2 demonstrates an inferior performance when $\lambda$ is moderate to high. Further investigation is needed to fully understand why this is so. The NOP model does not overlap CPU with I/O, so the CPUs allocated to a job are idle when I/O operations are in progress and vice versa. Consequently, it demonstrates the worst performance. The I/O models that have CPU-I/O overlap demonstrate superior performance, but doing a smaller number of I/O operations (as in the O1 model) seem to give better performance at high $\lambda$ and low $F_i$. The performance of NOP is observed to be inferior to O1 even when the values of $n_i$ and I are increased to 40 and 20, respectively, while keeping $n_d=10$ for both models.

## 4.0 Data Distribution Policies

Three classes of data distribution strategies are investigated: Write Anywhere Read Anywhere ("Replicated"), Fixed Read and Write ("FixedRW") and Fixed Read ("FixedR"). The Replicated and FixedR policies are further subdivided into Centralized (Replicated-C and FixedR-C) and Distributed (Replicated-D and FixedR-D). In the centralized approach, a centralized dispatcher monitors the status of all devices (busy or idle) and requests are always sent to an idle device. In the distributed approach, automatic routing of an I/O request to a device is done without regard or knowledge of the current device status (busy or idle). The centralized approach is appropriate for medium scale shared memory systems or smaller distributed memory systems. In larger systems, especially in larger distributed memory system, a high cost is associated with maintaining such a centralized database so a non-centralized (eg. distributed) approach for I/O management may be preferable.

The Replicated class replicates only the data that is read by applications. The data written by the applications are *not* replicated. This lack of write data replication would be appropriate for scientific applications where the output results are written to I/O devices and this data written by one thread are not needed by the other threads in the application. Because read data is replicated, any device can service a read request. Write data is not replicated and can be written anywhere so any device is allowed to service a write request.

The FixedRW class has no data replication. Read data is available only on specific devices and only one copy of written data is maintained so that a read or write operation must be directed to a specific I/O device. Similarly, the FixedR class also does not use any data replication, so reads must be directed to specific devices but any I/O device can be used to service a write request.

Visual representations of the Replicated and FixedR policies are shown in Figure 3. FixedRW is similar to FixedR-D except that the write requests are also handled by a fixed router rather than a distributed router. A more detailed description of each of the data distribution policies follows.

**FIGURE 3. Illustration of data distribution policies**

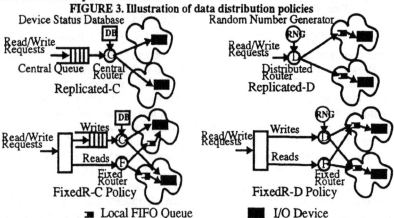

In *Replicated-C*, all I/O requests are inserted into a central FIFO queue. A central router which knows the busy/idle status of every I/O device sends an I/O request to the first idle I/O device the router finds. If no device is idle, then all requests remain in the queue until a device becomes free. In the *Replicated-D* policy, no central record of device status is maintained so each request is sent immediately to one of the I I/O devices chosen at random with probability 1/I. At the device, requests are then placed into a FIFO queue maintained and accessed only by the local I/O device. If the device is idle, then the request is processed immediately.

The two *FixedR* policies do not use any data replication so data can be written onto any device but data can only be read from specific devices. All the read requests for the FixedR class of policies are sent immediately to the specified device which has the desired data regardless of the current device state. The read requests are placed into a local FIFO queue maintained by the device. In the *FixedR-C* policy, write requests are maintained in a central queue from which a central router which has access to the device status database routes a write request to a device. For the *FixedR-D* policy, write requests are sent immediately to a device chosen at random with probability 1/I. Both the read and write requests wait on a FIFO queue local to the device if the device is busy. When the device becomes free, a request is removed from the local queue for servicing.

The *FixedRW* class does not replicate any data and data can be written only to specific devices and data can be read only from specific devices. This set of I/O devices correspond to the devices onto which the read data has been distributed apriori and onto which data will be written. For FixedRW and FixedR, the I/O devices are allocated in one of the two following ways: Round Robin and Random. Note that the policy called Fixed in [Maju95] is called FixedRW(Rand) in this report.

With Round Robin device allocation (or equivalently, Round Robin data distribution), parallelism in I/O is maximized so that $\min(I, n_i)$ different devices are used by an NOP application and $\min(I, n_d)$ are used by an O1 application. Data for the first I/O operation is assumed to be placed on device number 'k' chosen at random. The data for the remaining I/O operations are assumed to be placed on device number 'k+1', 'k+2' and so on in a round robin fashion. When all the devices have been chosen once, they may be reselected again. Such an organized allocation of application input data attempts to maximize the parallelism in I/O for an application but this may not always be possible. On a general purpose multiprogrammed system in which the amount of data read or written by different applications can vary a great deal, imbalance in stored data may result; certain devices may become full while other devices may be relatively empty. In such a situation, an application may end up using a smaller number of I/O devices than ideally possible. This type of environment is simulated with the help of Random device allocation (data distribution) where the input data for a job's I/O operations are placed on devices chosen at random. Consequently, some devices can possibly be chosen multiple times whereas some devices are not chosen at all. The reason for comparing these two device allocation policies is to find out whether or not motivation exists to reorganize the stored data from time to time so that the Round Robin allocation can be used.

## 5.0 Performance of the Data Distribution Policies

The performances of the Round Robin and Random device allocation schemes in the context of the FixedRW strategy are first analyzed by computing the mean job response times using NOP and O1 workloads against increasing $\lambda$ with the degree of I/O parallelism $n_i$ set equal to $2n_d$. The results show that for both job models, the performance of the Random allocation scheme is inferior to the Round Robin scheme. The difference is seen to be more significant for NOP than for O1.

The performance difference between the two device allocation schemes can be rationalized as follows. Random device allocation randomly assigns a device set to a job and so can potentially reduce the parallelism in I/O. Even though the system may have enough devices, some devices may be used more often than necessary while some devices are not selected at all for use by a given job. This causes the I/O workload to be concentrated on only a few devices even if other devices may be available. In contrast, Round Robin device allocation distributes its data across as many devices as possible so that a given job is able to make use of as many devices as possible in parallel for its I/O, thus improving I/O parallelism. Note that for NO jobs, the choice between FixedRW(Rand) and FixedRW(RR) policy is irrelevant because this model only has one read operation and one write operation so that only one device is needed at any time to do either the read or write.

The relative performances of the data distribution strategies are presented for both NOP and O1 workloads. Results for O1 are presented first (see Figure 4). Replicated-C policy produces the best performance. At $CV_i$ =1.0, the FixedR-C policies perform very closely to Replicated-C policy, at both low and high λ. With Random device allocation, FixedRW(Rand) is inferior to Replicated-D at high λ while FixedR-D(Rand) is indistinguishable from Replicated-D. Interestingly, with Round Robin allocation, FixedRW(RR) is better than Replicated-D while FixedR-D(RR) lies between Replicated-D and FixedRW(RR).

**FIGURE 4. R vs λ for O1 workload and two different device allocation policies**

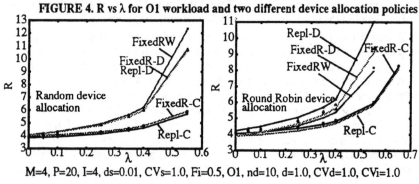

M=4, P=20, I=4, ds=0.01, CVs=1.0, Fi=0.5, O1, nd=10, d=1.0, CVd=1.0, CVi=1.0

**FIGURE 5. Performance of Data distribution and device allocation policies with NOP**

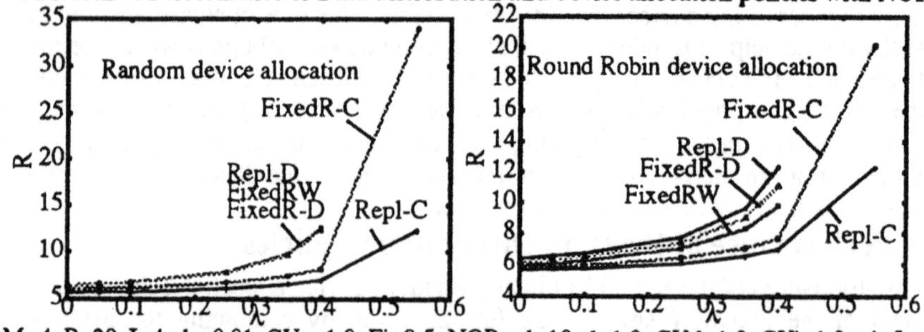

M=4, P=20, I=4, ds=0.01, CVs=1.0, Fi=0.5, NOP, nd=10, d=1.0, CVd=1.0, CVi=1.0, ni=5

Results using NOP workload show slight differences from O1 in the relative behaviours between the data distribution policies (see Figure 5). For both device allocation policies, FixedR-C policies rapidly diverge from Replicated-C when λ is high. With Random device allocation, the FixedRW(Rand), FixedR-D(Rand) and Replicated-D are indistinguishable, even when $n_i$ is increased from 5 to 20. With Round Robin allocation, however, FixedRW(RR) is noticeably better than FixedR-D(RR) and Replicated-D.

## 5.1 Discussion

The simulation results reveal that centralized routing, where feasible (eg. when the cost of communicating with a central server and the costs of managing the central database is low), is beneficial to system performance. Replicated-C performs much better than Replicated-D even though both policies replicate read data on all devices. Replicated-D randomly routes I/O requests to devices without knowing the devices' existing I/O workload thereby causing a load imbalance between I/O devices. Consequently, I/O requests may wait longer than necessary for service because they are queued behind other requests even though the system has idle devices that can service the waiting requests. Performance of FixedRW and FixedR-C policies is worse than Replicated-C because having I/O requests serviced only by specific I/O devices may cause some requests to be sent to busy devices even though other devices are idle. This does not happen with Replicated-C because any idle device can service an I/O request.

Interestingly for moderate $CV_i$, the centralization of the writes in the FixedR-C policy for O1 workload has a stronger effect than the choice of device allocation policy as its performance is very similar to Replicated-C for both Random and Round Robin device allocation. FixedR-C is superior to the FixedRW policies as well as the distributed policies (FixedR-D and Replicated-D). This can be attributed to the centralized router spreading the I/O workload across I/O devices by always sending an I/O write request to an idle device, thus reducing the I/O wait times.

In the FixedRW policy, the reads and writes have to be routed to specific devices. This policy demonstrates very poor performance when Random device allocation is used but performs better than both Replicated-D and FixedR-D when Round Robin allocation is used. The general improvement in performance with respect to Replicated-D when Round Robin device allocation is used (e.g. in FixedRW or FixedR class policies) can be attributed to the spreading of I/O workload across I/O devices which increases I/O parallelism and reduces device bottlenecks and I/O wait times.

Although the FixedR-D policy sends its write requests to a randomly chosen device, it performs slightly better than Replicated-D when it uses Round Robin device allocation to spread the read workload across a large number of devices. This distribution of the read operations seems to compensate for the load imbalance caused by the distributed handling of write requests.

## 6.0 Conclusions

This paper describes a computer simulation based investigation of the performance of several I/O models and several I/O management strategies for a multiprogrammed parallel system. For a given number of I/O devices, increasing the parallelism of I/O and/or having CPU-I/O overlap can give improved job performance. Where centralized management is feasible, policies such as Replicated-C and FixedR-C perform better than the other policies. Replicated-C is better than FixedR-C but the former requires replication of input data whereas the latter does not use any data replication. The central routing of I/O requests can compensate for the potential poor device allocation for the FixedR-C read requests. Where I/O management cannot be centralized, little motivation exists for input data replication and distributed routing. Instead, fixed routing with FixedRW(RR) using Round Robin device allocation demonstrates better performance than the other distributed policies. With FixedRW(RR), no data replication is needed. Future research work into management of parallel I/O includes: studying I/O scheduling policies; studying I/O of real applications to refine the application models described in this paper.

**Acknowledgements**

This research is supported by the Natural Sciences and Engineering Research Council of Canada and Carleton University. Help from Istabrak Abdul-Fatah in preparing the manuscript is gratefully acknowledged.

# References

[Corb93] P.F. Corbett, D.G. Feitelson, J.-P. Prost, S.J. Baylor, "Parallel Access to Files in the Vesta File System", Proc. Supercomputing '93 Conf., 1993, pp. 472-481.

[Cyph93] R. Cypher, P. Messina, "Architectural Requirements of Parallel Scientific Applications with Explicit Communication", Proc. International Symp. on Computer Architecture, 1993.

[Delr93] J.M. Del Rosario, R. Bordawekar, A. Choudhary, "Improved Parallel I/O via a Two-Phase Run-Time Access Strategy", ACM Computer Architecture News, Vol. 21, No. 5, December 1993, pp. 31-38.

[Delr94] J.M. Del Rosario, A. Choudhary, "High Performance I/O for Massively Parallel Computers", IEEE Computer, March 1994, pp. 59-68.

[Jain93] R. Jain, K. Somalwar, J. Werth, J.C. Browne, "Scheduling Parallel I/O Operations", ACM Computer Architecture News, Vol. 21, No. 5, December 1993, pp. 47-54.

[Kim86] M.Y. Kim, "Synchronized Disk Interleaving", IEEE Trans on Computers, vol 35, November 1986, pp. 978-988.

[Kotz94] D. Kotz, N. Nieuwejaar, "Dynamic File Access Characteristics of a Production Parallel Scientific Workload", Proc of Supercomputing '94, November 1994, pp. 640-649.

[Kotz95] D. Kotz, N. Nieuwejaar, et al.,"File-Access Characteristics of Parallel Scientific Workloads", Tech Report PCS-TR95-263, Dept. of Math. and Comp. Science, Dartmouth College, Hanover, U.S.A, 1995.

[Kwon96] P. Kwong, "Management of Parallel I/O in Multiprogrammed Parallel Systems", M. Eng Thesis, Carleton University, Ottawa, Canada. *To be available in the Fall of 1996.*

[Leut90] S. Leuttenegger and M. Vernon, "The Performance of Multiprogrammed Multiprocessor Scheduling Policies", Proc. 1990 ACM SIGMETRICS Conf. on Measurement and Modeling of Computer Systems, Boulder (CO), May 1990, pp. 226-236.College, Hanover, U.S.A.

[Livn87] M. Livny, "Multi-Disk Management Algorithms", Proc. 1988 ACM SIGMETRICS Conf. on Measurement and Modeling of Computer Systems, May 1987, pp. 69-77.

[Maju88] S. Majumdar, D.L. eager, and R.B. Bunt, "Scheduling in Multiprogrammed Parallel Systems", Proc 1988 ACM SIGMETRICS Conf on Measurement and Modeling of Computer Systems, Santa Fe, New Mexico, May 1988, pp. 104-113.

[Maju91] S.Majumdar, D.L.Eager and R.B.Bunt, "Characterization of Programs for Scheduling in Multiprogrammed Parallel Systems", Performance Evaluation, Vol. 13 (1991) Elsevier North-Holland.

[Maju94] S. Majumdar, Y.M. Leung, "Characterization of Applications with I/O for Processor Scheduling in Multiprogrammed Parallel Systems", Proc. Sixth IEEE Symp. on Parallel and Distributed Processing, Dallas, 1994, pp. 298-307.

[Maju95] S. Majumdar, F. Shad,"Characterization and Management of I/O on Multiprogrammed Parallel Systems", Proc. seventh IEEE symposium in Parallel & Distributed Processing, San Antonio, Oct. 1995.

[Patt88] D.A. Patterson, G. Gibson, R.H. Katz, "A Case for Redundant Arrays of Inexpensive Disks (RAID)", Proc. ACM SIGMOD Conference, June 1988, pp. 109-116.

[Patt94] Y.N. Patt, "The I/O Subsystem: A Candidate for Improvement", IEEE Computer, March 1994, pp. 15-16.

[Redd89] A.L.N. Reddy, P. Banerjee, "An Evaluation of Multiple-Disk I/O Systems", IEEE Trans. on Computers, Vol. 38, No. 12, December 1989, pp. 1680-1690.

[Sevc94] K.C. Sevcik, "Application Scheduling and Processor Allocation in Multiprogrammed Parallel Systems", Performance Evaluation, 1994.

# An Experimental Evaluation of the Parallel I/O Systems of the IBM SP and Intel Paragon Using a Production Application*

Rajeev Thakur, William Gropp, and Ewing Lusk

Mathematics and Computer Science Division
Argonne National Laboratory
9700 S. Cass Avenue
Argonne, IL 60439, USA
{thakur, gropp, lusk} @mcs.anl.gov

**Abstract.** We present the results of an experimental evaluation of the parallel I/O systems of the IBM SP and Intel Paragon using a real three-dimensional parallel application code. This application, developed by scientists at the University of Chicago, simulates the gravitational collapse of self-gravitating gaseous clouds. It performs parallel I/O by using library routines that we developed and optimized separately for the SP and Paragon. The I/O routines perform two-phase I/O and use the parallel file systems PIOFS on the SP and PFS on the Paragon. We studied the I/O performance for two different sizes of the application. In the small case, we found that I/O was much faster on the SP. In the large case, open, close, and read operations were only slightly faster, and seeks were significantly faster, on the SP; whereas, writes were slightly faster on the Paragon. The communication required within our I/O routines was faster on the Paragon in both cases. The highest read bandwidth obtained was 48 Mbytes/sec., and the highest write bandwidth obtained was 31.6 Mbytes/sec., both on the SP.

## 1 Introduction

It is widely recognized that, in addition to fast computation and communication, parallel machines must also provide fast parallel I/O. Researchers have proposed many different types of architectures and file systems for parallel I/O, a few of which are being used in current-generation parallel machines. There is no consensus, however, as to what is the best type of parallel I/O architecture or parallel file system.

---

* This work was supported by the Mathematical, Information, and Computational Sciences Division subprogram of the Office of Computational and Technology Research, U.S. Department of Energy, under Contract W-31-109-Eng-38; and by the Scalable I/O Initiative, a multiagency project funded by the Advanced Research Projects Agency (contract number DABT63-94-C-0049), the Department of Energy, the National Aeronautics and Space Administration, and the National Science Foundation.

To better understand this issue, we evaluated the performance of the parallel I/O systems of two different state-of-the-art parallel machines, with a real application workload. The two machines we considered are the IBM SP at Argonne National Laboratory and the Intel Paragon at Caltech. These machines are also the two testbeds for the Scalable I/O Initiative[2]. The application we used is a three-dimensional production parallel code developed by scientists at the University of Chicago to study the gravitational collapse of self-gravitating gaseous clouds. The application performs parallel I/O by using library routines that we developed and optimized separately for the SP and Paragon. We instrumented the I/O routines, ran two different sizes of the application on both systems, and analyzed the resulting trace files. We found that, in the small case, all I/O operations (open, close, read, write, seek) were much faster on the SP. In the large case, open, close, and read operations were only slightly faster, and seeks were significantly faster, on the SP; whereas, writes were slightly faster on the Paragon. The communication required within our parallel I/O routines was faster on the Paragon in both cases.

The rest of this paper is organized as follows. Section 2 provides an overview of related work. Section 3 describes the configurations of the two machines, the application, and the parallel I/O routines used in the application. Section 4 provides details of the experiments performed. We present performance results in Section 5 and draw overall conclusions in Section 6.

## 2 Related Work

We discuss related work in the area of I/O characterization of parallel applications and performance evaluation of parallel file systems.

Nieuwejaar et al. [17] performed a tracing study of all file-related activity on the Intel iPSC/860 at NASA Ames Research Center and the Thinking Machines CM-5 at the National Center for Supercomputing Applications. They found that file sizes were large, I/O request sizes were fairly small, data was accessed in sequence but with strides, and I/O was dominated by writes. Crandall et al. [7] analyzed the I/O characteristics of three parallel applications on the Intel Paragon at Caltech. They found a wide variety of access patterns, including both read-intensive and write-intensive phases, large as well as small request sizes, and both sequential and irregular access patterns. Baylor and Wu [3] studied the I/O characteristics of four parallel applications on an IBM SP using the Vesta parallel file system. They found I/O request rates on the order of hundreds of requests per second, mainly small request sizes, and strong temporal and spatial locality. Acharya et al. [1] report their experience in tuning the performance of four applications on an IBM SP. Del Rosario and Choudhary [9] provide an informal summary of the I/O requirements of several Grand Challenge applications.

Researchers have also studied the performance of parallel file systems. Bordawekar et al. [4] performed a detailed performance evaluation of the Concurrent

---

[2] See http://www.cacr.caltech.edu/SIO/ for information on the Scalable I/O Initiative

File System (CFS) on the Intel Touchstone Delta. Kwan and Reed [15] measured the performance of the CM-5 Scalable File System. Feitelson et al. [10] studied the performance of the Vesta file system. Nieuwejaar and Kotz [16] present performance results for the Galley parallel file system. Several researchers have measured the performance of the Concurrent File System (CFS) on the Intel iPSC/2 and iPSC/860 hypercubes [5, 11, 18].

In an earlier work, we studied the I/O characteristics of a different application on the SP and Paragon [20]. For that study, we used a two-dimensional astrophysics application that performs sequential I/O (only processor 0 performs all I/O) using the Unitree file system on the SP and the PFS file system on the Paragon. In this paper, we consider a completely different three-dimensional application that is much more I/O intensive and performs parallel I/O (two-phase I/O) using the parallel file systems PIOFS on the SP and PFS on the Paragon.

# 3 Machine and Application Description

We describe the SP and Paragon systems, the application, and the parallel I/O routines used in the application.

## 3.1 Machine Specifications

We used the IBM SP at Argonne National Laboratory and the Intel Paragon at Caltech, which are the two testbeds for the Scalable I/O Initiative.

**IBM SP.** The SP at Argonne was configured as follows during our experiments. There were 120 compute nodes, each an RS/6000 Model 370 with 128 Mbytes of memory, and eight I/O server nodes, each an RS/6000 Model 970 with 256 Mbytes of memory. All 128 nodes were interconnected by a high-performance omega switch. The operating system on each node was AIX 3.2.5. IBM's parallel file system PIOFS provided parallel access to files. Each I/O server node had 3 Gbytes of local SCSI disks, resulting in a total PIOFS storage capacity of 24 Gbytes. Users were not allowed to run compute jobs on the I/O server nodes.

PIOFS distributes a file across multiple I/O server nodes. A file is logically organized as a collection of *cells*: a cell is a piece of the file stored on a particular server node. A file is divided into a number of *basic striping units* (BSUs), which are assigned to cells in a round-robin manner. Cells in turn are assigned to server nodes in a round-robin manner. The default number of cells is equal to the number of server nodes, and the default BSU size is 32 Kbytes.

**Intel Paragon.** The Paragon at Caltech was configured as follows during our experiments. There were 512 compute nodes and 16 I/O nodes, each an Intel i860/XP microprocessor with 32 Mbytes of memory. The nodes were connected by a two-dimensional mesh interconnection network. The operating system on the machine was Paragon/OSF R1.3.3. Each I/O node was connected to a 4.8-Gbyte RAID-3 disk array, and Intel's Parallel File System (PFS) provided parallel access to files. As on the SP, users were not allowed to run compute jobs on the I/O nodes.

A PFS file system consists of one or more *stripe directories*. Each stripe directory is usually the mount point of a separate Unix file system. Just as a RAID subsystem collects several disks into a unit that behaves like a single large disk, a PFS file system collects several file systems into a unit that behaves like a single large file system. PFS files are divided into smaller *stripe units* and distributed in a round-robin fashion across the stripe directories that make up the PFS file system. During our experiments, the Paragon had 16 stripe directories, and the default stripe unit was 64 Kbytes.

## 3.2 The Application

The application we used is a production parallel code developed at the University of Chicago. This application simulates the gravitational collapse of self-gravitating gaseous clouds due to a process known as Jeans instability. This process is the fundamental mechanism through which intergalactic gases condense to form stars. The application solves the equations of compressible hydrodynamics with the inclusion of self-gravity. It uses the piecewise parabolic method [6] to solve the compressible Euler equations and a multigrid elliptic solver to compute the gravitational potential.

The application uses the Chameleon library for communication [13], which is portable. Originally, the application also used the Chameleon library for I/O [12], but we found that the Chameleon I/O routines were not well optimized for parallel I/O on the SP and Paragon. We therefore wrote special I/O routines, described below, with the same interface as the Chameleon I/O library, but separately optimized for the SP and Paragon. The application performs all I/O via calls to these optimized routines; therefore, it is directly portable across the two machines. The application is written in Fortran, whereas the I/O routines are in C.

The application uses several three-dimensional arrays that are distributed in a (block,block,block) fashion among processors. All arrays fit in memory, but every few iterations, several arrays must be written to files for three purposes: data analysis, checkpointing (restart), and visualization. The application reads data only while being restarted from a previously created checkpoint. The storage order of data in all files is required to be the same as it would be if the program were run on a single processor.

The data-analysis file begins with six variables (real numbers) that have the same values across all processors, followed by six arrays appended one after another. The arrays are stored in column-major (Fortran) order. The restart file has the same structure as the data-analysis file. The application performs all computation in double precision, but writes single-precision data to the data-analysis and restart files. The visualization data is written to four separate files. Each of those files begins with six variables (real numbers) that have the same value across all processors, followed by one array of character data. The application creates one restart file in all and new data-analysis and visualization files in each dump.

## 3.3 Parallel I/O Routines

Recall that, in this application, three-dimensional arrays are distributed among processors in a (block,block,block) manner. Each array must be written to a single file such that the data in the file corresponds to the global array in column-major (Fortran) order. The original Chameleon I/O routines perform this task by having all processors send their data to processor 0, and only processor 0 actually writes data to the file. This approach is inefficient for two reasons: the sequential nature of I/O and the communication bottleneck caused by the all-to-one communication pattern.

To overcome these limitations, we wrote new routines that have the same interface as the Chameleon I/O routines, but perform I/O in parallel from all processors. Since the interface did not change, we did not have to change the application code. The new routines use PIOFS on the SP and PFS on the Paragon. We optimized the routines separately for the two systems; for example, on the Paragon, the routines use the **gopen()** call for faster opens and the **M_ASYNC** mode for faster reads and writes.

In this application, the local array of each processor is not located contiguously in the file. Therefore, an attempt by any processor to read/write its local array directly would result in too many small read/write requests. We eliminated this problem by using two-phase I/O [8], a technique for reading/writing distributed arrays efficiently. In two-phase I/O, as the name suggests, a distributed array is read or written in two phases. For writing a distributed array, in the first phase, the array is redistributed among processors such that, in the new distribution, each processor's local data is located contiguously in the file. In the second phase, processors write their local data at appropriate locations in the file concurrently, with a single write operation each. To read a distributed array, each processor reads a contiguous block in the first phase and then redistributes it in the second phase. This method eliminates the need for several small I/O requests and also has a fairly balanced all-to-many communication pattern.

Figure 1 illustrates how our I/O routines use two-phase I/O to read/write a three-dimensional array distributed as (block,block,block). The write routine first redistributes an array from (block,block,block) to (*,*,block). In other words, after the first phase, the array is distributed along the third dimension only. In the second phase, all processors write their local data simultaneously to the file. Conversely, in the read routine, all processors first read their local data assuming a (*,*,block) distribution and then redistribute it to the required (block,block,block) distribution.

We note that the PIOFS file system also supports logical partitioning of files. A processor can specify a logical view of its local array in the global array file and then read/write the local array with a single operation, even though the local

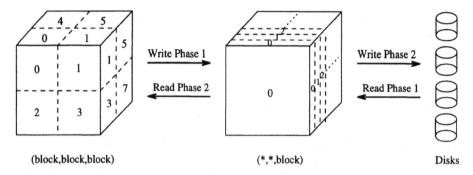

**Fig. 1.** Two-phase I/O for reading/writing a three-dimensional array distributed as (block,block,block) and stored in column-major (Fortran) order

array may not be located contiguously in the file. However, we found that this feature can be mainly used for arrays distributed in two dimensions (including three-dimensional arrays distributed in two dimensions). We were unable to use it in this application, because the arrays are distributed in three dimensions. Therefore, we used our two-phase I/O routines even on the SP.

The application also requires six variables (real numbers), with the same values across all processors, to be written in each dump and also read during restart. We wrote these variables by collecting all of them into a single buffer on processor 0 and then writing the buffer to the file, from processor 0 only, in a single operation. We read the variables by reading all of them in a single operation from processor 0 only and then broadcasting them to other processors.

## 4 Details of Experiments

To study the I/O behavior of the application, we instrumented the I/O routines by using the Pablo instrumentation library [2, 19]. We instrumented all open, close, read, write, and seek calls, and also all communication required within the I/O routines. We ran the instrumented code on both the SP and Paragon and collected trace files. The traces were visualized and analyzed by using Upshot [14], a tool for studying parallel program behavior.

The application only performs writes except when restarting from a checkpoint. To be able to measure the read performance as well, we restarted the code from a checkpoint each time. The application is iterative, and a complete run to convergence could take more than 10,000 iterations. To keep the trace files manageable, we ran the code only for a few iterations, as specified below. The I/O behavior in the remaining iterations is assumed to be similar to that in the first few iterations.

We considered two sizes of the application:

1. **Small.** For this case, we used a $128 \times 128 \times 64$ mesh on 8 processors. We restarted the code from a previously created restart file and ran it for 20

iterations, with all dumps performed every five iterations. The data analysis and restart files were 24 Mbytes each, and the visualization files were 1 Mbyte each.

2. **Large.** For this case, we used a $256 \times 256 \times 128$ mesh on 64 processors. Since only 120 compute nodes were available on the SP and the application runs only on a power-of-two number of processors, we could run it on a maximum of 64 processors on the SP. For a fair comparison, we used the same number on the Paragon. We restarted the code from a previously created restart file and ran it for five iterations, with all dumps performed after the fifth iteration. The data analysis and restart files were 192 Mbytes each, and the visualization files were 8 Mbytes each.

During our experiments, we did not have exclusive use of the system. To eliminate spurious results due to interference from other users' jobs and system-related activities, we ran the application several times and recorded only the run which took the least time.

## 5   Performance Results

We first discuss the results on the SP, followed by the results on the Paragon, and then compare the results on the two systems.

### 5.1   Results on SP

Table 1 shows the total number and total time for each type of I/O operation on the SP for the small case. We calculated the average time per processor as the total time across all processors divided by the number of processors. There were 200 open and close calls. The open calls were fairly expensive; close calls were not. There were 1225 seek calls that took a total time of 0.052 sec. In other words, the time for an individual seek operation was almost negligible. There were a small number of read operations during the restart. Write operations dominated the I/O, as the application is write intensive. Note that the write timings represent the time taken for the write calls to return. Data may or may not have reached the disks at the end of each write call, depending on the caching policy used by the file system. Communication for I/O (that is, the communication performed within our I/O routines) took even more time than the write operations. This was not the case on the Paragon, however, as we discuss in Section 5.2.

Table 2 shows the distribution of the sizes of individual read and write operations in the small case. Most of the reads and writes were large, since we used two-phase I/O. The few small requests were due to the reading and writing of six variables at the beginning of files. As explained in Section 3.3, these variables were read/written in a single operation by processor 0 only. The aggregate read bandwidth across all processors, computed as the total data read by all processors divided by the average read time per processor, was 48 Mbytes/sec. The aggregate write bandwidth, computed similarly, was 31.6 Mbytes/sec. We guess

**Table 1.** I/O operations on the SP for the small case—128 × 128 × 64 mesh on 8 processors, 20 iterations

| Operation | Total Count (all procs.) | Total Time (sec.) (all procs.) | Average Time (sec.) (per proc.) |
|---|---|---|---|
| Open | 200 | 31.35 | 3.919 |
| Close | 200 | 1.693 | 0.217 |
| Read | 49 | 4.001 | 0.500 |
| Write | 536 | 52.67 | 6.584 |
| Seek | 1225 | 0.052 | 0.006 |
| Communication (for I/O) | 5608 | 83.39 | 10.42 |

**Table 2.** Details of read and write operations on the SP for the small case

| Operation | Size Distribution | | | Total Data Transferred (MB) | Aggregate BW (MB/sec.) |
|---|---|---|---|---|---|
| | 24 B | 128 KB | 512 KB | | |
| Read | 1 | 0 | 48 | ≈ 24 | 48.00 |
| Write | 24 | 128 | 384 | ≈ 208 | 31.59 |

that the file system may be using a read-modify-write algorithm to implement write operations, resulting in the lower write bandwidth.

Tables 3 and 4 show the results for the large case on the SP. The overall trend in the results was similar to that in the small case. Open operations were again very expensive. Close operations took a small amount of time, and seek operations took negligible time. The most expensive operations were communication for I/O and write. The sizes of individual read and write operations were the same as in the small case: although the mesh size was eight times larger, the number of processors was also eight times larger. The aggregate read bandwidth (33.9 Mbytes/sec.) and the aggregate write bandwidth (17.4 Mbytes/sec.) were both lower than in the small case. The lower I/O bandwidth may be because, in the large case, the ratio of compute nodes to I/O server nodes was 8 : 1, whereas, in the small case, the ratio was 1 : 1.

## 5.2 Results on Paragon

Tables 5 and 6 show the results for the small case on the Paragon. The counts and sizes of I/O operations were the same as on the SP. Opens were very expensive; close and seek operations were inexpensive. Communication for I/O took less time than write operations, contrary to that on the SP. The aggregate read bandwidth was 28.6 Mbytes/sec., and the aggregate write bandwidth was 17.1 Mbytes/sec. As on the SP, the write bandwidth was lower than the read bandwidth.

**Table 3.** I/O operations on the SP for the large case—256 × 256 × 128 mesh on 64 processors, 5 iterations

| Operation | Total Count (all procs.) | Total Time (sec.) (all procs.) | Average Time (sec.) (per proc.) |
|---|---|---|---|
| Open | 448 | 358.5 | 5.601 |
| Close | 448 | 26.96 | 0.421 |
| Read | 385 | 362.5 | 5.664 |
| Write | 1030 | 1533 | 23.95 |
| Seek | 3235 | 0.138 | 0.002 |
| Communication (for I/O) | 109888 | 2142 | 33.47 |

**Table 4.** Details of read and write operations on the SP for the large case

| Operation | Size Distribution | | | Total Data Transferred (MB) | Aggregate BW (MB/sec.) |
|---|---|---|---|---|---|
| | 24 B | 128 KB | 512 KB | | |
| Read | 1 | 0 | 384 | ≈ 192 | 33.90 |
| Write | 6 | 256 | 768 | ≈ 416 | 17.37 |

**Table 5.** I/O operations on the Paragon for the small case

| Operation | Total Count (all procs.) | Total Time (sec.) (all procs.) | Average Time (sec.) (per proc.) |
|---|---|---|---|
| Open | 200 | 90.37 | 11.29 |
| Close | 200 | 7.586 | 0.948 |
| Read | 49 | 6.712 | 0.839 |
| Write | 536 | 97.16 | 12.15 |
| Seek | 1225 | 6.938 | 0.867 |
| Communication (for I/O) | 5608 | 70.17 | 8.771 |

**Table 6.** Details of read and write operations on the Paragon for the small case

| Operation | Size Distribution | | | Total Data Transferred (MB) | Aggregate BW (MB/sec.) |
|---|---|---|---|---|---|
| | 24 B | 128 KB | 512 KB | | |
| Read | 1 | 0 | 48 | ≈ 24 | 28.61 |
| Write | 24 | 128 | 384 | ≈ 208 | 17.12 |

Tables 7 and 8 show the results for the large case on the Paragon. The overall trend in the results was the same as in the small case. Opens were again very expensive. The aggregate read bandwidth (33.6 Mbytes/sec.) and the aggregate write bandwidth (18.6 Mbytes/sec.) were higher than in the small case, contrary to that on the SP. The reason may be that the Paragon had more I/O nodes (16) to service requests from 64 compute nodes.

**Table 7.** I/O operations on the Paragon for the large case

| Operation | Total Count (all procs.) | Total Time (sec.) (all procs.) | Average Time (sec.) (per proc.) |
|---|---|---|---|
| Open | 448 | 402.5 | 6.289 |
| Close | 448 | 36.68 | 0.573 |
| Read | 385 | 365.7 | 5.714 |
| Write | 1030 | 1429 | 22.33 |
| Seek | 3235 | 68.97 | 1.078 |
| Communication (for I/O) | 109888 | 1020 | 15.94 |

**Table 8.** Details of read and write operations on the Paragon for the large case

| Operation | Size Distribution | | | Total Data Transferred (MB) | Aggregate BW (MB/sec.) |
|---|---|---|---|---|---|
| | 24 B | 128 KB | 512 KB | | |
| Read | 1 | 0 | 384 | ≈ 192 | 33.60 |
| Write | 6 | 256 | 768 | ≈ 416 | 18.63 |

### 5.3  Comparison of SP and Paragon Results

In the small case, all I/O operations (open, close, read, write, and seek) were much slower on the Paragon. The aggregate read and write bandwidths on the Paragon were 60% and 55% of the bandwidths on the SP, respectively. However, the communication required within the I/O routines was faster on the Paragon.

In the large case, open, close, and read operations took only slightly longer on the Paragon. Seeks took significantly longer on the Paragon. On the other hand, writes were slightly faster, and communication for I/O was twice faster, on the Paragon.

On both machines, the time for opening common files from all processors was very high in both the small and large cases. We do not know the reason for the high open time, since it is related to the underlying implementation of the PIOFS and PFS file systems. On the SP, the read and write bandwidths obtained were higher in the small case, whereas, on the Paragon, they were higher in the large case, possibly because there were 16 I/O nodes on the Paragon versus only 8 on the SP.

## 6  Conclusions

We have presented the results of an experimental evaluation of the parallel I/O systems of the IBM SP and Intel Paragon using a production parallel application. We found that the relative performance of the two systems depends on the problem size. For the small case, all I/O operations were much faster on the SP. For the large case, open, close, and read operations were only slightly faster, and seeks were considerably faster, on the SP. Writes, however, were slightly faster on the Paragon. In both cases, communication for I/O was faster on the Paragon.

We note that the results in this paper are specific to the I/O access pattern of this application and should not be interpreted as a general performance comparison of the two systems. For some other access patterns, the results may be different. We also note that the results are for the particular hardware and software configurations specified in Section 3.1.

In all our experiments on both systems, we found that the time for opening common files from all processors was very high. Therefore, we recommend that parallel-file-system designers must also aim to reduce file-open time, in addition to reducing read and write times.

### Acknowledgments

We thank Andrea Malagoli for giving us the source code of the application and Ruth Aydt for helping us understand how to use Pablo.

## References

1. A. Acharya, M. Uysal, R. Bennett, A. Mendelson, M. Beynon, J. Hollingsworth, J. Saltz, and A. Sussman. Tuning the Performance of I/O Intensive Parallel Applications. In *Proceedings of Fourth Workshop on Input/Output in Parallel and Distributed Systems*, pages 15–27, May 1996.
2. R. Aydt. A User's Guide to Pablo I/O Instrumentation. Technical report, Dept. of Computer Science, University of Illinois at Urbana-Champaign, December 1994.
3. S. Baylor and C. Wu. Parallel I/O Workload Characteristics Using Vesta. In R. Jain, J. Werth, and J. Browne, editors, *Input/Output in Parallel and Distributed Computer Systems*, chapter 7, pages 167–185. Kluwer Academic Publishers, 1996.
4. R. Bordawekar, A. Choudhary, and J. del Rosario. An Experimental Performance Evaluation of Touchstone Delta Concurrent File System. In *Proceedings of the 7th ACM International Conference on Supercomputing*, pages 367–376, July 1993.

5. D. Bradley and D. Reed. Performance of the Intel iPSC/2 Input/Output System. In *Fourth Conference on Hypercube Concurrent Computers and Applications*, pages 141–144, 1989.

6. P. Colella and P. Woodward. The Piecewise Parabolic Method (PPM) for Gas-Dynamical Simulations. *Journal of Computational Physics*, 54(1):174–201, April 1984.

7. P. Crandall, R. Aydt, A. Chien, and D. Reed. Input-Output Characteristics of Scalable Parallel Applications. In *Proceedings of Supercomputing '95*, December 1995.

8. J. del Rosario, R. Bordawekar, and A. Choudhary. Improved Parallel I/O via a Two-Phase Runtime Access Strategy. In *Proceedings of the Workshop on I/O in Parallel Computer Systems at IPPS '93*, pages 56–70, April 1993.

9. J. del Rosario and A. Choudhary. High Performance I/O for Parallel Computers: Problems and Prospects. *IEEE Computer*, pages 59–68, March 1994.

10. D. Feitelson, P. Corbett, and J. Prost. Performance of the Vesta Parallel File System. In *Proceedings of the Ninth International Parallel Processing Symposium*, pages 150–158, April 1995.

11. J. French, T. Pratt, and M. Das. Performance Measurement of the Concurrent File System of the Intel iPSC/2 Hypercube. *Journal of Parallel and Distributed Computing*, 17(1–2):115–121, January and February 1993.

12. N. Galbreath, W. Gropp, and D. Levine. Applications-Driven Parallel I/O. In *Proceedings of Supercomputing '93*, pages 462–471, November 1993.

13. W. Gropp and B. Smith. Chameleon Parallel Programming Tools User's Manual. Technical Report ANL–93/23, Mathematics and Computer Science Division, Argonne National Laboratory, March 1993.

14. V. Herrarte and E. Lusk. Studying Parallel Program Behavior with Upshot. Technical Report ANL–91/15, Mathematics and Computer Science Division, Argonne National Laboratory, August 1991.

15. T. Kwan and D. Reed. Performance of the CM-5 Scalable File System. In *Proceedings of the 8th ACM International Conference on Supercomputing*, pages 156–165, July 1994.

16. N. Nieuwejaar and D. Kotz. Performance of the Galley Parallel File System. In *Proceedings of Fourth Workshop on Input/Output in Parallel and Distributed Systems*, pages 83–94, May 1996.

17. N. Nieuwejaar, D. Kotz, A. Purakayastha, C. Ellis, and M. Best. File-Access Characteristics of Parallel Scientific Workloads. Technical Report PCS–TR95–263, Dept. of Computer Science, Dartmouth College, August 1995.

18. B. Nitzberg. Performance of the iPSC/860 Concurrent File System. Technical Report RND-92-020, NAS Systems Division, NASA Ames, December 1992.

19. D. Reed, R. Aydt, R. Noe, P. Roth, K. Shields, B. Schwartz, and L. Tavera. Scalable Performance Analysis: The Pablo Performance Analysis Environment. In *Proceedings of the Scalable Parallel Libraries Conference*, pages 104–113, October 1993.

20. R. Thakur, E. Lusk, and W. Gropp. I/O Characterization of a Portable Astrophysics Application on the IBM SP and Intel Paragon. Technical Report MCS–P534–0895, Mathematics and Computer Science Division, Argonne National Laboratory, Revised October 1995.

# Switcherland - A Scalable Interconnection Structure for Distributed Computing

Hans Eberle

Swiss Federal Institute of Technology (ETH), Institute of Computer Systems,
CH-8092 Zurich, Switzerland
eberle@inf.ethz.ch

**Abstract**: This paper describes a scalable interconnection structure for distributed computing systems. The interconnection structure is scalable in that it can serve as an I/O interconnection structure of a workstation as well as a network interconnection structure for a group or cluster of workstations.

Switcherland implements a communication model based on a distributed shared memory architecture. With it, local communication within a workstation and remote communication within a cluster of workstations translate to load and store operations which are applied to a distributed memory which resides in a single address space.

Switcherland offers quality of service (QoS) in that memory can be accessed at guaranteed rates and access times are bounded. This feature is an essential prerequisite for the integration of video and audio into a workstation environment and allows systems to treat video and audio like standard data types.

**Keywords:** interconnection structure, quality of service, distributed shared memory, loosely-coupled parallel computing.

## 1. Introduction

Current workstation architectures provide only limited support for applications that manipulate time-dependent data such as video and audio. The main shortcomings are I/O bandwidth limitations and a lack of real-time guarantees.

Eventually, processors will treat video and audio data like standard data types since they will be powerful enough to do operations such as compression and decompression without the help of special-purpose hardware. A recent trend in processor implementations is to add instructions to speed up software compression and decompression. An example of such an implementation is the PA-RISC 7100LC CPU chip [9] which, for example, allows to perform MPEG decompression in software with a resolution of 352 by 240 pixels at 30 frames per second in real time. In addition to powerful processors, interconnection structures will be required that can handle the data rates of uncompressed video and audio. To illustrate the bandwidth required for processing video data, broadcast TV standards are considered. CCIR 601 specifies the transmission of video signals with a maximum resolution of 864 by 625 pixels and a frame rate of 25 frames per second. With a pixel depth of 16 bits this corresponds to a continuous data rate of 21 MByte/s. CCIR 709 specifies the transmission of high resolution video signals at a resolution of 1920 by 1080 pixels and a frame rate of 24 frames per second. At 16 bits per pixel this corresponds to a data rate of 100 MByte/s. These numbers have to be multiplied by the number of video streams that are processed simultaneously. To contrast these numbers with the bandwidth provided by modern busses, we take the PCI bus as an example. The 32-bit PCI bus, which is the fastest standard workstation bus in use today, is specified at a peak transfer rate of 132 MByte/s. The numbers presented clearly demonstrate the limitations of current bus-based systems.

An even more serious problem when processing time-dependent data is the lack of communication channels with guaranteed bandwidths and bounded end-to-end transmission delays. Not being able to predict the time it takes to transfer data from one system component to another makes the use of current architectures for audio and video applications unsatisfactory. In such a system, data is produced, transmitted and reproduced at unpredictable rates, with high delay jitter and with possible loss of data.

Recent developments in local area networks recognize the need for real-time support. So-called asynchronous transfer mode (ATM) networks distinguish between two classes of traffic: variable bit rate (VBR) traffic and constant bit rate (CBR) traffic. VBR traffic refers to the transfer of datagrams and CBR traffic refers to the transfer of time-dependent data. While VBR traffic is handled in the traditional way, CBR traffic requires novel mechanisms for computer network architectures. The main additional mechanisms required are connections with reserved bandwidths and guaranteed latency bounds. Unfortunately, the real-time properties of ATM networks do not extend into the workstations connected to them. The real-time guarantees provided by the network are lost as soon as the data enters the workstations. One of our goals is to investigate how some of the ideas developed for ATM networks can be applied to workstation interconnection structures.

One way to provide real-time guarantees when transferring data inside a workstation is to also use an ATM network switch to interconnect the components of the workstation system. This idea was investigated by the Desk-Area Network project at the University of Cambridge [4]. The Desk-Area Network, actually, carries this idea to the extreme in that ATM switches are not only used as an I/O interconnection structure but also as a memory interconnection structure. A typical node connected to this interconnection structure may contain a processor, memory or an I/O device. A processor node does not contain any local memory except for some cache memory, and has to use the switch interconnection structure to access memory.

The use of ATM switches to connect the components of a workstation might become attractive since the increasing popularity of this technology could result in the availability of low-priced switching equipment. Technically, however, ATM switching technology is not well-suited for this task since its design goals are different. Important considerations when designing a network architecture are scalability and tolerance to malfunctioning links and nodes. ATM networks are designed to support large numbers of nodes spread out over a large geographical area. Transmission faults have to be expected frequently since links can be long. Further, few assumptions can be made about the nodes since interoperability among products of different vendors is important. Therefore, supervisory functions are in place to ensure that the nodes function properly and, in particular, do not exceed their resource allocations.

An interconnection architecture designed for connecting the components of a workstation or a small cluster of workstations has to fulfill less stringent requirements. While ATM networks can support thousands of nodes, a cluster interconnection structure only consists of a few hundred nodes. While the links of an ATM network might span a few kilometers, the length of the links found in a cluster of workstations is limited to a few meters. Further, in a cluster it is legitimate to assume that the nodes comply with the rules that say how the network may be used. For example, while the switches of an ATM network ensure that the nodes do not exceed their bandwidth or buffer allocations, the switches of a cluster interconnection structure can trust the nodes in that they do not have to check whether the nodes keep their resource allocations. Switcherland is tailored specifically towards a cluster of a small number of trusted nodes, thus, the implementation can be simpler and cost less compared with an ATM-based interconnection structure.

In addition to the Desk-Area Network project, several other projects are exploring alternative interconnection structures. Other projects with goals similar to ours are the Scalable Coherent Interface [3], the Telegraphos system [7] and the TNet [5]. The common objective of these efforts is scalability and a simple communication model based on a distributed shared memory architecture. We are, however, not aware of any projects that try to provide QoS for such a communication model.

This paper describes the organization of the Switcherland interconnection structure. Section 2 gives an overview. Section 3 explains the main design decisions that underlie the Switcherland interconnection structure. Section 4 describes the implementation. Section 5 gives a short report on the status of the project. Finally, Section 6 contains some concluding remarks.

## 2. Overview

Figure 1 shows an example of a distributed computing system based on the Switcherland interconnection structure. A port of a switch (S) can be connected either to a *node* or to another switch. A node corresponds to a processor (P) with local memory (M) or to an I/O device (I/O). Examples of typical I/O devices are frame buffers and disk interfaces. As shown, a workstation can contain one or several switches.

The switches have two purposes. Within a workstation, they serve as an I/O interconnection structure and, within a cluster, they are used as a network interconnection structure. By using the same interconnection structure for inter- and intra-workstation communication the boundaries of the workstations are less clear than in a traditional networked system since the logical grouping of nodes can easily be different from the physical arrangement.

By cascading switches any arbitrary topology is possible. The aggregate bandwidth of such a system can be many times the bandwidth of a single switch. By adding switches and links, the aggregate bandwidth can be increased as required. Also, availability can be improved by adding redundant links and switches.

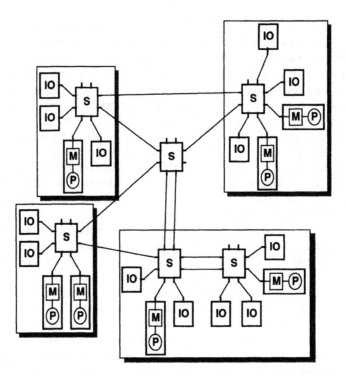

**Figure 1**: Topology of a Distributed Computing System

## 3. Design Decisions

This section describes the main design decisions that characterize the Switcherland interconnection structure.

### 3.1 Switches vs. Busses

In most workstation systems the components are interconnected by a single shared link or bus. The main attraction of the bus is its low cost and low complexity thanks to the use of a shared medium. The drawbacks are limited extensibility and scalability. The number of nodes is fixed and only short distances can be spanned. These limitations become even more evident at high speeds due to the electrical properties of busses. Further, the bandwidth is fixed and cannot be increased when new nodes are added. A possible alternative to a bus is an interconnection structure based on switches. Since such an interconnection structure uses multiple links rather than one shared link, it cannot compete in terms of cost. However, an interconnection structure based on switches is attractive because of its high bandwidth, scalability and availability.

Compared with busses, switches provide higher bandwidth because multiple links can be used simultaneously. Since switches can be clustered easily, the aggregate bandwidth can be many times the link bandwidth and also many times the switch bandwidth.

Availability is higher for a switch than for a bus since there is no single point of failure. With a bus all communication fails if the shared link fails. If a link of a switch-based interconnection structure fails, typically only a subset of the nodes is affected. Further, redundant links can be added to achieve higher availability.

## 3.2 Serial Links

Recently, several serial I/O interconnection structures have been proposed. The most prominent examples are the Serial Storage Architecture, the FireWire and FibreChannel. These serial interconnection structures provide data rates in the range of 100 Mbit/s up to 1 Gbit/s. They are mainly intended for interconnecting distributed storage systems. Simple packaging and, with it, low cost are the main motivation behind these proposals.

Serial point-to-point links have some advantageous properties when compared with parallel shared links. A point-to-point link can be implemented as a nearly ideal transmission line with a defined load. With a shared link this is not possible since the load varies with the number of nodes connected. The result are reflections which have to be compensated by reducing the transfer rate. Further, transmitting data in parallel causes skew since the propagation delays of signals traveling along several parallel wires will vary slightly. Again, this effect has to be compensated by reducing the transfer rate.

Since parallel links need more wires and wider connectors, they are more expensive and also less reliable than serial links.

Switcherland uses serial links only. All switch ports are serial and serial point-to-point links are used for connecting switches with other switches as well as for linking switches with nodes. Twisted-pair cabling is used for the short links, which are typically found inside a workstation. Longer links could be implemented with fiber cables, though the prototype system uses metallic cables only. Switcherland links implement the physical layer of the FibreChannel specifications. To give an idea of the physical span of a FibreChannel link, the specifications give an operating range of up to 25 m for coax cabling and up to 10 km for fiber cabling at a data rate of 1062.5 Mbit/s [8]. For twisted-par cables the range is 50 m at a data rate of 265.625 Mbit/s.

## 3.3 Load/Store Architecture

Switcherland implements a load/store architecture. This means that local communication within a workstation and remote communication within a cluster of workstations translate to load and store or read and write operations. These operations are applied to a distributed memory which resides in a single address space. With it, the mechanisms to access local and remote memory are the same giving the programmer a uniform model for inter- and intra-workstation communication. Of course, the latency differs with local accesses taking a fraction of the time required for accesses to remote memory.

While it is not our goal to design a tightly-coupled architecture for running parallel applications, we want to provide for a modest amount of support for running distributed applications. For this purpose, two mechanisms are provided: a synchronization primitive in the form of an atomic *compare_and_swap* operation and a local *flush* operation.

The atomic compare_and_swap operation corresponds to a pair of operations, a read followed by a conditional write operation. These operations are executed atomically without being interrupted by other memory operations. While the read operation is executed unconditionally, the write operation is executed only if the value returned by the read operation is equal to an expected value. The compare_and_swap operation is typically used to implement critical regions.

The flush operation is used to synchronize the nodes' memories in that it propagates all outstanding write operations to memory. The flush operation is a local operation, that is, if a memory location is shared by several processors, every processor has to locally execute this operation. Looking at a link interface of a node there will, typically, be outstanding write operations that either have been requested but not acknowledged or have not yet been requested since they are still waiting in a write buffer. Of course, the possibility to allow several outstanding write requests and the availability of write buffers are dependent on the actual implementation of the link interface. The flush operation causes the link interface to empty the write buffers in that the corresponding requests are sent to remote memory. The flush operation terminates after all write operations have terminated.

It should be noted that without additional precautions the scheme described can only be used to synchronize shared memory that is uncached. Switcherland provides no hardware support for cache consistency. This means that shared data has to be uncached or that, if shared data is cached, a consistency protocol realized in software is needed. In its simplest form such a protocol implements an ownership protocol in that only one processor is allowed to cache a memory location.

It is worth noting that the described mechanisms are required not only for running distributed applications on several processors, but also for efficiently implementing DMA transfers between an I/O device and a processor. The handshaking between the nodes constituting the DMA source and destination use compare_and_swap operations and the transfer of the data is made visible with the help of a flush operation.

We have chosen a rather simple addressing scheme for accessing local as well as remote memory. Memory addresses are physical addresses which are split into two parts whereby the higher address bits identify a node and the lower address bits represent the address offset within the node.

## 3.4 Transfer Types

The data transferred by the load and store operations forms either CBR or VBR traffic. The traffic classes differ in the guarantees provided by the switches. For CBR traffic, the switches provide bandwidth guarantees and bounded transmission delays. For VBR traffic, a certain amount of buffering is preallocated in the switches, thereby guaranteeing that cells belonging to this class are never dropped due to overflowing buffers. When a switch becomes heavily loaded, VBR cells may be arbitrarily delayed without an upper bound while CBR connections remain unaffected.

Typically, CBR connections are used for transferring isochronous data. Transfers of such data require delivery times which are bounded by a minimum and a maximum delay. An example is the transmission of video frames at a given rate. VBR connections are used for transmitting asynchronous data. The transfer of these data is characterized by variable delays. An example might be an interactive application with a user generating requests to read sectors on a disk. In this scenario, data is transmitted in bursts making it difficult to specify any bandwidth and latency requirements.

A request to reserve bandwidth can be translated into reserving buffer space. As will be shown in Section 4 the output ports of the switches contain separate buffer queues for VBR and CBR cells. To describe the bandwidth allocation scheme, we introduce the notion of a *frame* made up of $n$ *slots*. A slot corresponds to the time taken to transmit a cell. The number of slots in a frame is equal to the number of cell buffers in a CBR output queue and determines the granularity with which link bandwidth can be reserved. If $b$ is the total link bandwidth, bandwidth can be reserved in multiples of $b/n$. If an application successfully sets up a CBR connection with a reserved bandwidth $r \cdot b/n$, cells may be sent by the source at a maximum rate of $r$ cells every $n$ slots. Since CBR cells have priority over VBR cells when leaving the output buffer, it can be guaranteed that a CBR cell remains in the output buffer for at most $n$ slots.

| |
|---|
| 4-byte header |
|       15-bit connection identifier |
|       1-bit CBR/VBR |
|       4-bit command (read, write, |
|             compare_and_swap) |
|       1-bit request/acknowledge |
|       1-bit acknowledge requested/ |
|             acknowledge not requested |
|       4-bit payload length |
|       6-bit tag |
| 60-byte payload |

**Table 1**: Cell Format

## 3.5 Cell Format

Switcherland transfers cells, that is, small packets with a fixed length. Table 1 shows the cell format. Cells consist of a 4-byte *header* and a 60-byte *payload*. The information contained in the header is used mainly to determine the routing path and the memory operation. The routing path is given by the *connection identifier*, which is used by the switches to decide to which output port a cell has to be forwarded. Each output port contains separate buffer queues for CBR and VBR cells. The queue is chosen according to the *CBR/VBR* flag. The memory operation is specified by a *command* field. Three commands are currently supported: read, write and compare_and_swap. A memory operation translates into a *request* and an *acknowledge*. We say that requests are sent by *clients* and received by *servers*, while acknowledgments are sent by servers and received by clients. While the request of a read or compare_and_swap operation always demands an acknowledge, the write operation does so only optionally. This option exists for VBR write requests only, since CBR write operations are never acknowledged. In the case of VBR requests, the acknowledgment is used not only to transfer the result of an operation, but also to help the client decide whether an operation was successfully executed.

All operations operate on multiples of 32-bit words. The *payload length* field says how many words a write request wants to write and how many words a read request wants to read. The compare_and_swap operation always processes single words.

The *tag* field is used for flow control and error detection as is explained in more detail in Section 3.6.

We have omitted the inclusion of a checksum since the transmission code specified by the FibreChannel standard already provides good error detection capabilities. FibreChannel uses a DC-balanced 8B/10B code that transmits 8-bit characters as 10-bit sequences [11].

As shown, the length of the cells is 64 bytes. We want the cell length to be a power of two to allow for simple buffer management in the switches. Though ATM cells have a length of 53 bytes, there are no fundamental differences and, therefore, our cells can be viewed as ATM cells.

Transferring data in the form of cells with a fixed small size rather than with a variable, possibly large size is particularly advantageous when transferring time-dependent data at high data rates.

Choosing a fixed length mainly simplifies the hardware of the switches and the nodes. Fixed-length cells simplify the control logic and datapaths. The timing of control signals is fixed and datapaths can be allocated at fixed time intervals. With it, processing cells in a node or switch can be implemented with a pipelined hardware structure that can be operated at high data rates. Also, managing buffer memory is significantly simpler since buffer space can be split up into units with a fixed length. In addition, fixed-length cells allow for a simple bandwidth reservation scheme as has been shown in Section 3.4.

Choosing a small size reduces buffer space in the nodes. Little buffer space is needed since the data can be sent shortly after it was produced and since it can be consumed shortly after it was received. Further, a short forwarding delay results in a short end-to-end latency. This is of particular importance when transmitting audio and video data. In terms of bandwidth allocation, a small cell size is advantageous since it allows for a fine-grained bandwidth allocation scheme.

### 3.6 End-to-end Flow Control

Congestion which can possibly lead to the loss of data can be avoided by using flow control. Flow control is only required for preventing the loss of VBR cells. CBR cells cannot be lost since they are guaranteed to be forwarded by the switches with an upper bound on the forwarding delay. Our flow control scheme only prevents the switches and not the nodes from loosing VBR cells due to buffer overflow. The nodes are not covered by flow control since they are expected to be fast enough to keep up with the interconnection structure. Of course, the bandwidth and buffer allocations of the switches should be chosen according to the capabilities of the connected nodes.

Flow control is performed end-to-end and works as follows. Every flow-controlled connection uses a full-duplex path and every memory operation translates into a request and an acknowledge. For every request sent over a connection, an acknowledge is received. The bookkeeping required to manage the buffer allocations is rather simple. At connection set up time, a credit counter is initialized to $m$ whereby $m$ represents the number of buffers available along the path of this connection. Every time a request is sent, the credit counter is decremented, and every time an acknowledge is received, the counter is incremented. Requests can be sent as long as the value of the counter has not reached zero. With it, there can be at most $m$ outstanding requests.

For memory efficiency reasons, link-by-link flow control is, typically, not only used by LAN networks, but also by cluster interconnection structures. Examples are Myrinet [1], Telegraphos [7] and TNET [5]. We can use end-to-end flow control since we assume that the diameter of a Switcherland system is small, that is, that any path connecting two nodes includes up to ten switches only. With it, the round trip time for a connection can be kept short. This allows for a small window size that requires relatively few buffers in the switches.

Flow control is further simplified since we assume that the nodes can be trusted in the sense that they never exceed their bandwidth and buffer allocations. Therefore, the switches are not required to contain any mechanisms for enforcing these allocations.

Every cell carries a tag which is used to detect its loss. Every client keeps track of the outstanding requests that it has sent by tagging them with a unique identifier. When a server receives a request, it generates an acknowledgment that contains the tag received in the header of the request and sends it back to the client. With the receipt of the acknowledgment, the client knows that the request has been received by the server. If an outstanding request is not acknowledged for a certain amount of time, it is timed out causing an error handler implemented in software to be notified. The error handler then performs the appropriate actions such as the retransmission of the unacknowledged request or notifying the task that issued the request [10].

### 3.7 Table-based Routing

Before data can be transferred between a client and a server, a routing path needs to be set up. The path is set up by the client in that it programs the routing tables in the switches along the chosen routing path. Routing decisions in the switches are done by table lookup, which is a simple and fast hardware operation. The table is indexed with the connection identifier contained in the header of the cell. A table entry represents a port vector that specifies the output ports to which the cell has to be forwarded. By allowing a cell to be forwarded to several output ports simultaneously, multicast is realized in hardware with very low latency. Multicast is supported for CBR traffic only.

## 4. Switch Implementation

There are basically two ways to organize a switch. The difference is the location of the buffer memory. As shown in Figure 2 the buffers are either located near the input ports or near the output ports. The real difference between *input buffering* and *output buffering* is, however, not the location of the buffers since an output buffer could as well be seen as the input buffer of the downstream switch. It is the memory bandwidth required for implementing the buffers that differs. Assuming a $n$ by $n$ switch and a link bandwidth $b$ an input buffer needs to provide an input bandwidth $b$ and an output buffer needs to provide an input bandwidth $n \cdot b$ to not lose any data. Output buffers need to provide $n$ times as much input bandwidth as input buffers since at a given time data from all $n$ input ports can be forwarded to the same output port.

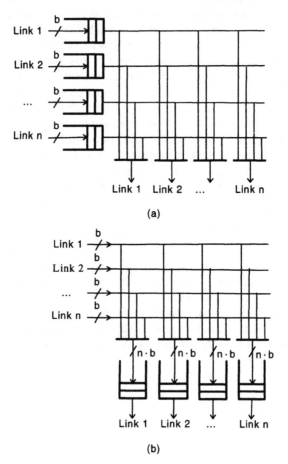

**Figure 2:** Input Buffering (a) vs. Output Buffering (b)

Logically, the implementation of the Switcherland switch represents a crossbar switch with output buffering. Physically, the output buffers are implemented with a single shared memory. Compared with an implementation that uses several output buffer memories the advantage of such an arrangement is that a single memory with an input bandwidth $n \cdot b$ can be used instead of $n$ memories each with an input bandwidth $n \cdot b$.

It is well known that output buffering yields much better performance than input buffering since cells can only be delayed when the bandwidth of the output link has been saturated and never due to internal contention. When FIFO queues are used as input buffers, a problem known as head-of-line (HOL) blocking occurs, which limits the output link utilization to 58% under a uniform workload [6]. Blocking happens when a cell at the head of a queue is blocked and all cells behind it are prevented from being transmitted even if they are destined for output ports which were available.

The disadvantage of output buffering is the cost of the memory. Since our switch contains a small number of ports, we chose output buffering, nevertheless, since it offers significantly higher link utilization as explained above. Also, scheduling CBR traffic for an output-buffered switch is simpler than for an input-buffered switch [2].

Figure 3 shows a block diagram of the implementation of the Switcherland prototype switch. It works as follows. From the input ports, the cells are transferred over a time-division multiplexed bus into buffer memory. The time-division multiplexing is fixed in that every $n$th access cycle to the buffer memory is assigned to the same input port. The port to the buffer memory provides $n$ times the bandwidth of one input link in order not to lose any arriving cells. There are two queues associated with each output port, one for CBR cells and one for VBR cells. When a cell arrives, an address of a free buffer is taken out of the *free list* and used for storing the cell in the *buffer mem-*

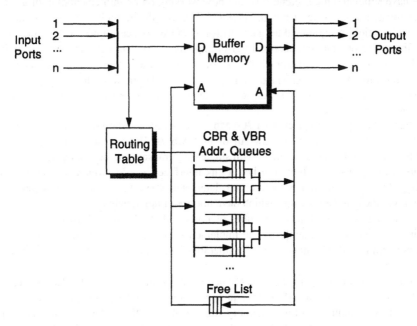

**Figure 3**: Block Diagram of the Switch Implementation

*ory*. The address of the cell buffer is then inserted into the appropriate *CBR* or *VBR* *address queue*. The output port to which the cell has to be forwarded and, with it, the address queue into which the buffer address has to be inserted, are determined by looking up a *routing table*. The routing table is indexed by the connection identifier contained in the header of the cell.

The output of the buffer memory feeds another time-division multiplexed channel. The multiplexing is again fixed. The addresses of the cell buffers to be read from memory are provided by the CBR and VBR address queues. When the content of a cell buffer has been completely transferred, the buffer is freed by writing its address into the free list.

CBR multicast is implemented in that the address of the cell buffer is written into multiple address queues. It should be noted that the cell itself is only stored once. A complication arises upon freeing a buffer used for a multicast cell since it needs to be determined when the last copy of the cell has left the buffer memory. A solution is to use a counter which is first set to the number of copies and then decremented every time a copy leaves the switch. Once the counter reaches zero, the buffer can be freed.

Even though the cells are small, cut-through is used to keep the cell forwarding time short. That is, the beginning of a cell can be accessed in the buffer memory and forwarded to the output port before the end of the cell has been written into the buffer memory.

## 5. Status

We have simulated the switches and are now working on an implementation of a 4 by 4 prototype switch as described in Section 4. We use off-the-shelf components and, in particular, field-programmable gate arrays (FPGAs) since rapid prototyping and flexibility are our main concerns. FPGAs implement the data path and control logic, and fast static RAMs realize the buffer memory. No dedicated processors are required for controlling the switches since operations such as determining the topology of the interconnection structure or setting up connections are achieved in cooperation with the processor nodes.

Each of the ports connects to a 200 Mbit/s full-duplex serial link. With it, a 4 by 4 switch offers an aggregate bandwidth of 800 Mbit/s. We use shielded twisted-pair cables for the links and drive them with single-chip transceivers originally designed for FibreChannel links. We have finished a link interface for a PC which will be used to debug the interconnection structure and, later, will serve for using PC hardware for providing those node functions which have not been implemented yet.

It should be noted that the number of ports and the bandwidth of the prototype switch are determined mainly by the implementation technology. With a custom implementation, wider switches and considerably faster links should be easily implementable.

Further, we are building a processor node and a frame buffer node. The processor node contains a MIPS R4700 CPU equipped with local DRAM memory. The frame buffer node contains a bitmap memory implemented with VRAM memory and the control logic required to interface a display monitor. A main feature of the frame buffer is its support for CBR traffic. In particular, CBR multicast is supported in that window positioning and clipping are performed by the frame buffer node. This is required for displaying the same video stream on multiple displays at different locations without any processor interaction.

## 6. Conclusions

Local area networks, such as ATM networks, provide real-time support for processing time-dependent data in the form of connections with guaranteed bandwidth. These guarantees, however, do not extend into current workstations. With the interconnection structure described in this paper, this gap is filled.

Switcherland is based on crossbar switches. Since the switches can be cascaded, the interconnection structure can be used not only for connecting the components of a workstation but also for interconnecting a cluster of workstations. Such a cluster can be viewed either as a group of tightly-coupled uniprocessor machines or as a loosely-coupled parallel machine. Switcherland offers tighter coupling than a typical network but looser coupling than provided by most parallel machines.

In addition to a uniform structure applicable at different system levels, the interconnection structure provides for a uniform access mechanism in the form of a load/store architecture and a single address space. This uniform model for inter- and intra-workstation communication simplifies overall system design considerably.

The presented interconnection structure offers high bandwidth and support for time-dependent data such as video and audio. It is the basis for a uniform treatment of conventional and time-dependent data. Video and audio will eventually become standard data types and, therefore, need to be able to pass through a system by using standard communication channels.

## Acknowledgments

Svend Knudsen and Erwin Oertli made many valuable contributions to the interconnection architecture presented in this paper.

## References

[1]   N. Boden, D. Cohen, R. Felderman, A. Kulawik, C. Seitz, J. Seizovic, W. Su: *Myrinet: A Gigabit-per-Second Local Area Network*. IEEE Micro, vol. 15, no. 1, Feb. 1995, pp. 29-36.

[2]   M. Goguen, *AN2: A Self-configuring Local ATM Network*. Proceedings of the National Communications Forum, vol. 46, 1992.

[3]   D. Gustavson, *The Scalable Coherent Interface and Related Standard Projects*. IEEE Micro, vol. 12, no. 1, February 1992, pp. 10-22.

[4]   M. Hayter, D. McAuley, *The Desk-Area Network*. ACM Operating Systems Review, vol. 25, no. 4, October 1991, pp. 14-21.

[5]   R. Horst, *TNet: A Reliable System Area Network*. IEEE Micro, vol. 15, no. 1, February 1995, pp. 37-45.

[6]   M. Karol, M. Hluchyi, S. Morgan, *Input versus Output Queuing on a Space-Division Packet Switch*. IEEE Transactions on Communications, vol. C-35, no. 12, December 1987, pp. 1347-1356.

[7]   M. Katevenis, *Telegraphos: High-Speed Communications Architecture for Parallel and Distributed Computer Systems*. Technical Report 123, Foundation for Research and Technology, Heraklio, Crete, 1994.

[8]   C. Jurgens, *FibreChannel: A Connection to the Future*. IEEE Computer, vol. 28, no. 8, August 1995, pp. 88-90.

[9]   R. Lee, *Accelerating Multimedia with Enhanced Microprocessors*. IEEE Micro, vol. 15, no. 2, April 1995, pp. 22-32.

[10]  J. Saltzer, D. Reed, D. Clark, *End-To-End Arguments in System Design*. ACM Transactions on Computer Systems, vol. 2, no. 4, November 1984, pp. 277-288.

[11]  A. Widmer, P. Franaszek, *A DC-Balalanced, Partitioned-Block, 8B/10B Transmission Code*. IBM Journal of Research and Development, vol. 27, no. 5, September 1983, pp. 440-451.

# Performance Aspects of Virtual Circuit Connections over a Local ATM Network

Franz Pucher, Hoang Anh Huy
Institute for Applied Information Processing and Communications Technology
Graz University of Technology
A-8010 Graz, Klosterwiesgasse 32/I, Austria.
Fax +43/316/873/5520
E-Mail: fpucher, hoang@iaik.tu-graz.ac.at

## Abstract

This paper proposes and discusses the results of performance measurements at the institutes local asynchronous transfer mode (ATM) network following the change of numerous communication parameters, especially Quality of Service (QoS) parameters, with the aim of giving a general view of ATM connections within a LAN. It compares the results with theoretically available data rates, and gives a conclusion of measurements of raw data rates which depend on QoS parameters with a given bandwidth for data exchange over a communication route, and values for the round trip time (RTT) for different application programming interfaces (API).

**Keywords:** Virtual Connection (VC), Application Programming Interface (API), Performance, Quality of Services (QoS).

## 1 Introduction

Over the last few years, there has been growing recognition that ATM will form the basis for the next-generation communication networks. The benefits of the ATM technique are its inherent scalability, statistical multiplexing, traffic integration, and network simplicity. While much of the early focus in ATM was on public network applications, the current demand for these new networks comes from computer-based parallel applications, which need higher bandwidth and shorter delays than current shared-access LANs are able to deliver.

ATM is a networking protocol with the potential to support applications with distinct tolerances for delay, jitter and cell loss, and distinct requirements for bandwidth and throughput. ATM is a packet-oriented transfer mode and it allows multiple logical connections to be multiplexed over a single physical interface. The information flow on each logical connection is organised into fixed-size packets, called cells. Logical connections in ATM are referred to as virtual channels (VCs), which is the basic unit of switching in B-ISDN.

A VC is set up between two end-users through the network, and a variable-rate, full duplex flow of fixed-size cells is exchanged over the connection. There is no link-by-link error control or flow control. Therefore, higher layer protocols have to handle communication problems, such as TCP/IP. These papers [1-6] demonstrate how TCP protocol software that performs well in a conventional LAN environment may perform poorly relatively in a high-speed ATM LAN environment. However, with carefully chosen parameter settings, the best throughput results for the current hardware configuration and software release for TCP/IP over AAL 5 are less than 50% of the theoretical value and medium utilisation [7]. The performance tools ttcp and netperf [8] have been used in [7] to show that the throughput increases as the message size increases.

The measurements have shown that network interface software overhead and processing power of the workstation rather than time on the wire is the larger part of the time needed to send messages between processes [9]. Bypassing the general-purpose TCP/IP protocols reduces overhead and lets a communications library take better advantage of high-speed ATM interconnections.

Prudent use of VC can improve communication performance significantly. In distributed parallel processing, excessive latency could result if a connection is established between source and destination for every individual message transmission. However, once a VC has been established, a cell may traverse an ATM switch in a few tens microseconds [10]. If certain processes communicate with one another repeatedly over an application's lifetime, performance improvements can be achieved by establishing VCs when a distribution application is started. If the potential communication patterns are known, a virtual topology of VCs can be constructed. In addition, the pipelining of cells across VCs reduces the effect of path length on message-transfer time. Also other factors influence the communication overhead. The above performance tools have not enough functionality, so that special programs have been implemented.

In this paper we discuss the performance of VCs over local ATM networks, mainly the end-to-end communication performance with different QoS parameters. The results depend on many parameters, such as AAL (ATM Adaptation Layer, in this paper we focus on AAL3/4 and AAL5) type, the dataflow type (simplex, duplex, multicast), the size of packet, and the QoS, such as peak bandwidth, mean bandwidth and mean burst length. Many VCs have been simultaneously opened, for example two VCs, three VCs, up to twelve VCs. The changes to given bandwidths, and to sending and receiving bitrates have been inspected. These values do not only depend strongly upon the number of parallel VCs but also depend on other ATM connection parameters, for example peak bandwidth. Moreover, round trip times (RTT) with different application programming interfaces have been measured, such as FSI API, TCP/IP and UDP/IP, PVM-ATM, and PVM-TCP [11]. Due to the lack of space not all figures could be included in this paper, but can be found in [12].

This paper is organised as follows. Section 2 describes the ATM network environment. Section 3 reviews the ATM connections and the Fore Systems Inc. application programming interface (FSI API). In Section 4 the results of the performance measurements are presented. Finally, we close this paper with a discussion of the measured results. An appendix shows the parameter settings used in figure 3 through 7.

## 2 ATM Network Environment

Figure 1 shows the local configuration of the ATM LAN network environment at the institute. Different local host architectures are used, all from Sun Microsystems

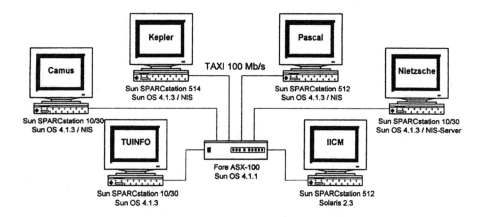

Fig. 1. Local IAIK-ATM cluster

running SunOS 4.1.3 and Solaris. These machines are equipped with Fore Systems Inc. ATM adapter cards ForeRunner SBA-200. The physical interface for the SBA-200 adapter cards is the 100 Mbit/s TAXI interface (FDDI fiber plant and signal encoding) over multimode fibers. The ATM switch is the ForeRunner ASX-100 also from Fore Systems Inc [11].

The SBA-200 adapter cards are equipped with an Intel I960 as an onboard processor. I960 takes over most of the AAL and cell related tasks, including segmentation and reassembling (SAR) functions for AAL 3/4 and AAL 5, and cell multiplexing. The host interfaces at the packet level feed lists of outgoing packets and incoming buffers to the I960, which then uses local memory to manage pointers to packets, and uses direct memory access (DMA) to move cells out of and into host memory. Cells are never stored in adapter memory. The host system software is described in the next section.

The ASX-100 switch is based on a 2.4 Gbit/s switch fabric and a RISC control processor. The switch supports four 4-port network modules where each module supports up to 622 Mbit/s. Two four-port 100 Mbit/s TAXI modules have been installed. Currently, the ATM switch is connected over Ethernet and a 100 Mbit/s FDDI-backbonering to the MAN and WAN. As shown in figure 2, future connections to other ATM switches within both the MAN and the WAN are planned. The ASX-100 supports Fore's SPANS (simple protocol for ATM network signalling) [13] protocol with the SBA-200 adapter cards, and can establish either SVCs or PVCs. The FSI API and the SPANS are proprietary, because ATM standards in this area are still incomplete.

## 3 ATM Connections

This section describes the host system software, which provides two protocol stacks [11]. On one side, the TCP/IP protocol stack for unmodified applications and operating system modules, and on the other side, new modules that Fore supplies with its ATM host interface. In the first case, any existing network application can utilise immediately the ATM LAN. In the second case, a new interface is required for ATM

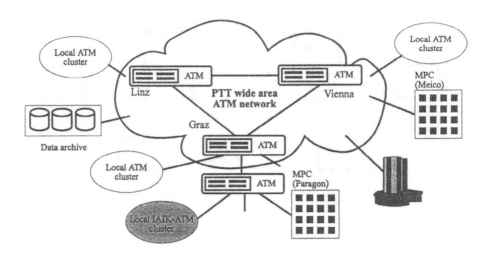

Fig. 2. Future wide area ATM cluster

applications that need to exploit capabilities not found in other LANs and protocols, such as guaranteed bandwidth reservation, selection of AAL type, multicasting, and other ATM-specific features. This section describes the proprietary FSI API and the pseudo code for the performance program used.

## 3.1 FSI API

With support from the underlying device driver, the user-level library routines provide a connection-oriented client server model for the FSI API. Depending on the platform, the subroutine library uses either a System V streams interface or a socket-based interface to the device driver. These details are hidden from the programmer, so that the FSI API is portable across platforms.

Before data can be transmitted, a VC has to be established between a client and a server. Both unidirectional and bi-directional point-to-point connections are supported, as well as multicast connections from one sender to multiple receivers. The resource reservation features of the SPANS signalling protocol can be accessed by the programmer.

The library routines provide a socket-like interface. Applications first use *atm_open()* to open a file descriptor and then bind a local application service access point (ASAP) to the file descriptor with *atm_bind()*. Each ASAP is unique for a given end-system and is composed of an ATM switch identifier and a port number in combination with *atm_listen()* and *atm_accept()* within the server process. The arguments to *atm_connect()* allow the application to specify the ATM address and ASAP of the destination, the desired and minimum acceptable resources, QoS, which AAL to use, and whether the data transfer is specified as simplex, duplex, or multicast.

These information is reserved at connection request to reduce the chances of buffer overflow, and will refuse the connection if insufficient resources are available. If QoS parameters are specified as zero, the connection is assumed to carry low-priority and loss-tolerant traffic. This connection request will not be refused due to lack of intermediate resources.

QoS parameters are reserved for each connection and contains:

- *Peak bandwidth*: This is the maximum (burst) rate at which the source produces data.
- *Mean bandwidth*: This is the average bandwidth expected over the lifetime of the connection, also measured in Kbit/s.
- *Mean burst length*: This is the average size of packets sent at peak bandwidth.

Data is transferred by giving *atm_send()* and *atm_receive()* a data buffer and waiting for the transfer to be completed. One protocol data unit (PDU) is transferred on each call. The maximum size of the PDU depends on the AAL selected for the connection and the constraints of the underlying UNIX sockets (BSD) or streams (System V) implementation. The data given with *atm_send()* is segmented by the appropriate AAL protocol. Each cell is prefixed with the outgoing VC identifier for its connection as it is transmitted. On the receiver side, the data is reassembled and delivered via the connection descriptor corresponding to the incoming VC identifier.

As mentioned above, the local ATM network also supports TCP/IP. Either AAL 3/4 or AAL 5 can be used to encapsulate IP packets. On the receiver side, the packet is implicitly demultiplexed. The host uses the identity of the VC to determine whether it is an IP packet. The bandwidth specified for IP connections is zero, which is interpreted by the switch control software as being lower priority than any other connection with non-zero reserved bandwidths.

## 3.2 Echo Program

For performance, measurement tools like ttcp and netperf have been used. But in this paper we concentrate on QoS parameters and multiple connections etc. in parallel. For these additional measurements, performance programs have been implemented, similar to the client/server program structure below:

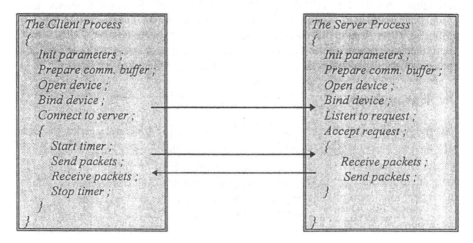

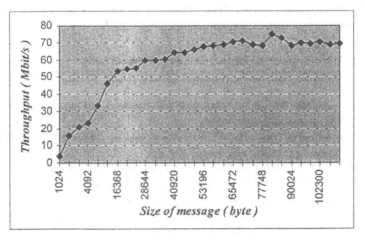

Fig. 3. Throughput versus message size

## 4 Performance Measurements

This section discusses and concludes the performance results and is divided into three parts: Firstly, the achieved throughput in this paper with performance tools, such as ttcp and netperf, is compared to the theoretical maximum. Secondly, the QoS parameter peak bandwidth will be discussed, where the peak bandwidth has been changed for multiple connections, which have been established in parallel. Thirdly, the round trip time has been measured for different programming interfaces, which supports the paper by O. Spaniol [9], claiming that the processing power of endstations limits the end-to-end performance in high speed networks.

Numerous communication parameters are changed with the aim of giving a general view of the performance characteristics of ATM connections in a local environment. This section is divided into four parts. Section 4.1 gives a short overview of throughput results for TCP/IP, UDP/IP, and FSI API. Section 4.2 shows the throughput for the QoS parameter peak bandwidth. Section 4.3 compares the RTT for different APIs. Section 4.4 concludes the performance measurements with a table describing the dependencies of data throughput and QoS parameters. The appendix at the end of the paper shows the parameter settings used in the following figures.

### 4.1 Throughput

The throughput for FSI API as well as UDP/IP over ATM increases as the message size increases and produces significantly better results than those produced with data transmission over TCP/IP, which achieves less than 50% of the theoretical value and medium utilisation. For the FSI API a maximum throughput value of over 84% of the theoretical maximum of 89% has been achieved. The throughput for UDP/IP is also over 74% of the theoretical maximum and shows only a difference of 10% compared to the FSI API as shown in figure 3. In order to improve throughput, the message size

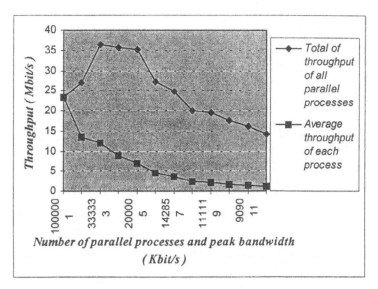

Fig. 4. Throughput varied by increasing the number of parallel
processes and associated peak bandwidth parameter.

has to be large enough, for example, bulk data transfer. A detailed discussion is given
in [7].

The measurements have shown that network interface software overhead and the
processing power of the workstation rather than time on the wire take up most of the
time needed to send messages between processes. Bypassing the general-purpose
TCP/IP protocols reduces overheads and allows a communications library to make
more high-speed ATM interconnections.

## 4.2 Peak Bandwidth

Observing the throughput with QoS parameters, the throughputs through an ATM
connection only depend on peak bandwidth parameters. The throughput is
demonstrated in figure 4 by changing the peak bandwidth for AAL5 using the echo
program from section 3.2. Figures 5 and 6 show the throughput for multiple
connections opened simultaneously.

Peak bandwidth parameters can be set to zero or to any other valid number:

(1)  Changing peak bandwidth with a value such as 100 Mbit/s divided by the number
     of parallel processes: This means that if four processes work simultaneously, a
     peak bandwidth of 100/4 = 25 Mbit/s is assigned. The total throughput increases
     with the associated peak bandwidth when there are up to three processes. But
     with four or more processes, the total throughput decreases dramatically (from 25
     down to 8,3 Mbit/s) over five parallel virtual channel connections (figure 4).

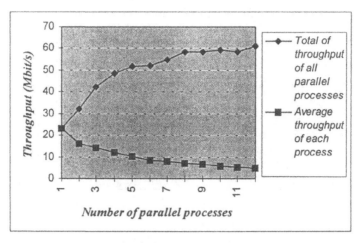

Fig. 5. Throughput varied by increasing number of parallel processes

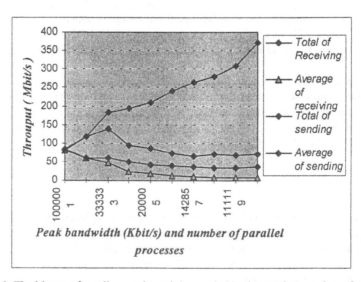

Fig. 6. The bitrate of sending and receiving varied by increasing number of parallel process and associated peak bandwidth parameter.

(2) Keeping peak bandwidth equal to 0: This means assigning the maximum available data rate with lowest priority to the virtual channel connections. The total throughput of all processes increases with the number of processes (figure 5).

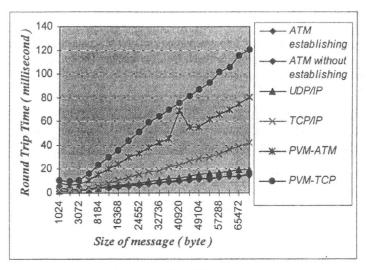

Fig. 7. RTT for different APIs.

## 4.3 Round Trip Time

The RTT is improved significantly by using the faster FSI API instead of TCP/IP. Establishing a connection at the start-up of the application and over longer distances is of particular interest. However, once a virtual circuit has been established, a cell may traverse an ATM switch in a few tens of microseconds [11]. Figure 7 shows that the RTT for PVM over the FSI API is better than over TCP/IP. But compared to the FSI API, there is a significant communication overhead in the PVM library, which leads to poorer performance and latency.

There is no difference between ATM establishing and ATM without prior establishing, because Fore System's software provides a caching mechanism, so that an ATM connection is only closed when the connection is quiet for approximately 15 minutes [11]. But over longer distances and using different switch vendors this could play a major factor.

With respect to distributed applications, an application running over the FSI API, must deal directly with the communication problems that a reliable protocol would have handled (e.g. retransmission, data flow, and so on). However, as a basis for new high-speed network protocols, the standardisation of ATM APIs, that would initially introduce less overhead than the IP over ATM protocol stacks, should be explored further.

## 4.4 Dependencies

These results have described implementations of ATM connections, following its parameters and given boundaries for each QoS parameter. The following table shows the dependencies for data communication with different QoS parameters:

| Parameters for an ATM connection | Throughput over communication route | Sending bitrate | Receiving bitrate |
|---|---|---|---|
| AAL type | Y | N | Y |
| Dataflow type | N | N | Y (*) |
| Size of packet | Y | Y | Y |
| Peak bandwidth | Y | Y | Y |
| Mean bandwidth | N | N | N |
| Mean burst length | N | N | N |
| Number of parallel processes | Y | Y | Y |

+ _Note :_ **Y** : Depend on

       **N** : Does not depend on.

+(*):   The sending and receiving time is much smaller than the transmitting time, therefore the communication route bitrate does not change if the receiving bitrate varies.

## 5 Conclusion

This paper has shown the results of performance measurements at the institutes local ATM LAN following the change of numerous communication parameters, especially Quality of Service (QoS) parameters. The results have been compared with the theoretical maximum and results from performance tools, such as ttcp and netperf. These measurements have shown that in order to improve throughput, the message size has to be large enough and that network interface software overheads and the processing power of the workstation rather than time on the wire take up most of the time needed to send messages between processes.

To measure the impact of QoS parameters, an echo program has been used. The results for different QoS parameters have shown that the throughput does not depend on dataflow (simplex, duplex or multicast), on mean bandwidth, or on mean burst length. But, the QoS parameter peak bandwidth has a major impact on throughput. Therefore, peak bandwidth has been changed for multiple connections, which have been established in parallel. The total throughput increases with the number of parallel processes from 1 to 3 and the associated peak bandwidth between 100 down to 33 Mbit/s, and decreases if the number of parallel processes and the associated peak bandwidth (from 25 down to 8,3 Mbit/s) is greater than 3.

Finally, the round trip time has been measured for different programming interfaces, which hase shown that the processing power of endstations limits the end-to-end performance in high speed networks.

## Acknowledgements

The authors gratefully acknowledge the support of Kapsch, Austria, who make it possible for us to use ATM equipment from Fore Systems Inc. free of charge.

## Reference

[1] Armitage G. J., Adams K. M.: How Inefficient is IP over ATM Anyway? IEEE Network, Volume 9, Number 1, January/February 1995.

[2] Cavanaugh J. D., Salo T. J.: Internetworking with ATM WANs. Minessota Supercomputer Center, Inc., December 1992. ftp://ftp.magic.net/ip-atm.ps

[3] Comer D. E., Lin J. C.: TCP Buffering and Performance Over an ATM Network., 1995 (to appear in Journal of Internetworking: Research and Experience). ftp://gwen.cs.purdue.edu/pub/lin/TCP.atm.ps.Z

[4] Comer D. E., Lin J. C.: Probing TCP Implementations. Proceedings of USENIX Summer Conference, 1994. ftp://gwen.cs.purdue.edu/pub/lin/probing.TCP.ps.Z

[5] Luckenbach T., Ruppelt R., Schulz F.: Performance experiments within local ATM networks. EFOCN'94, Twelfth Annual Conference on European Fibre Optic Communication and Networks, Heidelberg, Germany, June 22 - 24, 1994. ftp://ftp.fokus.gmd.de/pub/docs/nthp/tlrrfs-PERFEX-EFOC94.ps.Z

[6] Luckenbach T., Schulz F., Burak M.: Performance experiments with Inhouse ATM Technology. ICCS'94, Singapore, November 14 - 18, 1994. ftp://ftp.fokus.gmd.de/pub/docs/nthp/tlfsmb-PERFEX-ICCS94.ps.Z

[7] Matijasevic M., Posch R., Pucher F.: ATM LAN Throughput Measurements and Evaluation for BSD socket and FSI Application Programming Interface. Third IFIP Workshop on Performance Modelling and Evaluation of ATM Networks, Ilkley, 6. July 1995.

[8] Netperf: A Network Performance Benchmark, Revision 2.0, Information Networks Division, Hewlet-Packard Company, February 15, 1995. http://www.cup.hp.com/netperf/NetperfPage.html

[9] Spaniol O.: High Speed Network Interconnection: Concepts, Problems and Experiences. Papers of the SEACOMM'94, Kuala Lumpur, Malaysia, October 1994.

[10] Biagioni E., Cooper E., Sansom R.: Designing a Practical ATM LAN. IEEE Network, Volume 7, Number 2, March 1993.

[11] Geist G. A., Beguelin A., Dongarra J. J., Jaing W., Manchek R., Sunderam V.: PVM: Parallel Virtual Machine, A User's guide and Tutorial for Networked Parallel Computing, 1994.

[12] Pucher F., Hoang Anh Huy: Performance Aspects of Virtual Circuit Connections over a Local ATM Network; Report 419, IIG, TU-Graz, 1995.

[13] Fore Systems Inc.: SPANS: Simple Protocol for ATM Network Signalling, Release 2.3, 1994.

## Appendix: Parameter Settings

Parameter settings for figure 3: peak bandwidth = 0, mean bandwidth = 128 Kbit/s, mean burst length = 2 Kbit, AAL = AAL5 and dataflow = duplex.

Parameter settings for figures 4 and 5: AAL = AAL5, dataflow = duplex, size of packet is equal to the maximum transmission unit (MTU), mean bandwidth = 128 Kbit/s and mean burst length = 2 Kbit.

Parameter settings for figure 6: AAL = AAL5, dataflow = duplex, size of packet is equal to MTU, mean bandwidth = 128 Kbit/s and mean burst length = 2 Kbit.

Parameter settings for figure 7: Size of messages ranges from 1024 to 69564 byte in the following increments: from 1024 to 3072 byte with a 1 Kbyte increment, from 4092 (the MTU of an ATM connection in ATM signalling releases 2.3) to 69564 byte in 4 Kbyte increments.

# New Results of the Salzburg NTN-Method for the Radon Transform

Hausenblas Erika

Institute for Softwaretechnology
University of Salzburg

**Abstract.** The Radon transform arise in, if X-rays traverses a body, like in a computer tomograph. Thus, finding out the internal structure of a body in computer tomography corresponds to reconstruct a function from their Radon transform. This report deals with a parallelized numerical reconstruction algorithm, in particular the filtered backprojection. The filtered backprojection uses high dimensional integration. This integration is done by an equidistant grid and good lattice points. The results are discussed and presented. Further the corresponding program is described.

First we point out the mathematical background of the Radon transform. The second part deals with the program package we have implemented in C++. The intention of the program was to give the user a software tool for investigate backprojection methods by himself. Thus the program package is written as a C++ library. First, there is an instruction how to use the library. Then we give a list of the objects and an example. Further the paper treats the parallelized version and the speed up of the main functions. The last chapter presents some numerical results.

## 1 Introduction

Tomography, from the Greek $\tau\acute{o}\mu o\varsigma$, a slice, is associated with CAT scanner in medicine. In such applications, information is collected about the density distribution of a body. It is a technique to reconstruct internal structures of a body from data collected outside the body. This means, computer tomography provides a very good method to investigate the internal structure of an object without destroying it. Theoretically it is possible to reconstruct the internal structure without errors. There is only one problem - if the values of the Radon transform have been obtained by physical measurement, one cannot assume, that the data are complete. For example, the CAT scanner produces images of a two-dimensional sections of human patients from X-rays taken in a finite number of directions. Such a reconstruction is always only approximate, the accuracy depending on the number of X-rays, since no finite number of X-rays determines a density distribution uniquely. Therefore it is very important to find algorithms which yield to good approximation of the original object in spite of discrete or incomplete datas.

This paper deals with a resconstruction algorthm, the filtered backprojection algorithm. To reconstruct a point, a filter function is convoluted by the Radon transform. Thus, the result is determined by numerical integration. The common algorithm uses equidistant points for integration. But, instead of equidistant points, one can use also numbertheoretical methods explored by Korobov. We compared both methods by test images of superimposed ellipses, blury ellipses built up by smooth function and Bernoulli Polynoms.

The points of an image can be reconstructed independently. Therefore we parallelize the algorithm using PVM. We executed the computer experiment on a cluster of eight machines. The speed up enables us to create different sequences of images, varying the band parameter and the number of measurement points. Our observations are pointed out in the last chapter.

## 2 The Radon Transform

The Radon transform of a three dimensional body is the parallel projection of the physical density onto a plane. Considering the $IR^n$, the value $f(x)$ can be seen as the density at $x \in IR^n$ of a certain body. Therefor the body is described by the corresponding physical density function $f : IR^n \to IR, x \mapsto f(x)$.

### 2.1 The Radon Transform

A $n$ dimensional object can be described by a function $f(x) : IR^n \to IR$, where $f(x)$ is the physical density of the object in the point $x \in IR^n$. Considering the $IR^n$, the Radon transform maps a function $f : IR^n \to IR$ in a function $g = Rf : S^{n-1} \times IR \to IR$, where every point $[\theta, s] \in S^{n-1} \times IR$ describes uniquely a hyperplane orthogonal to $\theta$ with distant $s$ to the origin. The values of $Rf(\theta, s) = R_\theta f(s)$ is the integral taken over the hyperplane.

$$(Rf) : L^1(IR^n) \longrightarrow L^1(S^{n-1} \times IR)$$
$$f \longmapsto \int_{x\theta=s} f(x)\, dm(x) = \int_{\theta^\perp} f(s\theta + y)\, dy$$

where $L^1(IR^n)$ denotes the 1-time Lebesgue integrable function over $IR$ and $m(x)$ the Lebesgue measure on the $n-1$ dimensional hyperplane

### 2.2 The Inversion Formula of Radon

The problem is to reconstruct the object, respective its density $f(x)$, given the Radon transform. In 1917, Johann Radon showed that the density distribution in the plane is determined by the parallel projection taken in every direction. To prove this, Radon found in [Rad17] an explicit inversion formula for an integral transform now called the Radon transform. This formula can be derived in a few lines applying the inversion formula of the Fourier Transform. Before, some work must be done.

• The Radon and Fourier Transform or the Fourier Slice Theorem:

Let $f \in L^1(IR^n)$. We denote the Fourier Transform of $f$ by $\hat{f}$ and the inverse Fourier Transform by $\check{f}$. Therefore we have

$$\hat{f}(s\omega) = \frac{1}{(2\pi)^{n/2}} \int_{IR^n} e^{-ix\omega s} f(x) dx$$

hence, introducing coordinates in the hyperplane $x\omega = s$:

$$\hat{f}(s\omega) = (\widehat{R_\omega f})(s) \tag{1}$$

• $R$ can be seen as an operator from $L^1(IR^n)$ in $L^1(S^{n-1} \times IR)$. By a short calculation the adjoint or dual operator can be infered. We start out from the inner product:

$$\int_{S^{n-1}} \int_{IR} Rf(\theta, s)\, g(\theta, s)\, ds d\theta = \int_{S^{n-1}} \int_{IR} \int_{\theta\perp} f(s\theta + y)\, dy\, ds\, d\theta$$

$$= \int_{IR^n} f(x)\, R^\sharp g(x)\, dx$$

Therefore the duale Radon transform corresponds to integration of the function $g(\theta, s)$ over all hyperplanes passing through the given point $x \in IR^n$.

$$R^\sharp : L^1(S^{n-1} \times IR) \longrightarrow (Rf) : L^1(IR^n)$$

$$g \longmapsto \int_{S^{n-1}} g(\omega, \omega x)\, d\omega$$

Equation (1) and the Fourier inversion immediately imply the inversion for the Radon transform:

$$f(x) = \frac{1}{(2\pi)^{n/2}} \int_{IR^n} \hat{f}(\xi) e^{ix\xi}\, d\xi$$

$$= \frac{1}{(2\pi)^n} \int_{S^{n-1}} \int_0^\infty e^{ix\theta s}\, s^{n-1} \int_{IR} e^{-irs} R_\theta f(r)\, dr\, ds\, d\theta$$

Replacing $s$ by $-s$ and $\theta$ by $-\theta$ in the second integral, and using the fact that the Radon transform is even we can split the second integral into two parts:

$$= \frac{1}{(2\pi)^n} \int_{S^{n-1}} \left( \frac{1}{2} \int_0^\infty e^{ix\theta s} \int_{IR} s^{n-1} e^{-irs} R_\theta f(r)\, dr\, ds\, d\theta \right. \tag{2}$$

$$\left. + \frac{1}{2} \int_{-\infty}^0 e^{ix\theta s} \int_{IR} (-s)^{n-1} e^{-irs} R_\theta f(r)\, dr\, ds\, d\theta \right) \tag{3}$$

If $n$ is odd, $n - 1$ is even and we obtain immediately:

$$f(x) = \frac{1}{2} \frac{1}{(2\pi)^n} \int_{S^{n-1}} \int_{-\infty}^\infty s^{n-1} e^{ix\theta s} \widehat{R_\theta f}(s)\, ds\, d\theta$$

$$= \frac{1}{2} \frac{1}{(2\pi)^{n-1}} R^\sharp \frac{1}{i^{n-1}} \left( \frac{\partial^{n-1}}{\partial^{n-1}s} R_\theta f(s) \right)\, ds\, d\theta$$

If $n$ is even, the situation is more complicated. The Fourier transform is multiplied by $sgn(s)$, but multiplication of $\hat{f}$ by $i\, sgn(s)$ corresponds to applying the Hilbert transform to the function $f$ itself, i.e.

$$-i\, sgn(x)\, \hat{f}(x) = f \star \widehat{\frac{1}{x}} := Hf(s)$$

Returning to (2), we see for $n$ even,

$$f(x) = \frac{1}{2}\, \frac{1}{(2\pi)^{n-1}} R^{\sharp}\, \frac{1}{i^{n-1}}\, H\left(\frac{\partial^{n-1}}{\partial^{n-1}s} R_\theta f(s)\right)\, ds\, d\theta$$

Therefore the inversion formula is given by

$$f(x) = \frac{1}{2}\, (2\pi)^{1-n}\, R^{\sharp}\, i^{1-n}\, H^{n-1}\, \frac{\partial^{n-1}}{\partial^{n-1}s}\, g_\theta(s) \tag{4}$$

where $g_\theta(s) = R_\theta f(s)$ and the Operator $H^{n-1}$ is defined by:

$$H^{n-1} = \begin{cases} (-1)^{(n-2)/2}H, & n \text{ even} \\ (-1)^{(n-2)/2}, & n \text{ odd} \end{cases}$$

The fact that the operator $H$ shows up only for $n$ even has an important practical consequence. We see that the problem of reconstructing a function from its integrals over hyperplanes is, for odd dimension, local. This means, the function is determined at some point by the integrals along the hyperplanes through a neighbourhood of that point. This is not true for even dimension, since the Hilber transform is not local. Thus, in even dimension, the reconstruction algorithm is not local in the sense that computing the function at some point requires the integral along all hyperplanes meeting the support of the function. If there are available all values of $R_\theta(t)$, the inversion formula works quite well. But this formula leads to numerical instabilities, if the Radon transform is available in a finite number of directions, for example on a lattice $M_n = \{(s_i, \theta_i) \,|\, i = 1\ldots n\}$. Therefore it is of practical importance to find algorithms which yield a good approximation of the density function, utilizing only few number of points.

## 2.3  The Filtered Backprojection Algorithm

The filtered backprojection reconstruction is presently the most important algorithm, at least in the medical field. As we pointed out above, the inversion formula of Radon works only on continuous values. If we want a good approximation of the density by discrete data we have to add one step. The function value $f(x_0)$ at a point $x_0 \in IR^n$ can be represented by a convolution of $f$ with a delta function. If the function is available only on a finite set of points $\{x_i, i = 1\ldots n\}$, one can approximate the function $g$ by convolution of the sample function with an approximated delta function.

$$\tilde{g}_{appr}(x) = \delta_{appr} * \left(\frac{1}{n}\sum_i^n g(x_i)\right)(x)$$

Such an approximated delta function is mostly a low pass filter, because the approximation takes into account only the Fourier coefficients until a certain frequency and cut off the higher by convolution. It can be compared with smearing the exact value in the neighbourhood of each point. Now, the idea behind the filtered backprojection is to convolute the reconstructed function with an appropriate filter. Thus, the step we add is convoluting the function by a low-pass filter with cut-off frequency until a certain value b. An example is the following filter defined by

$$\widehat{W_b}(\xi) = \frac{1}{(2\pi)^{n/2}}\widehat{\Phi}(|xi|/b)$$

where

$$\widehat{\Phi}(s) = \begin{cases} 1 & \text{f } s < 1 \\ 0 & \text{if } s \geq 1 \end{cases}$$

It is easy to verify $W_b \to \delta$ for $b \to \infty$. The second important fact is given by the relation

$$W_b \star f = R^\sharp(w_b \star Rf), \quad \text{where} \quad W_b = R^\sharp w_b$$

Thus, to reconstruct the value, first the Radon transform is convoluted by $w_b$ and then the inversion formula for the Fourier transform is applied. The problem is now finding the function $w_b$ given the Fourier transform of the low pass filter $\widehat{W_b}$. Let $w \in L^1(IR^n)$ an arbitrary function. We obtain from the definition of $R^\sharp$ as a dual operator of $R$:

$$\int_{IR^n} R^\sharp f \, \hat{w}(x) \, dx = \int_{S^{n-1}} \int_{IR} g(\theta, s) \, R\hat{w}(\theta, s) \, ds \, d\theta$$

$$= \int_{S^{n-1}} \int_{IR} \hat{g}(\theta, s) \, \check{R}\hat{w}(\theta, s) \, ds \, d\theta$$

hence $\int f\hat{g}dx = \int \hat{f}gdx$. Further the identity $\widehat{R\hat{w}}(\theta, s) = (2\pi)^{(n-1)/2}w(s\theta)$ implies

$$= (2\pi)^{\frac{(n-1)}{2}} \int_{S^{n-1}} \int_{IR} \hat{g}(\theta, s) \, w(s\theta) \, ds \, d\theta$$

$$= (2\pi)^{\frac{(n-1)}{2}} \int_{IR^n} \left( \hat{g}(\frac{\theta}{|\xi|}, |\xi|) + \hat{g}(-\frac{\theta}{|\xi|}, -|\xi|) \right) w(\xi) \, |\xi|^{1-n} \, d\xi$$

This relation gives us the transformed filter function $w_b$. Since $\widehat{W_b}$ is a radial function we drop the first argument in $\hat{w}_b$. We obtain

$$\hat{w}_b(s) = \frac{1}{2}(2\pi)^{1/2-n} \, |s| \, \widehat{\Phi}(|s|/b)$$

The filtered backprojection algorithm is a version of (4), where the inner part is convoluted with the delta-function before the inversion formula is applied.

Later we will see that the integrals which arise by the convolution $w_b \star g$ and the operator $R^\sharp$

$$R^\sharp \left( w_b \star g(\theta_j, s) \right) = \int_{S^{n-1}} \int_{I\!R} g_\theta(s) w_b(s) \, ds \, d\theta \qquad (5)$$

can be replaced by the discrete approximations. Here, the quality of approximation depends on the size of the sample and on the filter function. In the paper we are considering the filter

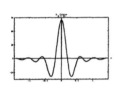

$$g_2 = b^2 \int_0^1 \cos\left(z\pi b u\right) u(1 - u^2) \, du$$

where $z = z_{x,y}(\theta, s) = x \sin(\theta) + y \cos(\theta) - s$ is a function of $(\theta, s)$ and denotes the distance of $L_\theta(s)$ to the intersection point of P, $b$ denotes the bandwith parameter.

## 3 Good Lattice Points and the Reconstruction Algorithm

The integration in (4), respective (5) can only be determined by numerical methods. Usually, this numerical integration is done on a grid with equidistant points:

$$\theta_i = \frac{i}{n} \pi \quad i = 1 \ldots n_\theta,$$

$$s_i = (2\frac{i}{n} - 1) \sqrt{2} \quad i = 1 \ldots n_s,$$

Reconstructing a $s$ dimensional object, a $s$ dimensional integral must be approximated by a intergration formula. In high dimensional integration it is worth while to use goog lattice points instead of an equidistant grid, because of gaining two advantages: First, the error is improved, second, you can decrease the number of points by smaller steps. In this section we give first a short summary of good lattice points and numbertheoretical integration. The second part deals with good lattice points applied to our special case, the backprojection method.

### 3.1 Mathematical Background

The method of good lattice points or numbertheoretical integration, explored by Korobov in 1954 (for further information see [Kor63]), arises by Monte Carlo methods (see [KH74]). Due to this fact we point out first the Monte Carlo Method and then introduce good lattice points.

**Monte Carlo Method** In simple terms the Monte Carlo Method may be described as a numerical method based on random sampling. What means a integral or approximating a integral? A integral $\int_X f(x)\, dx$ of a function $f$ over a bounded domain $X$ can be interpreted as the expectation $E[f]$ of the random variable $f(x)$, $x \in X$, where $x$ is uniform distributed in $X$. For simplification we consider the integral over the $s$-dimensional cube $[0,1]^s$. Now the problem of numerical integration is reduced to the problem of estimating the expectation value of $f$ by a random sampling.

$$\frac{1}{N} \sum_{i=1}^{N} f(x_i) \overset{N \to \infty}{\Longrightarrow} \int_{[0,1]^s} f\, d\lambda \tag{6}$$

where the $x_i$, $i = 1, \ldots, n$ are independent, uniform distributed points in $[0,1]^s$ and $\lambda$ denotes the Lebesgue measure. The strong law of large numbers guarantees the convergence of the sum in (6) almost surely.

**Discrepancy** By evaluating $E[f]$ on a computer the problem arises, how to generate a sequence of uniform distributed independent random variables by a computer ? A computer can only executes programs formulated in terms of deterministic algorithms, which is a contradiction to tossing a coin and the concept of randomness. Thus the requirement of 'the points should be uniform distributed' must be translated in a criterion for deterministic sequences. In ergodic theory one can infer, that if one observes a 'evenly distributed sequence of random points', the ratio of the number of points, falling in a certain subset of $[0,1]^s$ has the same order like the volume of the subset. This considerations leads to the concept of discrepancy. Roughly spoken the discrepancy can be viewed as a quantitative measure for the deviation from the uniform distribution. Let

$$B = \left\{ B = [a_1, b_1] \times [a_2, b_2] \times \cdots \times [a_s, b_s] \mid a_i < b_i,\ a_i, b_i \in [0,1],\ i = 1 \ldots s \right\}$$

the family of interval and $\xi = (x_i)_{i=1}^{\infty}$ a sequence in $[0,1]^s$. The discrepancy of the first $N$ points is given by

$$D_N(\xi) = \sup_{B \in B} \left| \frac{|(x_i)_1^N \cap B|}{N} - \lambda(B) \right| \tag{7}$$

where $|\cdot|$ denotes the number of $n$ with $1 \le n \le N$ and $x_n \in B$. We have to note that the discrepancy given by the family $B$ is a special case, called star discrepancy $D_N^*$. It is possible and worth while to replace $B$ by other families. This leads to other kinds of discrepancy. For example, if $B$ denotes the set of all convex subsets of $[0,1]^s$, the definition in (7) leads to the isotropic discrepancy $D_N^I$.

   Accordingly to a classical result in the ergodic theory, if the sequence $\xi = (x_i)_{i=1}^{\infty}$ is uniform distributed in $[0,1]^s$ then holds $\lim_{N \to \infty} D_N(\xi) = 0$ and vice versa. In this sense, the star discrepancy can be viewed as quantification of the definition of a uniformly distributed sequence.

Error Bounds The next important point is the error bound. Here we have to cite the classical result of Koksma and Hlawka, most inequalities base on. Let $f$ be of bounded variation in the sense of Hardy and Krause[1]. Now the error can be estimated by the following inequality of Koksma and Hlawka:

$$\left| \frac{1}{N} \sum_{n=1}^{N} f(X_n) - \int_0^1 f(x)\, dx \right| \le V(f)\, D_N^*(x_1, \cdots, x_N)$$

A proof is given in [Nie92] p. 18. What is the merit of this formula ? The error bound consists of two independent part. One only depending on the function and one depending on the sequence $\xi$. Thus it is possible to separate the influence of the function from the choice of the sequence.

If the function is not of bounded variation in the sense of Hardy and Krause then the absolute value of the error has an upper bound expressed in terms of the isotropic discrepancy of $\xi$. For more please see [Zar72] p.114.

Good Lattice Points Above in the section we have seen that the error depends on the variation $V(f)$ and the discrepancy of the nodes. Now there are two possibilities to reduce the error. Either to interpolate the function between the nodes by splines or other interpolation formulas, or to search for sequences of low discrepancy. The second possibility leads to good lattice points introduced by Koborov in 1959. A natural way obtaining sequences of low discrepancy arises by numbertheoretical methods, from which the expression 'numbertheoretical integration' derives. For example if $p$ is a prime number, there exists a point $g = (g_1, \cdots, g_s)$, called good lattice point, with $1 \le g_i \le p - 1$ such that the sequence $\xi = ((n/p)\, g)_{n=1}^p = (g_1\, n/p \bmod 1, g_2\, n/p \bmod 1, \cdots, g_s\, n/p \bmod 1)_{n=1}^p$ is of low discrepancy $D_p$. Koborov [Kor63] investigated in the relation of Fourier transform, convergence of the sum in (6) and good lattice points.

A special case are good lattice points generated by Fibbonaci numbers, whereas the n'th Fibbonaci number is given by the recursion:

$$F_0 = 1, \quad F_1 = 1, \quad F_n = F_{n-2} + F_{n-1}$$

Particularly, for two dimensions, a formula in terms of Fibbonacci numbers yields the lowest star discrepancy ([Zar72] p.119). The corresponding lattice is generated by the point $g = (1, F_{n-1})$, where the sequence runs up to $F_n$.

---

[1] The variation $V(f)$ in the sense of Hardy and Krause of a function $f : [0,1] \to I\!R$ is defined by

$$V(f) = \sup_{0 = t_1 < t_1 < \cdots < t_n = 1} \sum_{i=1}^{n-1} |f(t_{i+1}) - f(t_i)|$$

## 3.2 Fibbonacci Numbers and Equidistant Grid

The next step is to transform these points onto the state space of the distance $s$ and the angle $\theta$. Because we evaluate the Radon transform in the interval $[-1, 1]^s$, the state space is given by $[-\sqrt{2}, \sqrt{2}] \times [0, 2\pi]$. For illustrating the importance of good lattice points, we add a grid generated by randomly chosen points. Thus in the program we determine the Radon transform on the following points:

- In the case of equidistant points

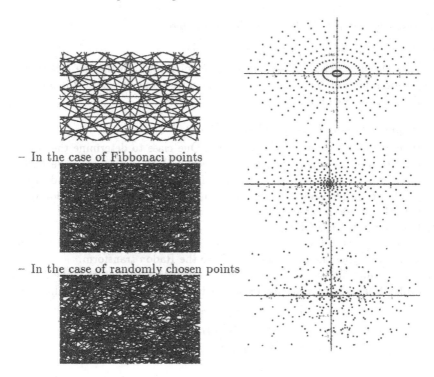

- In the case of Fibbonaci points

- In the case of randomly chosen points

## 4 Implementation of the Parallelized Algorithm

The program is written in C++ and is built up like a C++ library. The aim was to give the user a tool for research in the Radon transform. With the library the user can outline a program by himself with only a few lines. A detailed description is in [Hau94a] and [Hau94b].

### 4.1 The Structure of a Test Program

First the user design a phantom picture, which he will transform at the next step, i.e. evaluate the Radon transform. After, the inversion formula is applied. Now, the reconstructed image acn be compared with the original.

 The phantom picture is drawn by 150 × 150 pixels and on the range $[-1, 1] \times [-1, 1]$.

 This picture shows a reconstructed phantom picture. The numerical integration is done by $F_{10} = 144$ Fibonacci points.

The test algorithm is divided in the following steps:

1. Creating the Phantom Picture
   First the user defines a variable of type phantom. Further he creates the phantom picture, for example by adding ellipses one by one to the object.
2. Drawing the Phantom Picture

3. Transforming the Phantom Picture
   Here the user has two classes available. One class to determine the Radon transform on an equidistant grid, the second class to determine the Radon transform on good lattice points. The following two kinds of good lattice points are implemented: Fibonacci points and points chosen randomly by the C++ random generator.
4. Reconstructing the Object
   First, the user defines a picture of the same size like the original picture. Then he applies the inversion formula to the Radon transform.
5. Determining the Error The error of the reconstructed picture is the 2-norm of the difference between the reconstructed picture and the original.

$$error = \sqrt{\frac{1}{n_x} \frac{1}{n_y} \sum_{i=1}^{n_x} \sum_{j=1}^{n_y} \left(f(x_i, y_j) - f_{rec}(x_i, y_j)\right)^2} \qquad (8)$$

## 5  Parallel Virtual Machine (PVM)

The Parallel Virtual Machine is a software system that enables a collection of heterogeneous computers to be used as a coherent and flexible parallel computational resource. It can be used especially for the development and execution of large concurrent or parallel applications that consist of many interacting, but relatively independent components [GS92]. PVM was developed initially at the Emory University and Oak Ridge National Laboratory. The individual computers may be shared- or local-memory multiprocessors, vector supercomputers or scalar workstations that can be interconnected by a variety of networks (ethernet, FDDI, etc.). User programs written in C, C++ or Fortran are provided access to PVM through the use of calls to PVM library routines for functions such as process initiation, message transmission and reception. The PVM system handles message routing, data conversion for incompatible architectures and other tasks that are necessary for operation in a heterogeneous network environment. For more details see [Gei93].

## 5.1 Implementation with PVM and Load Balancing

Since the Radon transform or reconstruction for different points $(s_i, \theta_i)$ of the lattice for a point $(x_i, y_i)$ of the image are evaluated independently, the outer loop may be distributed among the processors. On a dedicated network, where the user disposes 100% of the machines' capacity on each node, this can be done by partitioning the lattice into equal parts for each node. If there are other processes running or if a heterogeneous network is used, a processor with high workload or a slower one would cause a delay in the whole computation. With a finer partitioning of the lattice it is possible to react on changes in the system performance. Therefore the algorithm is implemented using the master–slave paradigm and the asynchronous pool of tasks methodology.

## 5.2 The Program Package

The program of determining the Radon transform of a given phantom picture and reconstructing the image contains three time consuming procedures: the function for drawing the picture, the function for evaluating the Radon transform and the function for reconstructing the image given the discrete version of the Radon transform. Hence reconstructing the image is the step we are interested on, we give a short descritption of the parallelized structure.

By reconstructing a image, the physical density of each point in the unit square can be reconstructed independently. Therefore each slave can determine the value of the physical density in one point. But the amount of communication time increases if the tasks are to small. Because of this for casting the task each slave gets the task to reconstruct a column of the image. First the master distributes the Radon transform and the size of the image to reconstruct to all. After this each slave gets the number of the column he has to evaluate. The next step, after a slave finished his task, he will send back the result and get a new number of column if there are some left.

The rough structure of the master program:

enroll in PVM
get startparameters (number of processors (n) and so on)
invoke the slaves
send the Radon picture
if good lattice points are chosen
        send the angles and s-values
cast the tasks to the slaves (send each slave the number of the column, he has to evaluate)

```
loop (i=1) to number of the x_pixels
        wait until a vector arrives
        entry the values to the own reconstruction image
        if there is a column left
                send the number of the column to the slave
end loop
cast to all slaves −1
```

The rough structure of the slave program:

```
enroll in PVM
get the Radon picture
if good lattice points are chosen
        get the angles and s-values
get the size of the image to reconstruct
get the number of column to reconstruct
while (number of column >-1)
        evaluate the corresponding column of the reconstructed image
        send the image to the master
end loop
pvm_exit()
```

## 5.3   The Speedup of Executing Time

Because all time consuming functions are also implemented in PVM, you can neglect the amount of time needed by the other procedures. Further, the executing time of a program using PVM depends first and foremost on the number of hosts. Thus, the factor of the execution time of a sequential version to the parallelized version of the program is equivalent to the number of hosts. In our example, the computations dedicated to eight DEC 5000/33 Workstations. In order to demonstrate the speed up, we reconstruct pictures of 150 × 150 and 200 × 200 pixels by the function bild::pvm_new1_reconstruct( ). We vary the number of points evaluating the Radon transform between 60 × 60 and 100 × 100. The result is given in the table below.

| Pixels | Points | Time | | speed up |
|--------|--------|------|--|----------|
| | | parallelized version | sequential version | |
| 150 × 150 | 60 × 60 | 5 min | 38 min | 7.7 |
| | 70 × 70 | 7 min | 54 min | 7.8 |
| | 80 × 80 | 9 min | 1h 10 min | 7.8 |
| | 90 × 90 | 11 min | 1h 24 min | 7.6 |
| | 100 × 100 | 14 min | 1h 47 min | 7.7 |
| 200 × 200 | 60 × 60 | 9 min | 1h 10 min | 7.8 |
| | 70 × 70 | 11 min | 1h 26 min | 7.8 |
| | 80 × 80 | 16 min | 2h 4 min | 7.7 |
| | 90 × 90 | 19 min | 2h 25 min | 7.6 |
| | 100 × 100 | 27 min | 3 h 18 min | 7.8 |

# 6  Results and Conclusions

## 6.1  Reconstructed Images

In order to test the algorithm we reconstruct three different kinds of images. First we create phantom pictures built up by superimposed ellipses, second by blur ellipses and by Bernoulli functions. Further, one sequence can be divided into three kinds of reconstruction, where we uses different grids for the numerical integration - equidistance points - good lattice points generated by Fibbonaci numbers and randomly chosen points.

phantom 1      phantom 2      phantom 3

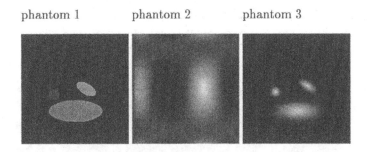

Further, there are presented pictures, reconstructed by equidistant points, random chosen points and Fibonacci points. We took the choice of the best band parameter.

You should not use \subparagraph in this style.

(The bandparameter is chosen to be 11)

(1)        (2)        (3)

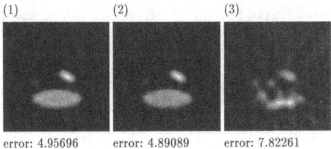

error: 4.95696    error: 4.89089    error: 7.82261

You should not use \subparagraph in this style.

The nuber of measurement points is $F_{12} = 377$.

### Fibbonnaci points

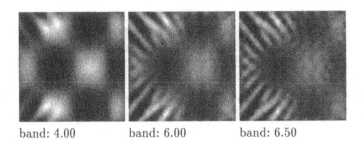

band: 4.00     band: 6.00     band: 6.50

### equidistant grid

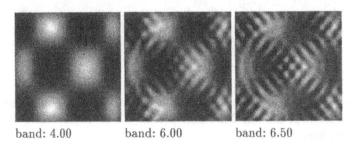

band: 4.00     band: 6.00     band: 6.50

You should not use \subparagraph in this style.

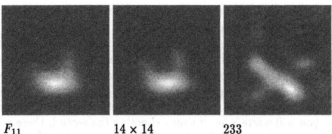

| $F_{11}$ | $14 \times 14$ | 233 |
|---|---|---|
| error: 0.197490 | error: 0.191615 | error: 0.420542 |
| band: 2.75 | band: 2.5 | band: 1.5 |

At smooth function we observe, that the images reconstructed by good lattice points are better than the images reconstructed by an equidistant grid. The assumption could be verified. The following images show a reconstruction with $F_9 \sim 10 \times 9$ measurement points of phantom 3. Though the error is lower in the second sequence, a black spot arises above the reconstructed object, a artefact caused by the regularity of the grid. A person, considering the reconstructed image without knowing the original, will assume above the center a black whole. At the first column the choice of the band parameter is done by minimalizing the error.

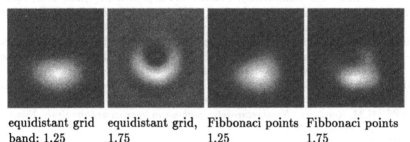

| equidistant grid | equidistant grid, | Fibbonaci points | Fibbonaci points |
|---|---|---|---|
| band: 1.25 | 1.75 | 1.25 | 1.75 |

## 6.2 Conclusions

At function with unbounded variation the algorithm based on equidistant grid and Fibbonaci numbers yields to the same error rate. The next step was extending the software tool by a new class of differentable function and comparing the algorithms phantom pictures generated by smooth function.

First we get the suspicion that using a only few points, the algorithm based on Fibbonaci number leads to a lower error rate than the second algorithm. Verifying the idea it turned out that the assumption is true. Although often a image reconstructed by a grid of good lattice points is more blury, there arises no artefact and the observer identifies more quickly the original. At an equidistant grid the observer often get the impression of a black whole or spot where is nothing in reality. Thus a reconstructed image based on the first algorithm is much more realistic than an image based on the second.

Further putting objects in the center of the image, the beams generated by Fibbonaci numbers scan better than the beams generated by an equidistant grid.

Therefore the first algorithm reconstructs objects near the center with a better quality than the second.

Adding some points improves the error rate. At randomly chosen points, you can add one point by one until the error is low enough. For adding $m$ points at an equidistant grid, you have to chose between three possibilities: to cast the old points and to measure new $n + m$ points, to have a grid, which consists no more of equidistant points, or to go by steps of order $n^2$. Choosing the first alternative, you will waste a lot of time - choosing the second, there will appear artefacts because the domain of integration is not covered uniformly. Thus the third alternative is the only left. If you use Fibonacci points, you have also to determine the points a second time, but you can raise up the number of points by smaller steps.

# References

[Gei93]   A. Geist. PVM3 beyond network computation. In J. Volkert, editor, *Parallel Computing*, volume 73 of *Lectures Notes in Computer Sience*, pages 194–203. Springer Verlag, Stuttgart, 1993.

[GS92]   A. Geist and V.S. Sunderam. Network based on concurrent computing on the PVM system: Concurrency. *Practice and Experience*, 4(4):293–3115, 1992.

[Hau94a]   Erika Hausenblas. The Salzburg NTN-Method for the Radon Transform. Technical report, Institute of Softwaretechnology, 1994.

[Hau94b]   Erika Hausenblas. The Salzburg NTN-Method for the Radon Transform: Introduction and Description of the Radon Software Tool. Technical report, Institute of Softwaretechnology, 1994.

[KH74]   L. Kuipers and Niederreither H. *Uniform Distribution of Sequences*. Pure and Applied Mathematics. John Wiley and Sons, 1974.

[Kor63]   N.M. Korobrov. *Numbertheoretic methods in approximate analysis*. Fitzmatgiz, Moskau, 1963.

[Nie92]   Harald Niederreither. *Random Nuber Generation and Quasi-Monte Carlo Methods*, volume 63 of *CBMS-NSF, Regional Conference Series in Applied Mathematics*. Society for industrial and applied mathematics, 1992.

[Rad17]   Johann Radon. Ueber die Bestimmung von Funktionen durch ihre Intergralwerte laengs gewisser Mannigfaltigkeiten. *Berichte der Saechsische Akademie der Wissenschaften, Leipzig, Math.-Phys.*, 69:262–267, 1917.

[Rev90]   Michael Revers. *Anwendung zahlentheoretischer Methoden fuer die Numerik der Computertomographie*. PhD thesis, University of Salzburg, 1990.

[Rev94]   Michael Revers. Numeric Integration of the Radon Transform on Classes $e_s^\alpha$ in multiple (finite) dimensions. preprint, 1994.

[Zar72]   S.K. Zaremba, editor. *Applications of Number Theory to Numerical Analysis*. Academic Press London, 1972.

# Parallel Computation of Optimal Parameters for Pseudo Random Number Generation [*]

D. Brunner[1] and A. Uhl[2]

E-mail: {dbrunner,uhl}@cosy.sbg.ac.at

[1] Department of Mathematics, Salzburg University, Austria
[2] Research Institute for Softwaretechnology and Department of Computer Science and System Analysis, Salzburg University, Austria

**Abstract.** Two systematic search methods are employed to find multipliers for linear congruential pseudo-random number generation which are optimal with respect to the discrepancy of pairs of successive pseudo-random numbers. These two methods are compared in terms of their suitability for parallel computation. Experimental results of a MIMD workstationcluster–implementation and an evaluation of the calculated parameters using the spectral-test are included.

## 1 Introduction

The statistical properties of the most commonly used pseudo-random numbers (PRN), namely of those generated by the linear congruential generator (LCG), depend strongly on the choice of parameters in the method. In this paper we introduce two systematic search techniques which yield optimal multipliers relative to the discrepancy of pairs of successive PRN. Due to the enormous computational demand of these search techniques parallel processing is necessary to accelerate the execution time – we compare our techniques in terms of efficiency and scalability when implemented on a parallel system.

We now briefly recall the definition of linear congruential PRN. Let $m \geq 3$ and $r$ be integers, let $y_0$ be an integer in the least residue system modulo $m$, and let $\lambda$ be an integer co-prime to $m$ with $2 \leq \lambda \leq m$ and $(\lambda - 1)y_0 + r \not\equiv 0 \pmod{m}$. A sequence $y_0, y_1, \ldots$ of integers in the least residue system modulo $m$ is generated by the recursion

$$y_{n+1} \equiv \lambda y_n + r \pmod{m} \quad n = 0, 1, \ldots$$

and the sequence $x_0, x_1, \ldots$ in $[0, 1]$ defined by $x_n = \frac{y_n}{m}$ for $n = 0, 1, \ldots$ finally is a sequence of linear congruential PRN. In this context, $m$ is referred to as the *modulus*, $\lambda$ as the *multiplier*, and $r$ as the *increment*. One distinguishes between the inhomogeneous case $r \not\equiv 0 \pmod{m}$ and the homogeneous case. The sequence $x_0, x_1, \ldots$ is purely periodic in both cases, we denote by $\tau$ the length of the least period in the sequence.

---

[*] The first author was supported by the Austrian Science Foundation (FWF) project P11009 MAT.

The parameters $m, \lambda$ and $r$ have to be chosen in such a way, that the resulting PRN passes appropriate statistical tests for "randomness". The modulus $m$ is selected in accordance with machine capabilities, typical choices being a large prime number such as the Mersenne prime $m = 2^{31} - 1$ or a large power of two such as $m = 2^{30}, 2^{32}$ or $2^{35}$. The increment $r$ has only a secondary influence, so that the properties of the sequence are mainly governed by the choice of the multiplier $\lambda$. For more general information on linear congruential PRN see [12] and [10].

## 2  Theoretical background

For given $s \geq 2$ the amount of statistical independence among $s$ successive terms in a sequence of PRN can be measured by the $s$-dimensional discrepancy $D_N^{(s)}$. This expression arises from the theoretical study of the so-called $s$-dimensional serial test as applied to linear congruential PRN. To carry out this test one takes the $s$-tuples $X_n = (x_n, x_{n+1}, \ldots, x_{n+s-1})$ for $n = 0, 1, \ldots$ and calculates the maximal deviation $D_N^{(s)}$ (discrepancy) between the uniform distribution on the $s$-dimensional unit cube and the empirical distribution of the $s$-tuples $X_0, X_1, \ldots, X_{N-1}$. The sequence of linear congruential PRN passes the $s$-dimensional serial test if $D_N^{(s)}$ is small for large $N \leq \tau$. In this case we may think of $s$ successive terms in the sequence of having good distribution behavior.

Thus it becomes clear that desirable multipliers relative to the $s$-dimensional serial test are obtained by minimizing $D_N^{(s)}$. If $m$ is a power of 2 it is customary to use a multiplier $\lambda \equiv 3, 5 \pmod 8$, if $m$ is a prime modulus we use a primitive root $\lambda$ modulo $m$ as a multiplier (this choice guarantees a large period). Beside inequalities for $D_N^{(s)}$ for general $s$, in the case $s = 2$ minimizing $D_N^{(2)}$ is facilitated by a useful connection between estimates of $D_N^{(2)}$ and continued fractions.

Consider the regular continued fraction expansion $\frac{\lambda}{m} = [a_1, \ldots, a_q]$ with $a_q = 1$ and put $K = K\left(\frac{\lambda}{m}\right) = \max(a_1, \ldots, a_q)$. For $m = 2^\alpha, \alpha \geq 3$ and $\lambda \equiv 5 \pmod 8$ we have

$$\tau D_\tau^{(2)} \leq 1 + \sum_{i=1}^{q} a_i \text{ and}$$

$$\tau D_\tau^{(2)} \leq 1 + C(K) \log \tau,$$

where $C(K) = 2/\log 2$ for $1 \leq K \leq 3$, $C(K) = \frac{K+1}{\log(K+1)}$ for $K \geq 4$. For a prime modulus $m$, $r = 0$ and a primitive root $\lambda$ modulo $m$ as a multiplier we have

$$\tau D_\tau^{(2)} \leq 2 + \sum_{i=1}^{q} a_i \text{ and}$$

$$\tau D_\tau^{(2)} \leq 2 + C(K) \log m.$$

These results lead to the question how small $K$ and $\sum_{i=1}^{q} a_i$ can be for a fixed modulus $m$. Thus we consider $K_m = \min_\lambda K$ where the minimum is extended over all $\lambda$ co-prime to $m$.

There is a conjecture of Zaremba [16] according to which $K_m \leq 5$ $\forall m$. This was verified by Borosh for $m \leq 10^4$ [1] and Knuth ($K_m \leq 3$) for $10^4 \leq m \leq 3.2 \, 10^6$. Moser conjectures [5] that for all primes $p$ $\exists a, b$, $p = a + b$, $\frac{b}{a} = [a_1, \ldots, a_n]$ and $\sum_{i=0}^{n} a_i \leq c \log p$. For more details on these conjectures and their implications on numbertheoretical numerics [6] see [15].

Niederreiter [11] established the following results by constructive proofs: if $m = 2^\alpha$ or $3^\alpha$, $\alpha \geq 1$, then $K_m \leq 3$ and $K_m = 2$ for infinitly many $\alpha$. If $m = 5^\alpha$, $\alpha \geq 1$, then $K_m \leq 4$ and $K_m = 3$ for infinitly many $\alpha$.

Metric considerations on these topics can be found in [3] and [13].

For the purpose of selecting optimal multipliers relative to the two-dimensional serial test, other quantities than $K_m$ are even more pertinent. For $m = 2^\alpha$, $\alpha \geq 3$ a relevant quantity is $Q_m = \min_\lambda K$ where the minimum is extended over all $\lambda \equiv 5$ (mod 8). A systematic search method for such multipliers is introduced by Borosh and Niederreiter [2].

For a prime modulus $m$ we have to consider

$$P_m = \min_\lambda K$$

where the minimum is extended over all primitive roots $\lambda$ modulo $m$. It is known that $P_m = O(\log m \log \log m)$ [10]. Since the computational complexity of calculations including a search for primitive roots is very high, neither a search for $P_m$ has been carried out in [2] nor since this time. We introduce two systematic search methods for $P_m$ for which we present concepts for MIMD parallelization and which are compared in terms of their efficiency and scalability.

## 3   Two search methods for $P_m$

As explained in the last section, we search for a given prime modulus $m$ the primitive roots $\lambda$ yielding the smallest $K$. If more $\lambda$'s with the same $K$ are being found, we choose the $\lambda$ having the smallest value for $\sum_{i=1}^{q} a_i$ as our multiplier. Basically there are two approaches to a search strategy:

1. **Algorithm Cantorset**: Find all numbers with appropriate $K$ (which is below a predefined threshold), subsequently test if they are primitive roots.
2. **Algorithm Primitive Root**: Compute all primitive roots modulo $m$, subsequently evaluate and compare their $K$.

### 3.1   Algorithm C

The main principle of this algorithm is the construction of a truncated Cantor set as introduced in [2]. Our strategy is first to find all numbers $a$ for which $K = K\left(\frac{a}{m}\right) = 2$.

Denote by $I_{a_1 \ldots a_l}$ the set of all reals in $(0, 1]$ whose continued fraction expansion is $[a_1, \ldots, a_l, \ldots]$. Clearly $I_{a_1 \ldots a_l}$ is an interval whose endpoints are

$[a_1, \ldots, a_l]$ and $[a_1, \ldots, a_{l-1}, a_l + 1]$ and whose length is $1/(q_l \, (q_l + q_{l-1}))$ if $[a_1, \ldots, a_l] = \frac{p_l}{q_l}$. Let

$$F_l = \{ I_{a_1 \ldots a_l} | a_i \in \{1, 2\}, \; i = 1, \ldots, l \}.$$

Each interval $I$ in $F_l$ yields two intervals of $F_{l+1}$ contained in $I$. This construction gives a Cantor set in the limit. However, we stop the subdivision of $F_l$ at a predefined depth $l$. In our specific case, the interval $(0, 1]$ is replaced by $[1, m-1]$ and the set $F_l$ is generated as a set of pairs, namely the endpoints of its elements.

Each number contained in the subintervals (the "elements") of $F_l$ is investigated further for its $K$. If the predefined threshold is met, the number is tested for being a primitive root in the least residue system modulo $m$. If a number meets the condition on $K$ and is a primitive root $\sum_{i=1}^{q} a_i$ is evaluated. Subsequently only numbers satisfying the condition on $K$ and improving $\sum_{i=1}^{q} a_i$ are tested for being a primitive root. The primitive root with lowest $K$ (and subsequently lowest $\sum_{i=1}^{q} a_i$) is the optimal multiplier $\lambda$. There is generally no unique result of this algorithm.

## 3.2  Algorithm P

The complete set of primitive roots in the least residue system modulo $m$ is computed using the following property: if a number $a \leq m$ is known to be a primitive root modulo $m$, the number $b \equiv a^c \pmod{m}$ is a primitive root modulo $m$ as well if and only if $c$ is co-prime to $m-1$ $((c, m-1) = 1)$. After having generated all primitive roots, they are investigated for meeting the threshold-condition on $K$. The primitive root with lowest $K$ (and subsequently lowest $\sum_{i=1}^{q} a_i$) is the optimal multiplier $\lambda$.

If not the optimal $\lambda$ for modulus $m$ is being sought but just a primitive root $\lambda$ meeting the condition on $K$ (or a threshold on $\sum_{i=1}^{q} a_i$), both algorithm C and P may be used and terminated if such a $\lambda$ is found.

# 4  MIMD Parallelization of $P_m$ search

Obviously both algorithm C and P are computational very demanding (see figure 1 for timings). Therefore we propose MIMD parallelization strategies which can be used for both shared and distributed memory architectures, respectively.

## 4.1  Parallel algorithm C

A straightforward parallelization strategy looks as follows: first the Cantor set is constructed, then the subintervals produced are distributed among the processor elements (PE) and are processed independently on a PE. Each PE proceeds in the same way as in the sequential implementation. If no load balancing is required, the subintervals are distributed evenly, in the case of load balancing

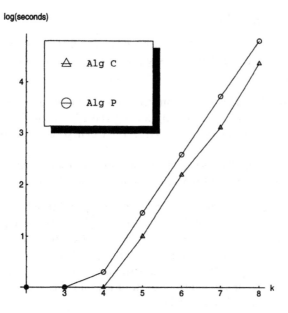

**Fig. 1.** Sequential timings of algorithms C and P for growing moduli (log-log plot; for a definition of the value $k$ see section 5)

the subintervals are used as a pool of tasks (which can be distributed dynamically). Unfortunately this technique leads to very bad run-time behavior for the following reasons:

- The most expensive operation is the test for being a primitive root. If a "new" primitive root is found (i.e. with better $K$ or $\sum_{i=1}^{q} a_i$) the number of candidates for being a primitive root is reduced since only such with even "better" properties are investigated. This results in a lot of overhead in the parallel execution since candidates are being tested concurrently that are not tested in the sequential version after a "new" primitive root is found.
- It often happens that only on PE still tests a candidate while all the others have already finished all their work.

Therefore we suggest two possibilities for parallelizing C:

1. **Algorithm C1:** We use the same parallelization as suggested in the beginning, but since it is not possible to evaluate the amount of work contained in a subinterval, the nodeprocesses are only allowed to run a fixed time. Afterwards they contact the hostprocess for new results of the other nodes. This timecomparison can be performed efficiently only after a primitive root test.
2. **Algorithm C2:** We use the sequential algorithm. If a number is to be tested for the primitive root property, this test is executed in parallel.

## 4.2  Parallel algorithm P

The most demanding part of the algorithm is identified as the calculation of the "initial" primitive root $a$. Again we suggest two possibilities for parallelizing this programpart:

1.  **Algorithm P1:** The initial primitive root is simply calculated by distributing the interval $[1, m-1]$ evenly among the PE. If the first primitive root $a$ is found all PE stop and proceed to the calculation of the other $\phi(m-1)$ primitive roots.
2.  **Algorithm P2:** The test for being a primitive root is parallelized and applied consecutively until the first primitive root $a$ is found.

The following procedures are the same for algorithm P1 and P2. Since we look for $b \equiv a^c \pmod{m}$ with $(c, m-1) = 1$ in the following, the range of the exponent $c$ is distributed among the PE in order to be able to investigate the primitive roots found for their $K$ and $\sum_{i=1}^{q} a_i$. The start value for the first PE is known trivially ($b \equiv a^1 \pmod{m}$), the second start value is evaluated recursively (by a recursive multiplication of $a$), all other $b \equiv a^x \pmod{m}$ for the other PE can be calculated trivially.

Now we give the pseudocode of a host/node implementation of algorithm P1:

*Structure of the hostprogram*

```
enroll in pvm
get size of tasks
get number of available processors n
invoke n nodes
send global parameters (modulus m)
send borders of subintervals to nodes
wait: get initial primitive root
partition range of c and form pool of tasks
while (pool of tasks is not empty)
        compute startvalue for next node
        send next task to that node
        receive result from a node (primitive root with lowest K
                                    in that range of c)
endwhile
terminate nodes
exit
```

*Structure of the nodeprogram*

```
enroll in pvm
receive global parameter
receive subintervalborders
```

```
'infinite loop'
        receive parameters
        search primitive root or search through subinterval of c
        send result
end loop
```

When there is no further work, the nodeprocess blocks at the receive–statement until it is terminated by the hostprocess.

## 5  Experimental Results

### 5.1  Efficiency of the parallelization

We have implemented the four different search methods on a workstationcluster consisting of eight DEC/AXP 3000/400 interconnected by FDDI, which makes communication as fast as possible for a configuration like this. Such a system can be interpreted as a moderate parallel distributed memory MIMD architecture with high communication cost. The host–node programming paradigm is applied using the parallel programming environment PVM ([14, 4]). In case of load balancing the asynchronous single pool of tasks method is used [8] (see figure 2).

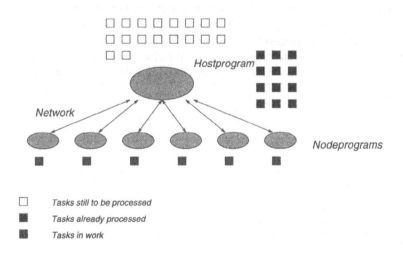

**Fig. 2.** Dynamic load balancing: asynchronous single pool of tasks method

In table 1 we present some optimal multipliers which have been calculated using one of the algorithms above. Let $P[k]$ be the $10^k$th prime and M the Mersenne prime $2^{31} - 1$. It should be noted that there are often more results having the same value for $K$ and $\sum_{i=1}^{q} a_i$ (see table 2) – in such a case the use of a different quality measure (see section experimental results) may help to decide which parameter to use.

| Prime modulus $m$ | Multiplier $\lambda$ | $K$ | $\sum_{i=1}^{q} a_i$ |
|---|---|---|---|
| $P[1] = 29$ | 18 | 2 | 7 |
| $P[2] = 541$ | 331 | 3 | 14 |
| $P[3] = 7919$ | 3325 | 2 | 19 |
| $P[4] = 104729$ | 43955 | 2 | 25 |
| $P[5] = 1299709$ | 818870 | 2 | 31 |
| $P[6] = 15485863$ | 6507610 | 2 | 36 |
| $P[7] = 179424673$ | 104026441 | 3 | 42 |
| $P[8] = 2038074743$ | 1289818712 | 2 | 47 |
| $P[9] = 22801763489$ | 9450445177 | 2 | 52 |
| $M = 2147483647$ | 1257471787 | 2 | 48 |

**Table 1.** Some optimal multipliers $\lambda$

Concerning efficiency algorithm C1 shows a very bad behavior. This parallelization may lead to a higher over-all computational demand than the sequential version. This happens if a node spends much time in a primitive root test while all the others yet work on tasks, which are computed in the sequential version with already updated parameters coming from a possibly positive primitive root test result. Algorithm P1 shows a similar speed up behavior than C2 but is clearly outperformed by algorithm P2. The reason for this is that a lot of computation is performed in vain by partitioning the data while searching for the initial primitive root. Figure 3 shows speedup with 2, 4, 6, and 8 processors using algorithms C2 and P2.

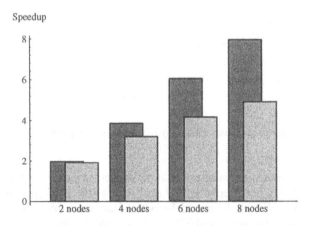

**Fig. 3.** Speedup of algorithms C2 (light) and P2 (dark) over algorithms C and P.

Algorithm P2 shows a linear speed up in the order of the number of PE whereas algorithm C2 only shows logarithmic speed up. This is easily explained by the relatively large sequential part of C2 (since only the test for being a primitive root is executed in parallel). Figure 4 shows the time demand for an increasing number of PE of algorithms C2 and P2.

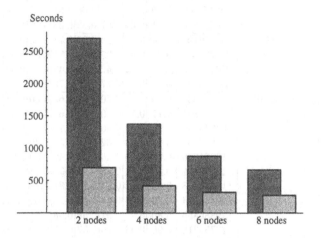

**Fig. 4.** Timings of algorithms C2 (light) and P2 (dark).

It can be easily derived that algorithm C2 is faster than P2 – as long as the number of PE is small enough. The linear speed up of P2 (in the range considered) suggests that this algorithm is better suited for massively parallel implementations. At a PE number between 20 and 30 the time demand of both algorithms is expected to be the same, for higher PE numbers algorithm P2 will exhibit its scalability and will outperform C2 (despite of the fact that algorithm C is at least twice as fast as P). This fact is subject to further experimental studies on massively parallel architectures.

## 5.2 Quality of the parameters

In order to rate the quality of the calculated LCG-parameters we performed a spectral-test which gives the maximal distance between adjacent parallel hyperplanes, the maximum being taken over all families of parallel hyperplanes that cover all overlapping tuple generated in dimensions $2 \leq s \leq 8$ (see [7, 9]). It should be noted that this test uses a different quality measure than discrepancy for judging the quality of LCGs – especially we investigate the behavior of the LCG sequences for dimensions $s \geq 2$. See the following normalized spectral-test results (values near 1 imply a "good" lattice structure, e.g. see the figures below for dimension $s = 2$):

It can be easily seen that we obtain excellent spectral-test results for dimension $s = 2$. For higher dimensions $s$ the results differ a lot – if more than one

| $k$ | $m$ | $a$ | $s=2$ | 3 | 4 | 5 | 6 | 7 | 8 |
|---|---|---|---|---|---|---|---|---|---|
| 1 | 29 | 18 | 0.86 | 0.71 | 0.89 | 0.72 | 0.77 | 0.80 | 0.80 |
| 2 | 541 | 331 | 0.77 | 0.64 | 0.78 | 0.61 | 0.66 | 0.74 | 0.79 |
| 3 | 7919 | 3325 | 0.73 | 0.68 | 0.32 | 0.49 | 0.63 | 0.74 | 0.73 |
| 4 | 104729 | 43955 | 0.92 | 0.64 | 0.12 | 0.21 | 0.30 | 0.38 | 0.44 |
| 5 | 1299709 | 818870 | 0.79 | 0.76 | 0.75 | 0.68 | 0.61 | 0.46 | 0.56 |
|  |  | 819599 | 0.79 | 0.76 | 0.75 | 0.68 | 0.61 | 0.46 | 0.56 |
|  |  | 940020 | 0.81 | 0.60 | 0.57 | 0.62 | 0.53 | 0.72 | 0.73 |
| 6 | 15485863 | 6507610 | 0.94 | 0.53 | 0.63 | 0.80 | 0.71 | 0.65 | 0.75 |
|  |  | 10906844 | 0.90 | 0.77 | 0.27 | 0.60 | 0.75 | 0.67 | 0.67 |
|  |  | 10906934 | 0.79 | 0.69 | 0.47 | 0.59 | 0.49 | 0.69 | 0.54 |
|  |  | 11205526 | 0.90 | 0.77 | 0.27 | 0.60 | 0.75 | 0.67 | 0.67 |
| 7 | 179424673 | 100600034 | 0.90 | 0.59 | 0.70 | 0.57 | 0.65 | 0.60 | 0.61 |
|  |  | 103380851 | 0.77 | 0.52 | 0.60 | 0.64 | 0.64 | 0.76 | 0.69 |
|  |  | 104026441 | 0.93 | 0.35 | 0.56 | 0.80 | 0.70 | 0.69 | 0.67 |
|  |  | 104287534 | 0.76 | 0.75 | 0.62 | 0.71 | 0.65 | 0.79 | 0.59 |
|  |  | 110061606 | 0.96 | 0.59 | 0.46 | 0.77 | 0.49 | 0.69 | 0.70 |
|  |  | 110898719 | 0.87 | 0.61 | 0.36 | 0.62 | 0.71 | 0.61 | 0.51 |
|  |  | 111265158 | 0.82 | 0.78 | 0.54 | 0.85 | 0.81 | 0.72 | 0.72 |
|  |  | 112843334 | 0.79 | 0.35 | 0.66 | 0.67 | 0.73 | 0.64 | 0.57 |
|  |  | 129386855 | 0.80 | 0.40 | 0.51 | 0.55 | 0.68 | 0.69 | 0.59 |
|  |  | 129755312 | 0.90 | 0.59 | 0.70 | 0.57 | 0.65 | 0.60 | 0.61 |
|  |  | 131238960 | 0.90 | 0.78 | 0.50 | 0.63 | 0.59 | 0.51 | 0.66 |
| 8 | 2038074743 | 1258180115 | 0.72 | 0.21 | 0.78 | 0.73 | 0.59 | 0.58 | 0.74 |
|  |  | 1289818712 | 0.72 | 0.21 | 0.78 | 0.73 | 0.59 | 0.58 | 0.74 |
| 9 | 22801763489 | 9450445177 | 0.88 | 0.69 | 0.70 | 0.55 | 0.59 | 0.56 | 0.67 |
| M | $2^{31}-1$ | 125747179 | 0.73 | 0.56 | 0.82 | 0.69 | 0.75 | 0.37 | 0.51 |

**Table 2.** Spectral-test results for dimensions $s \geq 2$.

solution for a given module has been found, the results help to decide which parametervalue to use. It has to be pointed out again that the method investigated does not lead to optimal parameters for arbitrary dimensions but most of the parameters found are better than average even for high dimensions. If the attention is restricted to the distribution of pairs of successive PRN we obtain optimal parameters in terms of discrepancy which perform excellent as well if a spectral-test is applied.

## 6  Conclusion

In this paper we propose two search methods for multipliers for linear congruential pseudo random number generators which are optimal with respect to the discrepancy of pairs of successive PRN. These search algorithms include search for primitive roots and fractions with small partial quotients in their continued fraction expansion. In our investigation it turns out that algorithm C (which is mainly based on the construction of a truncated Cantor set) is more efficient concerning sequential execution time. Concerning parallelization behavior we found that for moderate parallel architectures a parallelization of algorithm C is best suited, whereas for massively parallel architectures a parallelization of algorithm P (which is mainly based on a precalculation of the set of all primitive roots) is best. The quality of the computed LCG parameters is confirmed by using a two-dimensional spectral-test.

# 7 Acknowledgements

We thank K. Entacher and P. Hellekalek of the pLab-group (department of Mathematics, University of Salzburg) for their valuable suggestions and discussions and especially K. Entacher for providing his Mathematica spectral-test code.

# References

1. I. Borosh. Rational continued fractions with small partial quotients. *Notices of the American Mathemetical Society*, 23:A–52, 1976.
2. I. Borosh and H. Niederreiter. Optimal multipliers for pseudo-random number generation by the linear congruential method. *BIT*, 23:65–74, 1983.
3. T.W. Cusick. Continuants with bounded digits. *Mathematika*, 24:166–172, 1977.
4. G.A. Geist and V.S. Sunderam. Network based concurrent computing on the PVM system. *Concurrency: Practice and Experience*, 4(4):293–311, 1992.
5. R.K. Guy. *Unsolved Problems in Number Theory*. Springer, New York, Heidelberg, Berlin, 1981.
6. E. Hlawka, F. Firneis, and P. Zinterhof. *Zahlentheoretische Methoden in der Numerischen Mathematik*. Schriftenreihe der ÖCG. Oldenbourg, Wien, München, 1981.
7. D.E. Knuth. *The Art of Computer Programming, vol.2*. Addison-Wesley series in computer science and information processing. Addison-Wesley, 1981.
8. A.R. Krommer and C.W. Überhuber. Dynamic load balancing – an overview. Technical Report ACPC/TR92-18, Austrian Center for Parallel Computation, 1992.
9. P. L'Ecuyer. Efficient and portable combined random number generators. *Communications of the ACM*, 31:742–774, 1988.
10. H. Niederreiter. Quasi-monte carlo methods and pseudo-random numbers. *Bulletin of the American Mathemetical Society*, 84:957–1041, 1977.
11. H. Niederreiter. Dyadic fractions with small partial quotients. *Monatshefte für Mathematik*, 101:309–315, 1986.
12. H. Niederreiter. *Random Number Generation and Quasi-Monte Carlo Methods*. Number 63 in CBMS-NSF Series in Applied Mathematics. SIAM, Philadelphia, 1992.
13. J.W. Sander. On a conjecture of Zaremba. *Monatshefte für Mathematik*, 104:133–137, 1987.

14. V.S. Sunderam, G.A. Geist, J. Dongarra, and R. Manchek. The PVM concurrent computing system: evolution, experiences, and trends. *Parallel Computing*, 20:531–545, 1994.

15. A. Uhl. Zwei Vermutungen in der Theorie der Kettenbrüche und deren Bedeutung in der numerischen Analysis. Master's thesis, University of Salzburg, 1992.

16. S.K. Zaremba. *Applications of Number Theory to Numerical Analysis*. Academic Press, New York, 1972.

# Parallel Evaluation of Multi-join Queries *

Annita N. Wilschut and Jan Flokstra and Peter M.G. Apers

University of Twente
P.O.Box 217, 7500 AE Enschede, the Netherlands
Phone: +3153-894190
{annita, flokstra, apers}@cs.utwente.nl

**Abstract.** A number of execution strategies for parallel evaluation of multi-join queries have been proposed in the literature. In this paper we give a comparative performance evaluation of four execution strategies by implementing all of them on the same parallel database system, PRISMA/DB. Experiments have been done up to 80 processors. These strategies, coming from the literature, are named: *Sequential Parallel*, *Synchronous Execution*, *Segmented Right-Deep*, and *Full Parallel*. Based on the experiments clear guidelines are given when to use which strategy.

## 1 Introduction

For years now, research has been done on the design, implementation, and performance of parallel DBMSs. Teradata [CaK92], Bubba [BAC90], HC186-16 [BrG89], GAMMA [DGS90], and XPRS [SKP88] are examples of systems that actually were implemented. The performance evaluation of these systems is mainly limited to simple queries.

Recent developments in the direction of support of non-standard applications, the use of complex data models, and the availability of high-level interfaces tend to generate complex queries that may contain larger numbers of joins between relations. A number of parallelization strategies was proposed [CLY92,CYW92,HoS91,HCY94,ScD90] and their performance was evaluated via simulation. However, no comparative experimental performance evaluation is available. This paper describes the proposed strategies in a common framework. Four strategies are implemented on PRISMA/DB and a comparative performance evaluation is done. The results yield clear guidelines for the choice of a strategy.

### 1.1 Implementation Platform

PRISMA/DB was used to do the experiments. PRISMA/DB is full-fledged parallel, relational DBMS [ABF92]. A fully functional prototype is running on a 100-node multiprocessor machine. PRISMA/DB is used for research in various directions [Gre92, HWF93,Wil93,WiA91,WFA92]. PRISMA/DB is a main-memory DBMS and therefore the experiments described in this paper refer to a main-memory context.

---

* This is an extended abstract; the full paper appeared in Proc. ACM SIGMOD'94, Minneapolis, Minnesota, May 24–27, 1994

## 1.2 Optimization and Parallelization of Multi-join Queries

In System R [SAC79], join trees are restricted to linear trees, so that available access structures for the inner join operand can optimally be exploited. System R chooses the cheapest (in the sense of minimal total costs) linear tree that does not contain cartesian products.

Subsequently, it is remarked in [KBZ86] that the restriction to linear trees may not be a good choice for parallel systems. However, the space of possible join trees is very large if restriction to linear trees is dropped [LVZ93].

Obviously, when optimizing the response time of a complex query, it is not sufficient to optimize towards minimal total costs. Rather, the exploitation of parallelism has to be taken into account as well. However, the search space that results if all possible trees and all possible parallelizations for these trees are taken into account is gigantic. To overcome these problems, [HoS91] proposes a two-phase optimization strategy for multi-join queries. The first phase chooses the tree that has the lowest total execution costs and the second phase finds a suitable parallelization for this tree. The same strategy is used here.

## 1.3 Organization of Paper

This paper is organized as follows. Section 2 shortly introduces PRISMA/DB, it shows how the different parallelization strategies for the execution of multijoins can be implemented on PRISMA/DB, and it discusses some results from earlier research in the context of PRISMA/DB that are used to explain the results of this paper. Section 3 describes four execution strategies for multi-join queries and their trade-offs in detail. Section 4 describes a comparative performance evaluation and Section 5 summarizes and discusses the results of this paper.

## 2  PRISMA/ DB

PRISMA/DB has extensively been used for research in the area of parallel query processing [Wil93,ApW94]. Our previous research followed two lines. First, the system was used to experiment with large-scale intra-operation parallelism for single operation queries [WFA92]. Second, a theoretical study of the behavior of pure inter-operation parallelism in multi-join queries was done [WiA93]. The work presented in this paper combines those two lines of research: we study the use of both *inter-* and *intra-*join parallelism for the execution of multi-join queries via experimentation.

## 2.1  The System

PRISMA/ DB is a full-fledged parallel, main-memory relational DBMS, designed and implemented in the Netherlands. A goal of the PRISMA project was to provide flexibility in architecture and query execution strategy, to enable experiments with the functionality and performance of the system. This flexibility is used here to implement various strategies for the parallel evaluation of multi-join queries and to evaluate their performance. PRISMA/ DB currently run on a 100-node shared-nothing multi-processor.

Each node consists of a 68020 processor with 16 Mbytes of memory, a disk, and a communication processor. A full description of design, architecture, and implementation of PRISMA/ DB can be found in [Ame91,ABF92].

## 2.2 Results from Previous Research

**Parallel Execution of Single Operator Queries** [WFA92] studies the use of intra-operator parallelism for main-memory database systems. In that study, it is concluded that observed linear speedup for small numbers of processors cannot always be extrapolated to larger numbers of processors. This is caused by the fact that the overhead from starting on operations on processors —this overhead increases with increasing degree of parallelism— dominates the actual processing time —which decreases with increasing degree of parallelism— for a large degree of parallelism. The optimal number of processors to be used appears to be proportional to the square root of the size of the operands. As a consequence, larger problems allow a larger degree of parallelism. Also, it is concluded that the optimal number of processors for the parallel execution of an operation is smaller for a main-memory system than for a disk-based system.

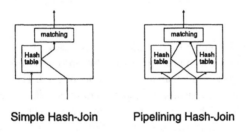

Simple Hash-Join      Pipelining Hash-Join

**Fig. 1.** Simple hash-join and Pipelining hash-join algorithm in a main-memory system

**The Pipelining Hash-join Algorithm** In [WiA91,WiA93] it is shown how special main-memory algorithms can be used that enhance the effective parallelism from pipelining. These pipelining algorithms aim at producing output as early as possible, so that a consumer of the result can start its operation. In particular, [WiA91,WiA90] proposes a pipelining Hash-Join algorithm. As opposed to the well-known two-phase, build-probe hash-join [ScD89,WiA91] (this algorithm is called simple hash-join in this paper), this symmetric algorithm builds a hash-table for both operands (See Figure 1). The join process consists of only one phase. As a tuple comes in, it is first hashed and used to probe that part of the hash table of the other operand that has already been constructed. If a match is found, a result tuple is formed and sent to the consumer operation. Finally, the tuple is inserted in the hash table of its own operand. Compared to the simple hash-join, the pipelining algorithm can produce result tuples earlier during the join process at the cost of using more memory to store a second hash-table. Using this algorithm, pipelining along both operands of the join is possible.

# 3 Parallel Execution Strategies for Multi-joins

The parallel execution strategies for multi-join queries that are dealt with in this paper all use known parallel algorithms to evaluate the constituent binary join operations. The difference between the various strategies lies in the way in which binary joins are allocated to processors. A lot of work was done on the use of intra-operator parallelism for the evaluation of binary join operations. It is generally agreed on that the parallel hash-join is the algorithm of choice [ScD89]. Two version of this algorithm are considered here: the simple hash-join and the pipelining hash-join (see Section 2.2).

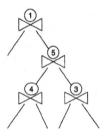

**Fig. 2.** The 5-way join tree that is used to explain the parallel multi-join strategies in this paper.

A parallel execution strategy for a multi-join query uses a parallel hash-join algorithm for the constituent binary joins. Apart from this *intra-operator parallelism*, also inter-operator pipelining or parallelism may or may not be used. The four strategies that are regarded here differ in the way in which *inter-operator parallelism* and *intra-operator parallelism* are used. Note, that we concentrate on adding inter-operator parallelism. This means that the available processors may have to be distributed over the operations in the join-tree. We do not allow a single processor to work concurrently on different join operations.

In the following, each of the strategies is described in detail. The 5-way join tree in Figure 2 is used as an example. The constituent joins in this tree are labeled with a number, which indicates the relative amounts of work in the join operations. So, the second join operation from the top needs five times the computation time of the top join operation.

## 3.1 Sequential Parallel Execution (SP)

The sequential parallel execution strategy does not use any inter-operator parallelism. The constituent joins are executed sequentially in parallel, using all available processors for each join operation. This strategy does not require pipelining between join operations, so the simple hash-join algorithm can be used.

The processors first work together on the join labeled with 4, then they work on the join labeled with 3 etc. This strategy does not need a cost function to estimate the costs of the join operation. Also, the idealized load balancing is perfect.

## 3.2 Synchronous Execution (SE)

This strategy uses inter-operator parallelism apart from intra-operator parallelism. The strategy was proposed in [CYW92]. The idea is to execute independent subtrees in the join tree independently in parallel. A join operation is started only after its operands are ready. The only inter-operation parallelism that is used in a join tree is the parallelism between independent subtrees of a bushy tree. An algorithm is proposed in [CYW92] that aims at equal processing time for both operands to be ready for joining. This is done by allocating a number of processors to a subtree that produces an operand, that is proportional to the total amount of work in the subtree. In this way, operands are supposed to be available at the same time so that no processors have to wait. This strategy does not require pipelining between join operations, so the simple hash-join algorithm is used.

The allocation algorithm needs a cost-function to estimate the processing costs for subtrees in the join tree. No perfect load balancing is achieved due to discretization errors (see Section 3.5) in the allocation of differently sized loads to a small number of processors.

## 3.3 Segmented Right-Deep Execution (RD)

In contrary to SE, segmented right-deep execution uses inter-operator pipelining in addition to intra-operator parallelism. This strategy is proposed in [CLY92], a paper which was inspired by [ScD90].

Schneider [Sch90,ScD90] describes the differences in possible parallelism between left-deep and right-deep linear join trees**, when the simple hash-join is used for the individual join operations. In a right-deep tree the build-phases of all join operations can be executed in parallel and after that probe-phases can be executed using extensive pipelining. Left-deep trees on the other hand only allow parallel execution of the probe phase of one join-operation and the build-phase of the next. It is concluded in this study that, due to the possibilities of extensive exploitation of pipelining right-deep trees perform better than left-deep trees.

The results of Schneider are extended in [CLY92] to bushy trees. That paper proposes to see a bushy tree as a segmented right-deep tree, which is a bushy tree that consists of right-deep segments. The right-deep segments can be evaluated using inter-operation parallelism as proposed in [Sch90,ScD90]. Each operation in a segment is assigned a number of processors that is proportional to the estimated amount of work in the join operation. Segments that have a producer-consumer relationship are evaluated sequentially. Independent segments, however, may be evaluated in parallel, using disjoint subsets of the available processors. In this approach, a left-deep tree is a bushy tree consisting of many small right-deep segments.

This strategy first uses all available processors to process the right-deep subtree that consists just of the join labeled with 4. Subsequently, the available processors are distributed over the other join operations, which also form a right-deep subtree. This last

---

** In this terminology the inner join-operand, which is used to build a hash-table, is called the left operand, and the outer join-operand, which is used to probe the hash-table is called the right operand.

subtree is executed in a pipelined fashion. Each of the join operations starts immediately hashing its left operand. However, during the probe-phase the join labeled with 3 (which has relatively few processors) cannot saturate the joins that are higher up in the pipeline so those operations cannot fully utilize their processor during the probe phase.

Again, this strategy needs a cost function to estimate the amount of work in each join operation. This strategy also does not yield perfect load balancing due to discretization errors in the allocation of work to a small number of processors and due to delays over the pipeline.

## 3.4   Full Parallel Execution (FP)

This strategy adds both inter-operator pipelining and inter-operator parallelism to intra-operator parallelism in the individual join-operations. The strategy was proposed in [WiA91,WAF91]. The idea behind this strategy is to allocate each join-operation to a private (set of) processors, so that all join-operations in the schedule are executed in parallel. Depending on the shape of the query tree, pipelining and independent parallelism are exploited. The strategy uses the pipelining hash-join algorithm (see Section 2.2). Because, this algorithm can exploit pipelining along both the right and the left operand, all individual join-operations can be executed in parallel. The available processors are distributed over all join-operations proportionally to the amount of work in each operation. Each join-operation starts working as soon as input is available.

The bottom two join operations start immediately on the processors allocated to them, as their operands are available as base-relations. The join operation labeled with 5 has to wait some time until its operands start producing output (see Section 3.5). The top join operation may start immediately hashing its left-operand. However, it has to wait for its right operand to become available, and therefore its processor is not fully utilized later during the join operation.

Again, this strategy depends on a cost function to estimate the amount of work in each join operation. It is clear that this strategy does not offer perfect load balancing either.

## 3.5   Tradeoffs

There are a number of barriers that prevent performance gain from parallelism. A general discussion of this issue can be found in [DeG92]. These barriers affect the execution strategies introduced above in a different way, resulting in a number of tradeoffs: startup, coordination, descretization error, and delay over pipelines.

Obviously, each of these four factors affects the execution strategies studied in a different way. Also, it is expected that the extent to which a strategy is affected by each of the factors depends on the shape of the query tree that is parallelized. For example, RD is expected to work fine for right-oriented trees, but not so well for e.g. a left-linear tree. Similarly, SE is expected to work better for bushy trees than for trees that are (almost) linear. SP, on the other hand, is not expected to be very sensitive to the shape of the query tree. Experiments are used to find out how these tradeoffs work out in reality.

# 4 Performance Evaluation

As stated in the introduction of this paper, we study the second phase of a two-phase optimization/parallelization strategy. The first phase, finds the join tree with minimal total costs for a given multi-join and the second phase generates a parallel execution strategy for this plan. To keep the problem manageable we decided to study one multi-join query. For this join query, we vary the *parallelization strategy*, the *number of processors used*, the *shape of the query tree*, and the *size of the problem*.

## 4.1 Test Data and Query

The join query studied in this performance evaluation consists of ten relations that contain equal numbers of Wisconsin tuples [BDT83]. These tuples consist of two unique integer attributes and a number of other attributes up to a total size of 208 bytes per tuple. The ten relations are joined one-by-one on their first integer attributes, and after each join they are projected to the second integer attributes and the remaining attributes of one of the operands, so that the result of each operation again is a Wisconsin relation equal in size to the operands. This test problem is similar to the problem used in [Sch90], in [ZZS93], and in [WiA93]. All possible join trees for this query have the same total execution costs. Also, the individual join operations are equal in costs and sizes of its operands. So, any differences in response time are caused by differences in the shape of the tree and the parallelization used. Therefore, such a regular tree is very suitable to study the effectiveness of the various parallelization strategies.

## 4.2 Experimental Setup

As said before, in our experiments, we vary the *parallelization strategy*, the *number of processors used*, the *shape* of the query tree, and the *size of the problem*. Each of three parameters is varied in the experiments. The following parameter values are chosen.

Four parallelization strategies used: SP, SE, RD, and FP. These strategies have been described above. Two problem sizes are used: the small experiment uses relations consisting of 5000 tuples each, so a total of 50000 tuples were involved in this query. The large experiment uses relations consisting of 40000 tuples each amounting to a total of 400.000 tuples in the query. These sizes will be referred to as the 5K and 40K experiments. For the 5K experiment, the number of processors used is varied from 20 to 80; for the 40K experiment we use 30 to 80 processors. The total size of the 40K query was too large to run on fewer than 30 processors. Finally, as explained in Section 3.5, we expect the strategies to perform differently for different query shapes. We are especially interested in the difference between (almost) linear and bushy trees, and in the difference between left and right-oriented trees. Therefore, the following 5 query shapes are used for this query: a right-linear, a right-oriented long bushy, a wide bushy, a left-oriented long bushy, and a left-linear tree.

## 4.3 Results

**Left Linear Join Tree** As a linear tree does not have any independent subtrees, SE allocates all available processors sequentially to each join. In this way, SE degenerates to SP for linear trees. Also, a left linear tree does not show any right-deep segments, and therefore RD allocates all available processors sequentially to each join operation. So, RD also degenerates to SP. The experiments indeed show coinciding performance for SP, SE, and RD, both for the 5K and for the 40K experiment.

Also, it is clear that SP (and for this case also SE and RD) works reasonable for small numbers of processors, but its performance degenerates for larger numbers of processors. The 5K experiment shows this effect stronger than the 40K experiment. This performance degradation is explained by the startup costs and coordination overhead. SP needs to start one operation process for each join on each processor. So, for the 80 processor case, 800 operation processes need to be initialized. Also, the coordination overhead for redistribution of operands may be large. The 5K experiment shows a more extensive performance degradation than the 40K experiment. This result corresponds to performance results for single operation queries (see Section 2.2).

FP execution of this query tree does show performance gain from parallelism. However, for the 40K experiment, its performance for a low degree of parallelism is not as good as SP.

**Left-oriented Bushy Join Tree**  The results for SP are similar to the results for the left linear tree. This fits with the expectation that SP is not very sensitive to the shape of the query tree.

The results show that SE and RD work much better than for the left linear case, but not as well FP (at least not for higher numbers of processors). The shape of this query is not very suitable for either RD or SE. RD profits from independent right-deep segments, which are very short for this tree. SE profits from independent subtrees, and those are very small. As a result, there is not much room for inter-join parallelism for RD and SE. This explains why the performance of both RD and SE for this tree is in between SP and FP.

The behavior of FP is similar to its behavior for the linear tree, but a close inspection of the data shows that its performance for small numbers of processors is slightly worse than for the linear tree.

**Wide Bushy Join Tree**  This query tree is very suitable for SE, because the tree is very wide resulting in nice independent subtrees. The results indeed show a good performance for SE. For the large experiment SE wins; for the small experiment SE is almost as good as FP.

FP performs well for the small experiment. This is caused by the fact that the operands are small, so FP does not suffer too much from delay over the pipeline. For a large number of operands, SE uses more operation processes than FP, so that the startup and coordination overhead dominates.

Like in the previous case FP suffers from pipeline delay for a small number of processors. This results in bad performance for a small number of processors and large operands, as explained for the previous case. Its speedup characteristics, however, outperform those of the other strategies and the performance for a large number of processors is good.

# Skew Handling in the DBS3 Parallel Database System*

Luc Bouganim[1,2], Daniela Florescu[1], Benoît Dageville[2]

[1] INRIA
Rocquencourt, France
firstname.lastname@inria.fr

[2] Bull
Grenoble, France
B.Dageville@frec.bull.fr

**Abstract:** *The gains of parallel query execution can be limited because of high start-up time, interference between execution entities, and poor load balancing. In this paper, we present a solution which reduces these limitations in DBS3, a shared-memory parallel database system. This solution combines static data partitioning and dynamic processor allocation to adapt to the execution context. It makes DBS3 almost insensitive to data skew and allows decoupling the degree of parallelism from the degree of data partitioning. To address the problem of load balancing in the presence of data skew, we analyze three important factors that influence the behavior of our parallel execution model: skew factor, degree of parallelism and degree of partitioning. We report on experiments varying these three parameters with the DBS3 prototype on a 72-node KSR1 multiprocessor. The results demonstrate high performance gains, even with highly skewed data.*

## 1 Introduction

DBS3 (Database System for Shared Store) [Ber91] is a parallel database system for shared-memory multiprocessors [Dew92a][Val93]. It has been implemented on an Encore Multimax with 10 processors and on a Kendal Square Research KSR1 with 72 processors. Although DBS3's run-time is designed for large shared-memory systems, the compiler supports a more general parallel execution model. During the EDS ESPRIT project (1989-1993), the compiler has been used to generate parallel code for the EDS shared-nothing parallel computer, the now Goldrush product from ICL.

In a shared-memory architecture, each processor has uniform access to the entire database through a global main memory. Thus, the *parallel scheduler,* which allocates processors to the query's operations, has much freedom for balancing the query load onto processors. However, query response time can be hurt by several barriers [Dew92a] which must be overcome by the scheduler:

- *start-up time:* before the execution takes place, a sequential initialization step is necessary. The duration of this step is proportional to the degree of parallelism and can actually dominate the execution time of low complexity queries. Thus, the degree of parallelism should be fixed according to the query complexity.
- *interference*: parallel access to shared software and hardware resources can create hot spots which increase waiting time. Parallel operations must be isolated, i.e., working on separated data sets, to minimize interference.
- *poor load balancing*: the response time of a set of parallel operations is that of the longest one. Thus, load balancing must deal with skewed data distributions and operations complexity.

* This work has been partially funded by the CEC under ESPRIT project IDEA.

A parallel execution plan is a graph of operations (filter, join, etc.) on database relations. Inter-operation parallelism is obtained by executing different operations in parallel. Intra-operation parallelism is obtained by executing the same operation on different relation partition. Relation partitioning can be done statically or at run-time.

With static partitioning, relations are physically partitioned using a *parallel storage model* based on a partitioning function like hashing. Relation partitioning typically dictates the degree of intra-query parallelism [Meh95]. This approach is very popular in research prototypes, e.g. Bubba [Bor90], Gamma [Dew90] and Volcano [Gra94], and commercial products, e.g. DB2, Informix, Tandem and Teradata. Static partitioning reduces interference between processors as they work on distinct data sets. It can scale up to large numbers of nodes, and works with either shared-memory or shared-nothing multiprocessors. However, static choices have a strong impact on performance as they influence load balancing and the degree of parallelism [Ham95]. In particular, start-up time may hurt the response time of low complexity queries.

Dynamic partitioning is advocated in XPRS [Hon92] and Oracle [Dav92] to overcome the problems of static partitioning. Relations are not stored using a parallel storage model but split, page by page among all the disks. Intra-operation parallelism is then obtained dynamically depending of the number of processors allocated for the operation. Thus, the degree of parallelism can be adjusted to the query complexity and the availability of memory and processors, to yield good load balancing. However, the fact that several processors may access the same data set (i.e. the entire relation) can yield high interference. Furthermore, this approach only works with shared-memory or shared-disk architecture.

Our solution in DBS3 tries to combine the advantages of static and dynamic partitioning. We use static partitioning to reduce interference and for compile-time query parallelization. We use dynamic allocation of processors to operations, independent of the degree of static partitioning, in order to control start up time and load balancing. This hybrid approach also simplifies database tuning since the degree of partitioning is not directly related to the degree of parallelism.

In this paper, we present the adaptative parallel query execution model of DBS3. To demonstrate the potential performance gains of our solution, we report on experiments varying the skew factor, the degree of parallelism and the degree of partitioning. The performance measurements were done on the KSR1 with 72 processors.

The paper is organized as follows. Section 2 presents DBS3's parallel execution model which is based on the parallel algebraic language Lera-par to represent parallel execution plans. Section 3 describes the implementation of the parallel execution model on a shared-memory system. Section 4 address the problem of load balancing in the presence of skewed data distributions. A simple analysis outlines three important factors that influence the behavior of our model: skew factor, degree of parallelism and degree of partitioning. Section 5 reports on experiments varying these factors with the 72-node KSR1 version of DBS3.

## 2   Parallel Execution Model

In DBS3, the compilation phase takes an ESQL query which is optimized [Lan94] and parallelized [Bol91]. The parallel execution plan produced by the compiler is expressed in Lera-par [Cha92] and captures the operations and their control.

Lera-par is a *dataflow* language whose expressive power is an extended relational algebra that supports ESQL. A Lera-par program is represented by a dataflow graph whose nodes are *operators* (like filter, join or map) and edges are *activators*. An activator denotes either a tuple (data activation) or a control message (control activation). In either case, when an operator receives an activation, the corresponding sequential operation is executed. Therefore, each activation acts as a sequential unit of work.

Lera-par's storage model is statically partitioned. Relations are partitioned by hashing on one or more attributes, and relation partitions are distributed onto disks in a round-robin fashion. Thus, the degree of partitioning can be independent of the number of disks. To obtain intra-operation parallelism, each node of the execution plan, whose input is a partitioned relation, gets as many instances as partitions. This yields an extended view of the Lera-par graph.

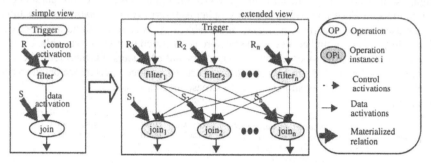

Figure 1: A parallel execution plan in Lera-par

*Pipelined* execution is an important aspect of Lera-par. It is expressed by using data activation between a producer node and a consumer node, which can then operate in parallel as soon as the consumer gets activated.

Figure 1 illustrates a simple execution plan which performs a selection (filter) on relation R followed by a join with S. A triggering activation is sent to all filter operation instances, which can then process their associated partition in parallel. The result tuples from the filter operation are pipelined to the next join operation. Each result tuple is sent to one join instance which is automatically activated to perform the join with the associated S partition.

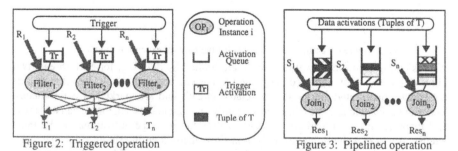

Figure 2: Triggered operation          Figure 3: Pipelined operation

To manage activations, a FIFO queue is associated to each operation instance. There are two kinds of queues, triggered or pipelined. A triggered queue is associated to an operation triggered by a control activation. It receives only one activation which starts the associated operation, e.g. the filter operation in our previous example (Figure 2)

A pipelined queue is associated to an operation which receives one operand in a pipeline fashion, e.g. the join operation in our example (Figure 3). In this case, each activation conveys one tuple and the queue will receive as many activations as pipelined tuples

# 3 Shared-Memory Implementation

In a shared-memory architecture, it is possible to uncouple the implementation of the parallel execution model from thread allocation. The typical thread allocation strategy would assign a single thread per operation instance. Instead, we allocate a pool of threads for the entire operation, independent of the operation instance. This is done by allocating the queues of an operation's instances in a shared-memory segment so all the threads of a pool can access all queues associated with the operation. Therefore, the threads can execute code for any activation in order to increase load balancing.

Figure 4 shows the basic data structures used for the implementation of our parallel execution model. Each node of the execution plan is described by an *operation* structure, which uses a table of activation *queues* and a table of *threads* to consume those activations. Because of parallel access, each structure is protected by a *mutex* variable. *Condition* variables are used to synchronize consumers and producers. Furthermore, there is an internal cache mechanism for activations in order to reduce interference between activation producers and consumers, and to increase locality of access.

operation:

| int | QueueNb | *Number of queues (instances) for this operation* |
| queue ** | QueueTbl | *Pointers to these queues* |
| int | CacheSize | *Size of thread's internal activation cache* |
| int | ThreadNb | *Number of consumer* |
| thread ** | ThreadTbl | *Consumer table (threads)* |
| void * | DBFunc | *Database function (ex: join, transmit, store...)* |
| Strategy | StrategyId | *Consumption strategy* |
| etc... | | |

queue:

| condition | NotFull | *Condition to wake producers* |
| mutex | Protect | *Protection mutex* |
| char * | Buffer | *Activation buffer* |
| etc ... | | |

thread:

| condition | NotEmpty | *Condition to wake consumer* |
| mutex | Protect | *Protection mutex* |
| bool * | MainQueue | *Table of boolean. Specifies if the $i^{th}$ queue is a main queue* |
| char * | IntCache | *Internal Cache buffer* |
| etc... | | |

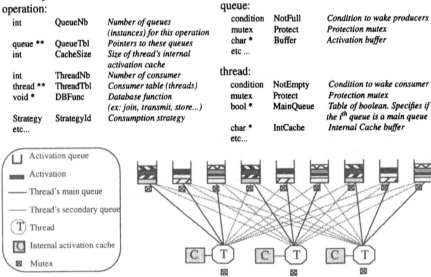

Figure 4: Basic data structures for the parallel execution model

Access conflicts to the activation queues are limited by defining, for each thread, two kinds of queues: main and secondary queues. For each operation, all activation queues are equally distributed among the associated threads and are marked as main queues. Therefore, each queue is the main queue of only one thread but each thread can have several main queues. A thread always tries to first consume the activations of the main queues. As there is a continuous activation flow, there is no interference for queue access. If all the main queues of a thread are empty, the thread would search in secondary queues. Thus, thread utilization is maximized as long as activations are available.

To summarize, this thread allocation strategy reduces the major barriers of parallel query execution by offering several means to adapt to the execution context. First, we can define the degree of parallelism independent of the degree of partitioning. Second, by controlling the number of threads per pool, we can achieve better balancing of CPU power between operations. Finally, each thread can dynamically choose in which queue to consume activations which should yields good load balancing.

# 4 Load Balancing with Skewed Data Distributions

Several solutions have been proposed to reduce the negative impact from skew. [Kit90] presents a robust hash-join algorithm for a specific parallel architecture based on shared-nothing. The idea is to partition each hash bucket in fragments and spread them among the processors (*bucket spreading*). Then a sophisticated network, the Omega network, is used to redistribute buckets onto the processors. The Omega network contains logic to balance the load during redistribution. [Omi91] proposes a similar approach in a shared-memory parallel system, using the *first fit decreasing* heuristic to assign buckets to processors. Finally, [Dew92b] suggests the use of multiple algorithms, each specialized for a different degree of skew, and the use of a small sample of the relations to determine which algorithm is appropriate.

The effects of non uniform data distribution (i.e. skew) on parallel execution [Wal91] are summarized in Figure 5.The example shows a filter-join query applied to two relations $R$ and $S$ which are poorly partitioned. Such poor partitioning stems from either the data or the partitioning function. Thus, the processing times of the two activations for triggering the operation instances *filter1* and *filter2* are not equal. The case of the join operation is worse. The uneven size of $S$ partitions yields different processing times for the activations from the filter operation. Furthermore, the number of activations received is different from one instance to another because of poor redistribution of the partitions of $R$ or variable selectivity according to the partition of $R$ processed.

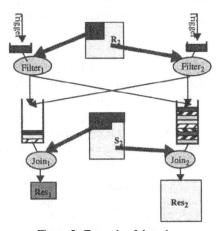

Figure 5: Example of data skew

Assuming all the data to be processed are main-memory resident, the problem of skewed data distribution reduces to that of optimizing CPU utilization. Thus, to obtain a query response time that is insensitive to skew, we must equally balance the load of each operation onto all the allocated threads. In the rest of this section, we consider the effect of skew on a single operation.

## 4.1 Analysis

We now analyze the effect of skew in our model on an operation execution. The objective is to derive an analytical formula that gives the overhead on the response time induced by skew. In DBS3, each thread can access all the activation queues of the operation. The default mode of queue consumption is random, i.e. the thread randomly chooses one queue among the non empty ones associated with its operation. Thus, thread utilization is maximum as long as activations are available. However, at operation end, when there is no more activation, threads become idle as they terminate until the last thread completes processing its activation.

Let us now consider an operation execution with $a$ activations and $n$ threads. $P$ indicates the average processing time for an activation. To maximize thread utilization, we must have $n \leq a$, otherwise, $n-a$ threads would be idle. In the worst case, one thread will consume the last activation when all other threads have terminated. During the processing of this last activation, only one thread is active and thread utilization is minimum.

Let $T_{ideal}$ be the ideal execution time for the operation, when all threads complete simultaneously, and $T_{worst}$ be the worst time. To compute $v$, the overhead of the worst time, we have the following equation for $T_{worst}$:

$$T_{worst} = (1+v) \times T_{ideal} = (1+v) \times \left(\frac{a \times P}{n}\right) \qquad (1)$$

The worst case scenario can be seen with two phases. In the first phase, all activations but the most expensive one are processed. Let $P_{max}$ be the time to process the last activation (i.e. the most expensive one), the execution time for the first phase is: $((a \times P) - P_{max})/n$ .

The second phase corresponds to the processing of the last activation whose time is $P_{max}$. Thus, we can compute $v$ as follows:

$$v \leq \frac{P_{max}}{P} \times \frac{(n-1)}{a} \qquad (2)$$

Equation (2) exhibits that the overhead depends on three factors: skew factor ($P_{max}/P$), degree of parallelism ($n$) and number of activations ($a$). For the latter, we have two interesting cases, depending on whether $a$ is high or low:

- *The number of activation is high.* This case corresponds to a pipelined operation with lots of tuples. $a$ is then equal to the cardinality of the pipelined relation. Thus, $v$ is quite small and the execution time of the operation is close to $T_{ideal}$. This good result is independent of thread consumption strategy and of skew.

- *The number of activation is low.* This case corresponds to a pipelined operation with few tuples or to a triggered operation. The overhead due to skew can then be quite serious. A solution is to use a consumption strategy that reduces this overhead, like LPT (Longest Processing Time First) which processes the most expensive activations with highest priority.

## 5 Experiments

In this section, we show though experimentation how our adaptative parallel execution model can be exploited to deal with a varying execution context. We first present the environment for the experiments, in particular, the KSR1 machine and the queries. Then we address the problem of load balancing in the presence of skewed data distributions. We report experiments by varying three important factors that influence the behavior of our model: skew factor, degree of parallelism and degree of partitioning.

### 5.1 The KSR1 Machine

DBS3 runs on a KSR1 multiprocessor at Inria. The KSR1 machine provides a shared-memory programming model in a scalable highly parallel architecture [Fran93]. It has a hybrid architecture in the sense that the memory is physically distributed and virtually shared using hardware mechanisms. Each processor has its own 32 Megabytes memory, called local cache. The Allcache memory system provides the user with a virtual shared-memory space which corresponds to the collection of all the local caches. When a processor accesses a data item which is not already cached, this item is shipped transparently to the local memory of this processor by the Allcache memory system. The configuration used for the experiments includes 72 * 40 MIPS processors for a total main memory of 2.3 Gb. As only one disk of the KSR1 was available to us, we simulate disk accesses to base relations with the following parameters:

| Disk Parameter | Value | Comment |
|---|---|---|
| Nb Disk | 1 per processor | Number of simulated disk |
| Rotation Time | 17 ms | Disk latency [Meh95] |
| Seek Time | 5 ms | |
| Transfer Rate | 6 MB/s | |
| I/O Cache Size | 8 pages | Buffer cache for sequential scans |

## 5.2 Databases and Queries

In all the experiments, we use the relations of the Wisconsin benchmark [Bit83]. These relations are partitioned based on hashing. In our experiments, we use two Lera-par execution plan: IdealJoin which indicates a parallel join where both operands (A and B') are partitioned on the join attribute in the same number of buckets, and AssocJoin where one operand (B') must be dynamically repartitioned before the parallel join (the other one (A) is partitioned on the join attribute). Figure 6 and 7 shows the parallel execution plans for these operations.

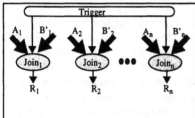

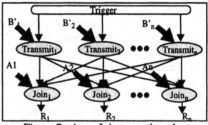

Figure 6: IdealJoin execution plan     Figure 7: AssocJoin execution plan

To do a thorough study of skewed data partitioning and high degree of partitioning, we had to generate a large number of databases (more than 50). The disk size available to us was relatively small (one Gigabyte). Therefore, measurements on large databases were avoided whenever possible. With small databases (i.e. 100 or 200 KTuples), index-based joins run too fast and make the result analysis difficult as the response time is of the same order of magnitude than measurement errors. Thus, when the join algorithm has no impact, we use a nested-loop join in order to slow down the execution time. In other cases, we use larger databases (500 Ktuples) and build indexes on the fly. We repeated each measurement six times and took the average result.

## 5.3 Expt 1: Varying the Skew

To get more practical insights on the previous analytical results, we performed several experiments with IdealJoin and AssocJoin for varying skews. We have created many databases for which we have varied the tuple distribution within partitions. To determine partition cardinality, we use a Zipf function [Zip49] which yields a factor between 0 (no skew) and 1 (high skew). Each database has two relations A and B' of 100K and 10K tuples, respectively. Each relation is statically partitioned in 200 partitions.

For each database (obtained by changing the skew of A), we have run the two queries AssocJoin and IdealJoin with 10 threads to obtain their response time. In the case of AssocJoin, B' is redistributed, so 10K tuples move through the pipeline. Figure 8 shows the relative performance degradation when skew is increased and confirms the analytical results. The execution time measured is quite constant whatever the skew (<2%). It also shows the graph for the worst case degradation according to the analytical formula. Even in the worst case, the maximum deviation is small (3%). Thus, this experiment shows that we obtain an ideal execution time, independent of the skew factor.

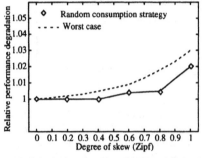

Figure 8: Degradation with AssocJoin

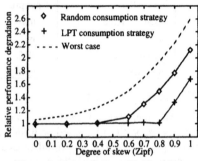

Figure 9: Degradation with Ideal Join

IdealJoin is a triggered operation. Thus, the number of activations is equal to the number of operation instances. Figure 9 shows the results of running this operation by varying the skew and changing the consumption strategy. For low skew factors, we obtain good results independent of the consumption strategy. Since the relation has 200 partitions, each partition is relatively small which yields good load balancing, even with Random. However, with a higher skew, LPT becomes better than Random, and remains insensitive to skew up to a skew factor of 0.8. The inflection after 0.8 is due to the execution time of the longest activation. This is because after 0.8, the execution time of this activation is higher than the ideal time of the whole operation, that is $P_{max} > (a \times P)/n$. With LPT, even if this activation is processed first, the operation response time is equal to the execution time of this first activation.

### 5.4 Expt 2: Varying the Degree of Parallelism

We now turn to the impact of increasing the degree of intra-operation parallelism on load balancing. We use similar databases, but with larger relations (200K and 20K tuples) in order to minimize error propagation in measurements. We ran the queries AssocJoin and IdealJoin (using nested loop) on a set of skewed databases. For each database, we vary the number of threads from 1 to 100 using 70 processors of the KSR1. Figure 10 and 11 show the speed-up results. With non skewed relations, the results are very good with a speed-up greater than 60 with 70 processors for both queries.

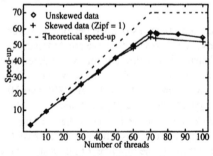

Figure 10: AssocJoin speed-up

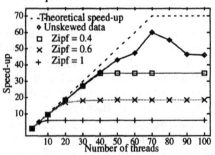

Figure 11: IdealJoin speed-up

With skewed relations, the results are different depending on whether the operation is pipelined or triggered. In the case of pipelined operation (AssocJoin), the high number of activations (20,000) can well absorb bad distributions, even with a high number of threads. Using Equation (2), we can analyze the behavior of AssocJoin. With 70 threads and the worst skew, the execution time is only 12% worse than the ideal time. Our measurements indicate that this worst case is overestimated since it never exceeds 5%.

In the case of triggered operation (IdealJoin), the results are not as good. With skewed relations, the speed-up reaches a ceiling of number of threads depending on the skew. Again, this is because of the longest activation $P_{max}$. When $P_{max} > (a \times P)/n$, the operation execution time is that of this single activation, independent of the number of threads. Thus, there is no gain in using a degree of parallelism greater than $n_{max} = (a \times P)/P_{max}$, i.e. the sequential execution time of the operation over the sequential time of the longest activation. The theoretical values of $n_{max}$ obtained from this formula are confirmed in Figure 11.

To summarize, the horizontal fragmentation of an operation into a high number of sequential units of work can absorb skewed data distributions and get much better performance than with small numbers of fragments.

## 5.5 Expt 3: Varying the degree of partitioning

The degree of relation partitioning on disks typically determines the degree of parallelism, hence the choice of full declustering [Meh95] or partial declustering [Cop88]. In DBS3, the degree of partitioning can be higher than the number of disks which is useful to reduce the effect of skewed data distribution. However, having more partitions than disks can induce some overhead since there are more queues to be created and accessed. In the rest of this section, we evaluate this overhead through experimentation and measure the improvement of a high degree of partitioning on skew.

### 5.5.1. Overhead of a High Degree of Partitioning

To study this overhead, we created several databases by varying the degree of partitioning of the two unskewed relations (of 100K and 10K tuples). We use the query IdealJoin for the overhead of a triggered join and AssocJoin for the overhead of a pipelined join. The measurements use 20 threads and a degree of partitioning varying from 20 to 1500.

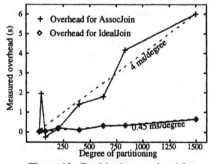
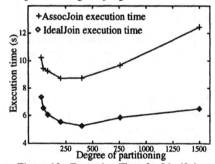

Figure 12: Partitioning overhead for IdealJoin and AssocJoin (No temp. index)

Figure 13: Execution Time for IdealJoin and AssocJoin (with temporary index)

Figure 12 shows the overhead for IdealJoin and AssocJoin without indexes. This overhead is computed as the difference of the measured time and the theoretical time[*]. Note that this difference does not depend on the join algorithm but on the kind of operation.

The overhead can be approximated with a straight line (dotted line), using the ratio 0.45 ms/degree for IdealJoin and 4 ms/degree for AssocJoin. The difference between these ratios has a simple explanation. In the case of IdealJoin, there is only one activation per partition and as many queues to create. In the case of AssocJoin, there are two groups of queues (one for the redistribution and one for the join) and 10K activations.

The overhead for a pipelined execution may be significant. However, it enables very high degree of partitioning (in the order of 1K) with little global overhead. The reason is that the gains obtained from algorithmic simplification can compensate the overhead due to partitioning. This is obvious for a nested loop join. It is less obvious when using indices. Thus, Figure 13 shows the results for the same queries using a temporary index with relations of 500K and 50K tuples. In this Figure, the overhead dominates the gain when d > 1000 for AssocJoin and d > 1400 for IdealJoin.

These experiments show the limited impact of the overhead incurred by a high degree of partitioning on unskewed relations.

### 5.5.2. Using a High Degree of Partitioning for Skewed Data

We now use this property of low impact overhead incurred by a high degree of partitioning to deal with skewed data distributions in the case of triggered operations. We run the IdealJoin query with 20 threads and relations of 500K and 50K tuples, and 100K and 10K tuples. The degree of partitioning varies from 20 to 1500. We ran the queries with a uniform distribution (Zipf = 0) and a skewed distribution (Zipf = 0.6). The consumption strategy for the threads is LPT. We used the measurements to compute the overhead $v$ of execution time ($T_{0.6}$) with respect to execution time without skew ($T_0$) obtained as follows: (see equation 1): $v_{0.6} = T_{0.6}/T_0 - 1$. Figure 14 shows the values of $v_{0.6}$ for IdealJoin with and without index. The two curves are almost identical. It confirms that the behavior of our model with data skew is independent of the join algorithm. The other graph shows the worst value of $v$ (equation 2).

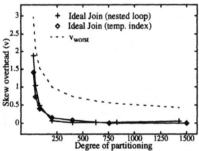

Figure 14: Skew overhead with IdealJoin

In the case of a triggered operation applied to skewed data, the advantage of a high degree of partitioning is clear. By increasing the degree of partitioning, the granule of the sequential unit of work gets smaller (one activation = one partition) and the LPT strategy can better balance the load on the threads.

In the case of a pipelined operation, the granule of sequential processing is very small (one activation = one tuple) and a higher degree of partitioning does not modify the overhead since the number of activations remains the same. We also verified this observation by experimenting with AssocJoin, and we obtained $T_{0.6} = T_0$ for any degree of partitioning ($v_{0.6} < 0.03$).

In general, complex queries will include both triggered and pipelined operations. A high degree of partitioning allows more efficient processing of skewed data distributions for triggered operations. However, it yields some overhead for pipelined operations which is well compensated by the gains obtained on triggered operations.

---

* Let $T^{20}$ be the time measured with a degree of partitioning 20, the theoretical time for degree d is obtained by $T^d = T^{20} \times (20/d)$ (Nested loop algorithm).

# 6 Conclusion

The barriers to parallel query execution are start-up time of parallel operations, interference and poor load balancing among the processors due to skewed data distribution. In this paper, we have described how these problems are addressed in DBS3, a shared-memory database system implemented on a 72-node KSR1 multiprocessor.

Our solution combines the advantages of static and dynamic partitioning. We use static partitioning of relations to reduce interference and dynamic allocation of processors to operations to reduce start-up time and improve load balancing. This adaptative approach also simplifies database tuning since the degree of partitioning does not dictate the degree of parallelism.

A major advantage of our solution is to be able to deal efficiently with skew by allowing each execution entity (thread) to dynamically choose which operation's instance it will execute and by increasing the degree of partitioning. To quantify the potential gains, we did a performance analysis and ran experiments on our prototype with different databases of the Wisconsin benchmark.

The behavior of our parallel execution model in front of skew depends heavily on the nature of the operation. In DBS3, pipelined operation are *naturally* insensitive to skew. This is because the high number of units of work (activations) produced by pipelined execution yields good load balancing even in difficult situations (high skew, high degree of parallelism).

For a triggered operation, the number of activations depends on the degree of partitioning of the operand relations. Heuristics can be used to reduce the overhead of skew. However, with high skew, the execution time is bounded by the time of the longest activation.Thus, there is no gain in increasing the degree of parallelism. An effective solution is to use a high degree of partitioning, since our models allow it with an insignificant overhead.

With a high degree of partitioning, our model is almost insensitive to skew and yields excellent performance. We obtained good speed-up using the 72 processors of the KSR1, even in presence of skew. These results are due to both our DBS3 hybrid model (static partitioning, dynamic processor allocation) and the hybrid architecture of the KSR1 (physically distributed, virtually shared-memory).

Since pipelined operations are insensitive to skew, a simple execution strategy would be to run as many operations as possible in pipelined mode. This strategy resists to bad data distributions but may yield high overhead, especially with limited memory size. The problem reduces to that of grain of parallelism. Coarse-grain parallelism (triggered operation) is bad with data skew but has limited overhead. Conversely, fine-grain parallelism (pipelined operation) makes the operation insensitive to skew but may yield high overhead. Future work in DBS3 will address this problem by allowing the choice of the grain of parallelism independent of the operation semantics.

**Acknowledgments:**

The authors thank Patrick Valduriez for his assistance in the preparation of this paper and Michael Franklin for his careful reading. They also want to thank J.P. Chieze and A. Clo who helped us manage the KSR1 at Inria, and finally, all the members of the DBS3 team for their cooperation.

# 7 References

[Ber91]    B. Bergsten, M. Couprie, P. Valduriez, "Prototyping DBS3, a shared-memory parallel database system". *Int. Conf. on Parallel and Distributed Information Systems*, Florida, 1991.

[Bit83]    D. Bitton, D. J. DeWitt, C. Turbyfill, "Benchmarking database systems - A systematic approach", *Int. Conf. on VLDB*, Firenze, 1983.

[Bor90]    H. Boral, W. Alexander, L. Clay, G. Copeland, S. Danforth, M. Franklin, P. Valduriez, "Prototyping Bubba, A highly parallel database system". *IEEE Knowledge and Data Engineering*, 2, 1990.

[Bol91]    P. Borla-Salamet, C. Chachaty, B. Dageville, "Compiling Control into Database Queries for Parallel Execution Management". *Int. Conf. on Parallel and Distributed Information Systems*, Florida, 1991.

[Cha92]    C. Chachaty, P. Borla-Salamet, M. Ward, "A Compositional Approach for the Design of a Parallel Query Processing Language", *Int. Conf. on Parallel Architectures and Language Europe*, Paris, 1992.

[Cop88]    G. Copeland, W. Alexander, E. Boughter & T. Keller, "Data Placement in bubba", *Int. Conf. ACM-SIGMOD*, Chicago, 1988.

[Dag94]    B. Dageville, P. Casadessus, P. Borla-Salamet, "The Impact of the KSR1 AllCache Architecture on the Behaviour of the DBS3 Parallel DBMS", *Int. Conf. on Parallel Architectures and Language Europe*, Athen, 1994.

[Dav92]    D. D. Davis, "Oracle's Parallel Punch for OLTP", *Datamation*, 1992.

[Dew90]    D. J. DeWitt, S. Ghandeharizadeh, D. Schneider, A. Bricker, H. Hsiao & R. Rasmussen, "The Gamma Database Machine Project", *IEEE Transactions on Knowledge and Data Engineering*, 2, 1990.

[Dew92a]   D.J. DeWitt, J. Gray, "Parallel Database Systems: the Future of High Performance Database Systems", *Comm. of the ACM*, 35 (6), 1992.

[Dew92b]   D.J. DeWitt, J.F. Naughton, D.A. Schneider, S. Seshadri, "Practical Skew Handling in Parallel Joins", *Int. Conf. on VLDB*, Vancouver, 1992.

[Fran93]   S. Frank, H. Burkhardt, J. Rothnie, "The KSR1: Bridging the Gap Between Shared-Memory and MPPs", *Compcon'93*, San Francisco, 1993.

[Gra94]    G. Graefe, "Volcano, An Extensible and Parallel Dataflow Query Processing System", *IEEE Transaction on Knowledge and Data Engineering*, 6, 1994.

[Ham95]    A. Hameurlain, F. Morvan, "Scheduling and Mapping for Parallel Execution of Extended SQL Queries", *Int. Conf. on Information and Knowledge Engineering*, Baltimore, 1995.

[Hon92]    W. Hong, "Exploiting Inter-Operation Parallelism in XPRS", *Int. Conf. ACM-SIGMOD*, San Diego, 1992.

[Hsi94]    H. Hsiao, M. S. Chen, P. S. Yu, "On Parallel Execution of Multiple Pipelined Hash Joins", *Int. Conf. ACM-SIGMOD*, Minneapolis, 1994.

[Kit90]    M. Kitsuregawa, Y. Ogawa, "Bucket Spreading Parallel Hash: A New, Robust, Parallel Hash Join Method for Data Skew in the Super Database Computer", *Int. Conf on VLDB*, Brisbane, Australia, 1990.

[Lan94]    R. Lanzelotte, P. Valduriez, M. Zait, M. Ziane, "Industrial-Strength Parallel Query Optimization: issues and lessons", *Information Systems*, 19 (4), 1994.

[Meh95]    M. Metha, D. DeWitt, "Managing Intra-operator Parallelism in Parallel Database Systems" *Int. Conf. on VLDB*, Zurich, 1995.

[Omi91]    E. Omiecinski, "Performance Analysis of a Load Balancing Hash-Join Algorithm for a Shared-Memory Multiprocessor", *Int. Conf on VLDB*, Barcelona, 1991.

[Val93]    P. Valduriez, "Parallel Database Systems: open problems and new issues.", *Int. Journal on Distributed and Parallel Databases*, 1 (2), 1993.

[Wal91]    C.B. Walton, A.G. Dale, R.M. Jenevin, "A taxonomy and Performance Model of Data Skew Effects in Parallel Joins" *Int. Conf. on VLDB*, Barcelona, 1991.

[Zip49]    G. K. Zipf, *Human Behavior and the Principle of Least Effort: An Introduction to Human Ecology*, Reading, MA, Addison-Wesley, 1949.

# Dynamic Declustering Methods
# for Parallel Grid Files*

Paolo Ciaccia[1], Arianna Veronesi[2]

[1] DEIS - CSITE-CNR, University of Bologna - Italy, pciaccia@deis.unibo.it
[2] CINECA, Casalecchio di Reno (Bologna) - Italy, veronesi@cineca.it

**Abstract.** Several declustering functions for distributing multi-attribute data on a set of disks have been proposed in recent years. Since these functions map grid regions to disks in a static way, performance deteriorates in case of dynamic datasets and/or non-stationary data distributions. We first analyze how declustering functions can be extended in order to deal with dynamic datasets without requiring periodic reorganizations. In order to support dynamic declustering, we propose to organize the directory as a parallel Multilevel Grid File. On this structure we experiment five dynamic declustering functions and two index-based allocation methods that only use locally available information. This first comparison among the two approaches reveals that methods based on local criteria always yield better results.

## 1  Introduction

Efficient management of large multi-attribute datasets is a key requirement for many advanced database applications dealing with scientific and statistical data, images, geographic maps, etc., stored on secondary memory devices. Since this requires to increase the overall performance of the I/O subsystem [DG92], a common and viable technique to reduce the response time of queries is to *decluster* data across a set of disks in order to exploit parallelism at the I/O level [PGK88].

Many algorithms for multi-attribute declustering, aiming to efficiently support multi-dimensional *range queries*, today exist. Methods based on *declustering functions* – DM [DS82], CMD [LSR92], FX [KP88], ECC [FM91], HCAM [FB93], and others – operate by first partitioning the data space into an orthogonal grid, and then mapping each cell of the grid to a specific disk. Since the mapping from space regions to disks is *static*, these methods cannot efficiently manage cases where either the size of the file or data distribution change over time. On the other hand, *index-based* methods, such as those proposed for R-trees [KF92], perform incremental (*dynamic*) declustering by mapping a new index node or data page to a disk according to some heuristic criterion that takes into account only local information.

In this article we propose a new approach to the declustering problem, which consists in using *dynamic* declustering functions (DDFs), able to adapt to data size and distribution. This implies that no *a priori* partitioning of the space and no reorganization is needed. After analyzing issues related to directory management, we argue that a parallel Multilevel Grid File, called "multiplexed" Grid

---

* This work has been partially supported by the ESPRIT LTR project no. 9141, HERMES, and by Italian CNR, Grant no. 95.00443.CT12.

File (MX-GF), is the best alternative to organize index nodes on disks. Because of the paged organization of MX-GF, we are also able to consider index-based declustering methods, namely *Round-Robin* (RR) and *Proximity Index* (PI). We experimentally compare the different methods and conclude that those based on local information are superior to the others. In particular, the PI method is the best choice for either small queries (regardless of data distribution) or uniform distributions (regardless of query size), whereas RR outperforms other methods in the case of medium-large queries on skewed distributions.

The rest of the paper is organized as follows. Section 2 provides basic background on declustering functions. Section 3 describes our approach in general terms. Section 4 introduces dynamic versions of specific declustering functions. Section 5 describes MX-GF and the two index-based methods. Section 6 presents experimental results.

## 2   Background and Motivation

In the following, for simplicity of exposition, we refer to a 2-dimensional space, but generalization to higher dimensions is immediate.

Consider a file of 2-dimensional points (records), and a set of $M$ disk units. When using a declustering function, the space is partitioned into an $S \times S$ orthogonal grid, so that each *cell* of the grid can be identified by its row-column coordinates, $I_1, I_2 \in [0, S-1]$. Each declustering method, *met*, maps cell identifiers (coordinates) into disk identifiers by using the $diskOf_{met}()$ function, that is:

$$diskOf_{met} : [0, S-1] \times [0, S-1] \to [0, M-1]$$

*Example 1.* The *disk modulo* (DM) method [DS82] is defined as:[3]

$$diskOf_{DM}(I_1, I_2) = (I_1 + I_2) \bmod M$$

whereas the *error correcting codes* (ECC) method [FM91], which requires $M = 2^m$ ($m \geq 1$) and $S = 2^s$, declusters grid cells by means of the parity check matrix of a binary code. Cell coordinates are represented using $s$ bits each, which are then interleaved to form the (binary) cell identifier, $Z(I_1, I_2)$, also called the *Z-value* of the cell [Ore86]. This is multiplied by the $m \times 2s$ parity check matrix, $\mathbf{H}_{2s}$, and the result, which is an $m$-bit vector, is the disk-id:

$$diskOf_{ECC}(I_1, I_2) = (\mathbf{H}_{2s} \cdot Z(I_1, I_2)')_2$$

where prime denotes vector transposition.[4] Figure 1 shows the mapping on 4 disks of a $4 \times 4$ grid generated by DM and ECC methods, respectively, the latter using the matrix $\mathbf{H}_4$ shown in the figure.                                    □

Performance of function-based declustering methods is usually evaluated with respect to the class of (orthogonal) range queries, by measuring how well they map cells to disks in such a way that approximately the same number of cells

---

[3] The more recent *Coordinate Modulo Distribution* (CMD) [LSR92] is a variant of DM which requires the grid size to be a multiple of $M$.

[4] In [KF92] a cell identifier is obtained by concatenating, rather than interleaving, the binary representations of its coordinates. This distinction is immaterial for the understanding of the ECC method.

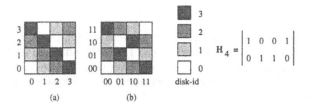

**Fig. 1.** The DM (a) end ECC (b) declustering methods.

satisfies the query on each disk. Let $q$ be a range query, and $C_i$ the number of cells that satisfy $q$ on the $i$-th disk , i.e. cells whose region intersects $q$. The *response time* of query $q$ is then defined as $\max\{C_0, C_1, \ldots, C_{M-1}\}$, to be compared to the *optimal response time* $\lceil \sum_i C_i / M \rceil$.

Experimental analysis has shown that no method is superior to the others for all the possible query and database scenarios (i.e. file size, number of disks, number of dimensions, size and shape of queries, etc.), with respect to the above performance metric [HS94]. The basic assumption which justifies a metric based on "counting the cells" is the existence of a 1-to-1 correspondence between cells and data pages (buckets), that is, between grid regions and data regions, so that the above-defined response time is indeed a measure of the (parallel) I/O complexity of a query. In practice, in order to avoid poor storage utilization, two or more cells can share a same data page, in which case the usual approach is to store the bucket in a randomly chosen disk (among those the sharing cells are mapped to) [ZSC94].

## 2.1 Limits of Static Declustering Functions

Parallel organizations based on known declustering functions are appropriate only for almost static datasets, for which neither file size nor data distribution change through time. When data distribution is non-stationary, even if the grid is initially designed to minimize data skew among cells [LRS93], this partitioning soon becomes obsolete. For stationary distributions, problems can arise if the size of the dataset changes, because the *granularity* of declustering cannot be explicitly controlled. When the file grows, data pages split. Since the regions of the new pages are included in the region of the split page, which is statically mapped to the $i$-th disk, the new pages are stored in disk $i$ as well. Thus, *the number of data pages which can correspond to a single cell of the declustered grid is unbounded*. If the file shrinks, merge of data pages easily leads to situations where no effective declustering control can be exerted, because of the above cited random assignment policy.

*Example 2.* Consider the ECC mapping of Figure 1 (b), and assume that each cell corresponds to a data page with $c = 2$ points. ECC (as well as any other method) is trivially optimal for each query that retrieves a single cell. However, if the file grows so that each of the 16 cells corresponds to, say, 4 data pages, this is no longer true. On the other hand, assume that file shrinks and only 4 data pages are needed, corresponding to four equally-sized square regions. Each of these data regions covers 4 cells, which are mapped by ECC to 4 different disks. Then, if assignment of data pages to disks occurs randomly, the method reduces to a pure random declustering strategy, which is known to perform poorly. □

## 3 The Approach

In order to remediate problems due to static declustering functions, we propose to extend them in such a way that they can gradually adapt to both changes in data distribution and file size, without requiring periodical reorganizations. As a first step, we define how a dynamic declustering function should operate on an orthogonal grid.

**Property 1** *The dynamic declustering function (DDF) based on method met, denoted $diskOf_{met+}()$, behaves like $diskOf_{met}()$, for each $S_l \times S_l$ grid such that $S_l = 2^l \times S_0$ ($l \geq 0, S_0 \geq 1$), that is:*

$$diskOf_{met+}(I_1, I_2) = diskOf_{met}(I_1, I_2)$$

$\forall l \geq 0, \forall I_1, I_2 \in [0, S_l - 1]$, *where l is the "grid level" and $S_0$ the initial grid size.*

Thus, we simply require that a DDF still correctly maps, according to the *met* criterion, all the grid regions which result from a doubling of the number of intervals on each dimension. In the following w.l.o.g. we assume that $S_0 = 1$.

*Example 3.* According to Property 1, if the $4 \times 4$ grid of Figure 1 (a) expands to an $8 \times 8$ grid, $diskOf_{DM+}()$ has to map the cells as shown in Figure 2, since this is the mapping of $diskOf_{DM}()$ for such a grid. □

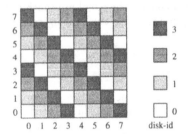

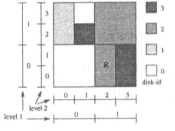

**Fig. 2.** An $8 \times 8$ grid declustered by the DM method.

**Fig. 3.** The DM$^+$ method.

For Property 1 to hold, and regardless of the specific *met*, when an interval $I$ is split, the two new subintervals have to be assigned values $2 \times I$ and $2 \times I + 1$. For instance, interval 2 in a $4 \times 4$ grid, corresponds to intervals 4 and 5 in a $8 \times 8$ grid. Any other numbering schema for the new (sub)intervals would not preserve the correspondence between interval values and their (relative) position in space, thus losing the basic property on which declustering functions are based. For instance, this is the case with the extension proposed in [ZSC94].

In the general case, where data regions of variable size are present, a DDF should provide a consistent way of mapping such regions to disks, thus avoiding as much as possible any form of "random assignment". Consider a region $R$, obtained by recursive binary partitioning of the space. Then, there is a single grid level, $S_{l_1}$, such that there exists an interval, $I_1 \in [0, S_{l_1} - 1]$, which exactly spans $R$'s extension on the first coordinate. The same holds for the 2nd coordinate, for which a level, $S_{l_2}$, and an interval, $I_2 \in [0, S_{l_2} - 1]$, are univocally identified. We call $l_1$ and $l_2$ the "grid levels" of region $R$. Then, we can generalize Property 1 as follows.

**Property 2** *Let R be a region, with coordinate values $(I_1, I_2)$, where $I_1 \in [0, S_{l_1} - 1]$, $I_2 \in [0, S_{l_2} - 1]$, and $l_1$ and $l_2$ are the grid levels of R. The dynamic declustering function (DDF) based on method met behaves like $diskOf_{met}()$, applied to the $S_{l_1} \times S_{l_2}$ grid.*

*Example 4.* Consider the regions in Figure 3. Region $R$ has coordinate values $I_1 = 2$ (at level $l_1 = 2$), and $I_2 = 0$ (at level $l_2 = 1$). Therefore, with $M = 4$ disks, the DM$^+$ method maps $R$ to disk $(2 + 0) \bmod 4 = 2$. Other disk-id values are obtained in a similar way. □

In order to characterize different DDFs, we introduce two requirements that a "good" DDF should satisfy. They are both related to the *smoothness* of the declustering process.

**Definition 1.** Consider a region $R$, currently mapped to disk $i$, which has to be split into two subregions. A DDF has the **Mem** (memory reuse) property if it maps back to disk $i$ at least one of the two subregions, and has the **Dec** (declustering) property if it maps the two subregions to different disks.

If a DDF has the **Mem** property, the disk space freed by $R$ is immediately reused, which is a desirable feature. The **Dec** property, on the other hand, guarantees that *each* split results in the declustering of the two new subregions. Figure 4 shows the ideal case where both **Mem** and **Dec** properties hold.

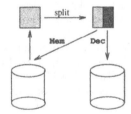

**Fig. 4.** The case where both **Mem** and **Dec** properties hold.

## 4 Dynamic Declustering Functions

In this Section we define and analyze the behavior of several DDFs. The first of them, DM$^+$, is analogous to static DM, the new feature being only the way new intervals are numbered. Figure 3 is an example of how DM$^+$ works. It can be observed that DM$^+$ enjoys the **Dec**, but not the **Mem** property. The table below summarizes results with respect to the **Mem** and **Dec** properties for all the methods we have analyzed.

| | DM$^+$ | Z$^+$ | HCAM$^+$ | ECC$^+$ | FX$^+$ |
|---|---|---|---|---|---|
| Mem | | | * | * | |
| Dec | * | * | * | * | * |

## 4.1 Fractal Methods: $Z^+$ and $HCAM^+$

Space-filling (*fractal*) curves visit each region of an $S_l \times S_l$ ($S_l = 2^l$) grid exactly once, thus establishing a linear ordering on regions. Declustering functions based on such methods rely on this ordering to map regions to disks in a round-robin fashion. The Z (or Peano) curve of order $l$, $Z_l$, is bit interleaving applied to binary representation of coordinate values. This generates so-called *Z-values* of length $2l$ [Ore86], which, interpreted as binary numbers, are then mapped to disks, i.e.: $diskOf_Z(I_1, I_2) = Z(I_1, I_2)_2 \mod M$ (see Figure 5).

A similar idea inspires the *Hilbert Curve Allocation Method* (HCAM) [FB93] which uses the Hilbert curve of order $l$, $H_l$ (see Figure 5), to visit regions and assign *H-values* to them: $diskOf_{HCAM}(I_1, I_2) = H(I_1, I_2) \mod M$.

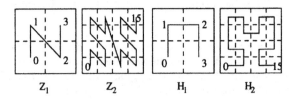

**Fig. 5.** Z and Hilbert curves of order 1 and 2.

The $Z^+$ DDF is obtained by allowing variable-length Z-values. Thus, for each region $R$ we consider the corresponding intervals $I_1$ and $I_2$ at levels $l_1$ and $l_2$, interleave them, interpret the result as a binary number, and take the modulus. Figure 6 (a) illustrates how $Z^+$ works. $Z^+$ does not have the **Mem** property, but it has the **Dec** property, since Z-values of regions originated by a split are consecutive integers.

The extension of HCAM is only a bit more involved. If a region $R$ has grid levels $l_1 = l_2 = l$, then its H-value is obtained from its position in $H_l$, the Hilbert curve of order $l$. The other possible case, considering that splits are done cyclically, is to have $l_1 = l_2 + 1$. Among the two square regions of $H_{l_1}$ which compose $R$, we select the minimum of the two H-values (see Figure 6 (b)). $HCAM^+$ does not have the **Mem** property. For instance, splitting the region $(0, 1)$, for which it is $H(0, 1) = 1$, yields regions $(00, 1)$ ($(00, 1) = 4$) and $(01, 1)$ ($(01, 1) = 6$), which are both mapped to different disks. If $M > 4$, no way to assign H-values to non-square regions can guarantee memory reuse. As to the **Dec** property, it holds provided $M \geq 4$ or, when $M \leq 3$, if the H-value of a non-square region is chosen on a per-case basis.

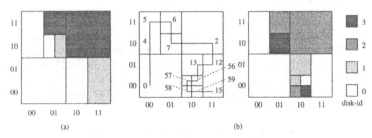

**Fig. 6.** The $Z^+$ (a) and $HCAM^+$ (b) methods.

## 4.2 ECC⁺

The ECC⁺ method works, as static $ECC$, with $M = 2^m$. It multiplies the Z-value of a region by a code check matrix. With variable-size regions, Z-values have variable length as well, and this implies using different check matrices (codes), one for each region size. The basic idea to achieve **Mem** and to avoid file reorganizations is derived by the technique used in [CTZ96] for the dynamic declustering of signature files. This suggests to extend the parity check matrix by *adjoining* non-zero $m$-bit column vectors to its right. Consider the split of region $R$, which originates regions $R_0$ and $R_1$, where $Z(R_0) = Z(R) \circ 0$ and $Z(R_1) = Z(R) \circ 1$ ("$\circ$" denotes concatenation). Let $\mathbf{H}_{l_1+l_2}$ be the check matrix used to allocate $R$, whose grid levels are $l_1$ and $l_2$. To allocate $R_0$ and $R_1$ we use a matrix $\mathbf{H}_{l_1+l_2+1} = [\mathbf{H}_{l_1+l_2}|\mathbf{h}]$, where $\mathbf{h}$ is a non-null vector. Then we have:

$$\mathbf{H}_{l_1+l_2+1} \cdot Z(R_0)' = \mathbf{H}_{l_1+l_2} \cdot Z(R)'$$
$$\mathbf{H}_{l_1+l_2+1} \cdot Z(R_1)' = \mathbf{H}_{l_1+l_2} \cdot Z(R)' \oplus \mathbf{h}$$

where $\oplus$ is sum modulo 2 (exclusive-or). This shows that the **Dec** property holds as well, since $\mathbf{h}$ is not null. Figure 7 (a) shows the effect of adding to the $\mathbf{H}_4$ matrix of Figure 1 (b) the column vector $\mathbf{h} = (1,0)'$.

## 4.3 FX⁺

The last method we consider is *Fieldwise eXclusive-or* (FX) [KP88]. It works with binary-valued coordinates, which are bitwise xor-ed and the result is taken modulo $M$: $diskOf_{FX}(I_1, I_2) = (I_1 \oplus I_2)_2 \bmod M$. For instance, for region $(3, 4)$ of an $8 \times 8$ grid, and $M = 4$ we get: $(011 \oplus 100)_2 \bmod 4 = (111)_2 \bmod 4 = 3$.

FX⁺ applies the same principle to allocate regions for which the grid levels are equal, $l_1 = l_2$. When $l_1 = l_2 + 1$, bit strings are aligned "to the left" before summing them. As an example, let $R = (110, 01)$. Aligning to the left yields, $(110 \oplus 010)_2 = (100)_2 = 4$, after which $4 \bmod M$ can be executed. Figure 7 (b) shows a complete example. FX⁺ has the **Dec** property (since regions originating

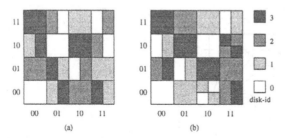

**Fig. 7.** The ECC⁺ (a) and FX⁺ (b) methods.

from a split differ only in the least significant bit of a coordinate value), but not the **Mem** property. To see this, let $M = 4$ and consider the split of region $R = (00, 01)$, mapped to disk 1. We get $R_0 = (000, 01)$ and $R_1 = (001, 01)$, which are respectively mapped to disks 2 and 3. Notice that, having we chosen to "align to the right" bit strings of different length, **Mem** would not hold as well. For instance, splitting region $R = (01, 10)$ (mapped to disk 3) yields $R_0 = (010, 10)$, which goes to disk 0, and $R_1 = (011, 10)$, mapped to disk 1.

# 5 The Directory: MX-GF

In order to support DDFs we analyze 3 basic design alternatives, on the assumption that the directory is too large to be kept in main memory, and has therefore to be efficiently declustered to evenly distribute the load on disks.

## 5.1 Global Flat Grid File

The *Global Flat Grid File* (GF-GF) uses a single (global) orthogonal grid, which is updated in front of file evolution. Addressing is based on a set of linear scales, one per dimension, which are resident in main memory and are used to address grid cells. The set of cells mapped to the $i$-th disk, denoted $C^i$, is then organized by some single-disk spatial access method (SAM), see Figure 8. In the dynamic case GF-GF has some major drawbacks, since it inherits problems of single-disk Grid File in managing skewed data distributions, for which the number of cells can become as large as $O(N^D)$ for $N$ points and $D$ dimensions. This is because many new cells have to be allocated in front of a single data page split which requires halving a scale interval. Furthermore, in a multi-disk environment the directory growth propagates to *all disks*, thus involving all local SAMs.

A semi-dynamic variant of GF-GF is obtained by dynamically declustering *only* data pages (using a DDF), whereas using a static set of global linear scales to partition the space. Thus, the SAM of disk $i$ organizes a *fixed* subspace, but it can provide access to data also stored in other disks. The major disadvantage of this approach is that it cannot efficiently distribute the access load to directory entries, since there is no control to balance the size of the directories.

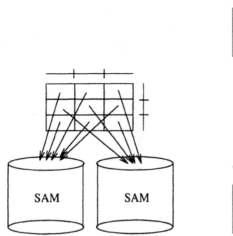

**Fig. 8.** The GF-GF organization.

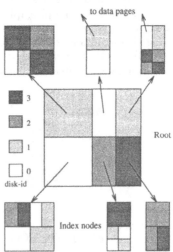

**Fig. 9.** MX-GF using FX⁺.

## 5.2 Multiplexed Grid File

The third alternative we analyze is based on hierarchical versions of the Grid File, in particular the *Multilevel Grid File* [WK85]. Each index node corresponds to a (hyper-)rectangular region and is stored on a disk page. Entries of the index node with region $R$ are binary-radix subregions of $R$, and are accessed through so-called "cross-disk" pointers, that is, pointers which can refer to a page stored in a different disk. Index nodes are declustered by applying to their region identifiers the same DDF used to allocate data pages, apart from the root which is kept in main memory. We term this organization *Multiplexed Grid File* (MX-GF), since it closely resembles a multiplexed R-tree [KF92]. Figure 9 shows how MX-GF organizes the data regions of Figure 7 (b) using the $FX^+$ DDF, and assuming that each node can store up to 6 entries.

MX-GF does not suffer any of the problems which plague GF-GF (as well its semi-dynamic variant): it can dynamically decluster both data and directory, a data page split leads to the insertion of a new index entry (rather than, possibly, of a new row or column in the global grid), and, apart from propagation of splits up to higher levels of the tree, only one disk is affected by directory growth. Search and maintenance algorithms are those of Multilevel Grid File [WK85], and therefore are not detailed here.

**Local Declustering: RR and PI.** Once we have chosen MX-GF as the way to implement the directory, index-based (local) declustering methods can be used as well. Consider the split of a page $P$ with region $R$, whose entry is stored in node $P_{father}$. When $P$ splits, a local declustering method decides on the allocation of the new pages, $P_0$ and $P_1$ (with regions $R_0$ and $R_1$), by only taking into account how other children of $P_{father}$ are mapped to disks. Thus, a good local declustering method should map "close" regions to different disks. We consider 2 local methods for the declustering of MX-GF pages: *Round-Robin* (RR) and *Proximity Index* (PI), the latter being an adaptation of a convenient criterion for the declustering of parallel R-trees [KF92]. In both methods we enforce the **Mem** property, that is, we impose $diskOf(R_0) = diskOf(R)$.

The RR method maps $R_1$ to the disk which has the minimum number of pages, by considering all and only the entries in $P_{father}$. This policy does not guarantee the **Dec** property, as Figure 10 demonstrates.

**Fig. 10.** The RR method with $M = 2$.    **Fig. 11.** The PI method with $M = 3$.

The PI method works by defining a "proximity measure" between regions. The measure we use is based on the distance between regions' centers, although more elaborated measures could be defined as well. Given region $R_1$ and the set of regions in $P_{father}$ which are mapped to disk $i$, $\mathcal{R}_i$, we map $R_1$ to the disk for which $\min_{R_j \in \mathcal{R}_i}\{distance(R_1, R_j)\}$ is maximized. With the possible exception of cases where "large" regions split (see Figure 11) this almost certainly guarantees that **Dec** holds .

# 6 Experimental Results

In this Section we present experimental results obtained from a prototype implementation of MX-GF. Without loss of generality we normalize input data to the unit hypercube and use Z-values for regions encoding.

For the implementation of static declustering methods we first define a square grid, which therefore establishes the "finest granularity" of declustering. Then, we use MX-GF to organize data and index pages, but we "freeze" the declustering process when splitting a region that has reached the chosen granularity level. Each experimental result is the average of the response time of 100 square range queries, uniformly distributed over the unit space and having a non-empty result. The response time of a range query $q$, denoted $R(q)$, is computed as the instant at which the last data page which satisfies $q$ is retrieved. We assume that each page retrieval incurs a (constant) unitary time cost and that CPU costs are negligible with respect to I/O costs. The (parallel) retrieval process of the pages which compose the *query tree* goes as follows. At each time $t \geq 0$ we have a queue $\mathcal{U}$ of (disk_id, page_id) page requests. A FIFO scheduling policy is used to solve conflicting requests which refer to two or more pages stored on a same disk. Entries of fetched pages are removed from $\mathcal{U}$. Incoming entries are first compared with $q$ and in case inserted in $\mathcal{U}$. The process halts when no more requests are waiting, that is, $\mathcal{U} = \emptyset$.

Unless otherwise stated, we use the following parameter values:

| Parameter | Description | Value |
|-----------|-------------|-------|
| $M$ | n. of disks | 8 |
| $D$ | n. of dimensions | 2 |
| $c$ | data page capacity (points) | 2 |
| $p\_size$ | disk page size (Kbytes) | 4 |

The low value of data page capacity, $c = 2$, is used to obtain, for a given number of points, $N$, the maximum number of index and data pages. The datasets used in the experiments are summarized in the table below.

| Dataset name | Description | N. points |
|--------------|-------------|-----------|
| 2D_unif_$xx$K | 2D uniform distribution | $xx \times 10^3$ |
| zip_codes | U.S. zip codes | 26,874 |
| fractal1.2 | "Lèvy's flight" | 20,000 |

The zip_codes dataset, available at URL http://www.census.org/ftp/pub/geo/www/tiger/zip_cent.txt, is from the TIGER database of the U.S. Census Bureau, and contains the centroids of all U.S. regions for which a ZIP code is defined. fractal1.2 is a highly skewed synthetic dataset (see Section 6.2).

## 6.1 DDFs vs Static Methods

In the first experiment we simulate a typical file growth scenario. Initially, the dataset size leads to define a $32 \times 32$ grid, which is the one still used by static methods when the file grows up to $10^4$ points (2D_unif_10K dataset). Since this requires 6,407 data pages, each grid region now corresponds to 6.25 data pages, on the average. Figure 12 shows that the relative response time of any static declustering method with respect to the corresponding dynamic version almost doubles with small queries. For larger queries the overhead decreases, because of the higher chance to get almost the same number of pages from each disk.

Figure 13 shows how performance of static organizations varies with dataset size, which is relevant to understand when they should be reorganized. We only consider the behavior of HCAM, but similar results have been obtained also with other static methods, as well as for other parameter values. The figure plots the ratio, $R_{HCAM}(q)/R_{opt}(q)$, of HCAM response time, for $0.02 \times 0.02$ square queries, to the "optimal response time", defined as:

$$R_{opt}(q) = \sum_{l=1}^{L} \left\lceil \frac{\text{n\_pages}_l(q)}{M} \right\rceil \tag{1}$$

where $L$ is the number of levels of MX-GF, excluding the root (which is cached in memory) and including data pages, and $\text{n\_pages}_l(q)$ is the total number of pages retrieved by query $q$ at level $l$.[5] For comparison, the relative response time of HCAM+ is also shown. It can be seen that performance of static methods considerably deteriorates with increasing dataset size, since the number of data pages which correspond to a single grid region grows without limits. For instance, when $N = 10^5$, there are about 64 pages per grid region. On the other hand, HCAM+ performance stabilizes around a value which only depends on the declustering method itself and on the query size.

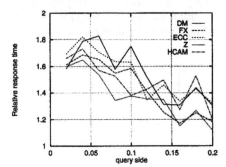

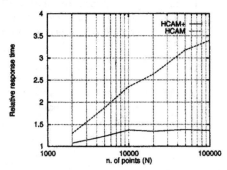

**Fig. 12.** $R_{met}(q)/R_{met+}(q)$ as a function of the size of query side.

**Fig. 13.** $R_{HCAM}(q)/R_{opt}(q)$ and $R_{HCAM+}(q)/R_{opt}(q)$ as a function of dataset size.

## 6.2 DDFs vs Index-Based Methods

In the next series of experiments we compare DDF and index-based (RR and PI) methods. Figure 14 plots the relative response time of dynamic methods with respect to optimal response time, using the uniform 2D_UNIF_10K dataset. The most remarkable observation concerns the PI method, which is observed to consistently outperform all the others. Although we used a simplified "similarity measure", as compared to the one proposed for R-trees [KF92], declustering

---

[5] For $L = 2$ the definition indeed corresponds to the optimal response time for query $q$. When $L \geq 3$, Eq. 1 can slightly overestimate the minimum theoretical response time, since it is possible to read in parallel pages at different levels of the query tree.

based on the analysis of local space configurations provides to be an excellent allocation criterion. At the other extreme we find that RR has almost the worst response time, whereas DDFs exhibit intermediate behaviors. Other experiments in which we considered larger (up to $0.6 \times 0.6$) and non-square queries confirmed that PI is the appropriate choice for declustering uniformly distributed datasets. This is consistent with the observations reported in [KF92].

We now turn to the case of non-uniform data distributions and restrict the analysis to the two index-based methods, RR and PI, and to two DDFs, namely $ECC^+$ and $HCAM^+$.

Figure 15 shows results obtained with the skewed zip_codes dataset, which requires $17,193$ data pages. Compared with the results in Figure 14, it appears that: 1) both index-based methods perform substantially better than DDFs; 2) RR outperforms PI for medium-large queries. As to the first point, we observe that, with skewed data distributions, the RR method achieves, by its very nature, a better balance than DDFs in allocating data regions to disks. This is shown in the table below, where, for each of the four methods, the standard deviation of the distribution of the number of data pages on disks is shown.

| $ECC^+$ | $HCAM^+$ | RR | PI |
|---|---|---|---|
| 31.6248 | 30.5541 | 19.8813 | 38.465 |

This is enough to guarantee that, on the average, RR has a lower response time than DDFs, with the only exception of very small queries (i.e. $0.005 \times 0.005$ in the figure), which lead to retrieve only a few data pages ($= 3.48$ on the average).

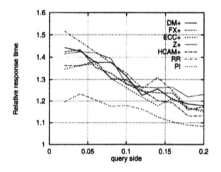

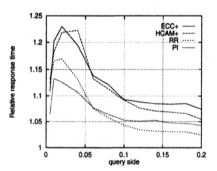

**Fig. 14.** $R_{met+}(q)/R_{opt}(q)$ of dynamic methods. Dataset: 2D_unif_10K.

**Fig. 15.** $R_{met+}(q)/R_{opt}(q)$ of dynamic methods. Dataset: zip_codes.

As to the reason why RR outperforms PI on medium-large queries, we argue that it is still due to the higher balance that RR can achieve. From the above table it appears that PI has the worst behavior as to uniformity of data allocation on disks, thus suffering from the presence of skewness in the dataset. Nonetheless, because of PI's smarter monitoring of local configurations, RR cannot do better than PI for small queries (i.e. up to 0.05 in the figure).

The last experiment examines the four methods on the $20,000$ points "fractal" distribution fractal1.2, represented in Figure 16. This corresponds to a so-called "Lèvy's flight" with fractal dimension 1.2 [Man77]. Figure 17 confirms that RR is the best choice for (highly) skewed data distributions. Also note that the improvement obtained by PI over RR in case of small queries has almost vanished.

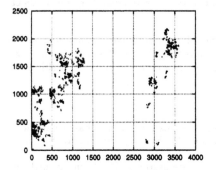

**Fig. 16.** The `fractal1.2` distribution.

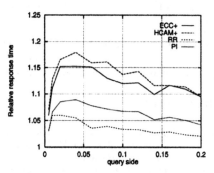

**Fig. 17.** $R_{met+}(q)/R_{opt}(q)$ of some dynamic methods. Dataset: `fractal1.2`.

## 7 Conclusions

In this work we have considered dynamic versions of well-known declustering functions. In order to support dynamic declustering functions (DDFs), we have introduced a "multiplexed" Grid File (MX-GF), that is, a Multilevel Grid File [WK85] whose index nodes and data pages are distributed over a set of disks. The paged organization of MX-GF allows the application of index-based declustering methods too, among which we have analyzed RR (Round-Robin) and PI (Proximity Index). Our experimental results can be summarized as follows:

1. DDFs can achieve good performance levels regardless of dataset size, whereas static declustering functions behave poorly when the dataset size does not fit the anticipated number of grid regions.
2. With uniform data distributions, the PI method is the clear winner, whereas RR has the worst performance. This confirms results obtained for parallel R-trees [KF92], even if we have used a different "similarity measure" for PI.
3. With skewed data distributions, RR rather surprisingly improves its effectiveness, it being the best method for medium-large queries. For small queries the advantage of using PI appears to be distribution-dependent. We note that these results do not have any counterpart with the analysis in [KF92], where only uniform distributions were considered.

Above results seem to suggest that DDFs are not worth implementing because of the better behavior of index-based methods. In favor of DDFs, however, there are some points, which would deserve further analysis, including a lighter CPU load – because the complexity of index-based methods depends on the number of entries in a node – and a mapping of data regions to disks which does not depend on the ordering of data input.

In this paper we have considered a single-processor multi-disk architecture. Our future work will deal with the problem of extending dynamic declustering methods to the case of multi-processor architectures, such as the shared-nothing distributed processing model. This requires to take into account also communication costs, in order to determine good trade-offs between the cost of moving data and the benefit of load balancing which dynamic declustering methods can achieve.

**Acknowledgments.** Fabio Grandi, Dario Maio, and Pavel Zezula read a preliminary version of the paper and contributed with useful suggestions. Paolo Tiberio strongly encouraged the first author to pursue the subject of this work.

# References

[CTZ96]  P. Ciaccia, P. Tiberio, and P. Zezula. Declustering of key-based partitioned signature files. *ACM Transactions on Database Systems*, 21(3), September 1996 (to appear).

[DG92]  D. DeWitt and J. Gray. Parallel database systems: The future of high performance database systems. *Communications of the ACM*, 35(6):85–98, June 1992.

[DS82]  H.C. Du and J.S. Sobolewski. Disk allocation for Cartesian product files on multiple disk systems. *ACM Transactions on Database Systems*, 7(1):82–101, March 1982.

[FB93]  C. Faloutsos and P. Bhagwat. Declustering using fractals. In *Proceedings of the 2nd International Conference on Parallel and Distributed Information Systems (PDIS'93)*, pages 18–25, January 1993.

[FM91]  C. Faloutsos and D. Metaxas. Disk allocation methods using error correcting codes. *IEEE Transactions on Computers*, 40(8):907–914, August 1991.

[HS94]  B. Himatsingka and J. Srivastava. Performance evaluation of grid based multi-attribute record declustering methods. In *Proceedings of the 10th International Conference on Data Engineering*, pages 356–365, February 1994.

[KF92]  I. Kamel and C. Faloutsos. Parallel R-tree. In *Proceeedings of the 1992 ACM SIGMOD International Conference on Management of Data*, pages 195–204, June 1992.

[KP88]  M.H. Kim and S. Pramanik. Optimal file distribution for partial match queries. In *Proceedings of the 1988 ACM SIGMOD International Conference on Management of Data*, pages 173–182, June 1988.

[LRS93]  J. Li, D. Rotem, and J. Srivastava. Algorithms for loading parallel grid files. In *Proceedings of the 1993 ACM SIGMOD Conference on Management of Data*, pages 347–356, May 1993. SIGMOD Record, 22(2), June 1993.

[LSR92]  J. Li, J. Srivastava, and D. Rotem. CMD: A multidimensional declustering method for parallel database systems. In *Proceedings of the 18th VLDB International Conference*, pages 3–14, August 1992.

[Man77]  B. Mandelbrot. *The Fractal Geometry of Nature*. W.H.Freeman, New York, 1977.

[Ore86]  J. Orenstein. Spatial query processing in an object-oriented database system. In *Proceedings of the 1986 ACM SIGMOD International Conference on Management of Data*, pages 326–336, May 1986.

[PGK88]  D. A. Patterson, G. Gibson, and R. H. Katz. A case for redundant arrays of inexpensive disks (RAID). In *Proceedings of the 1988 ACM SIGMOD International Conference on Management of Data*, pages 109–116, June 1988.

[WK85]  K.-Y. Whang and R. Krishnamurthy. Multilevel grid files. Research Report RC 11516, IBM Thomas J. Watson Research Center, Yorktown Heights, New York, November 1985.

[ZSC94]  Y. Zhou, S. Shekhar, and M. Coyle. Disk allocation methods for parallelizing grid files. In *Proceedings of the 10th International Conference on Data Engineering*, pages 243–252, February 1994.

# Encapsulation of Intra-operator Parallelism in a Parallel Match Operator

N.Biscondi[1], L.Brunie[2], A.Flory[1], H.Kosch[2]

[1] LISI, INSA de Lyon, 69621 Villeurbanne, France
E-mail: biscondi@lisiflory.insa-lyon.fr, flory@insa.insa-lyon.fr
[2] LIP, ENS de Lyon, 69364 Lyon Cedex 07, France
E-mail: (lbrunie, hkosch)@lip.ens-lyon.fr

**Abstract.** This paper presents a new concept for relational parallel query optimization. We propose to encapsulate the intra-operation parallelism in a *parallel match operator* realizing most binary relational operations. Our approach integrates the optimization of this operator : a comparative study of the three main match algorithms – Nested Loops, Sort-Merge and Hash – is presented for shared-nothing architecture. It shows that database systems could profit by the implementation of all these algorithms. Futhermore, our match optimizer can be used by the query parallelizer in order to determine an optimal parallel execution strategy for each binary relational operation.

**Keywords:** Parallel query optimization, match operator, algorithm complexity, shared-nothing architecture.

## 1 Introduction

Parallelism has been recognized as an attractive option for relational database systems. During the last years a parallel query optimization is an active area of database research. Optimizing a query consists in defining the inter-parallelism degree (i.e. the number of relational operations to be run in parallel), as well as the intra-parallelism degree (i.e. the number of processors dedicated to the execution of each operation), the task allocation on the processors, the synchronizations to be carried out.

Though many optimization strategies have been proposed, most of them were focused on a specific topic (communication [6], load balancing [19], index [9]...) or dedicated to specific platforms (e.g. hypercubes [1]).

This paper proposes to encapsulate the intra-operation parallelism in a *parallel match operator* realizing most binary relational operations : join, intersection, union et difference. Unlike the Volcano system [11] (which also relies on the notion of match operator), our approach integrates the optimization of this operator, i.e. we implement a specific module in charge of the choice, according to the execution parameters, of the best adapted match algorithm.

Futhermore, this match operator optimization module can be used by the query parallelizer in order to determine an optimal parallel execution strategy for each binary relational operation.

This paper is structured as follows. After some preliminary notes (section 2), our approach to optimization of a parallel match operator is presented (section 3). Section 4 deal with a theoretical comparative study of the three main parallel match algorithms. At last sections, 5 et 6 discuss this approach taking to account the previous works and point out future work.

## 2 Preliminary notes

**Match operator** The match operator, presented by Graefe in [11], realizes a variety of binary relational operations : join, intersection, union, difference. In all these operations, an item is included in the output depending on the result of a comparison between a pair of items. Thus, it sounded logical to implement them in one general and efficient module. The match operator for binary operations is based on the separation of the matching and non-matching tuples of two relations, and it produce the appropriate tuples of result relation, possibly after some transformation and combination as in the case of a join.

For ease of following presentation we define the match attribute as the set of attributes involved in the decision of matching two tuples, i.e. the join attribute for the join operation, all attributes of relation for intersection or difference (see [2] for more details).

In Volcano, the match operator is implemented only by two sequential algorithms, namely Sort-Merge and Hybrid Hash.

**Parallel join algorithms** During the last years, a significant amount of effort has been focused on developing efficient join algorihtms. Three main methods have been proposed [16], [17] :

- The **Nested Loops** technique consists in comparing each tuple of one relation with every tuple of the other. This algorithm is efficient either when indexes are available or when the number of available processors is high.
- The **Sort-Merge** acts in two steps : first, sorting parallely each relation, then merging them together on one single processor. This technique works well when the relations are already sorted.
- **Hash-Join** methods are based on three steps : first, each relation is distributed over the processors using a common hash function. Then the tuples of one relation are used to build a hash-table on each processor. Finally, the tuples of the second relation are probed against this hash-table to find the matching tuples. Based on this general framework, several alternative techniques have been proposed (e.g. Grace-Hash, Hybrid-Hash...)

Basically, the same techniques as those used for implementing the join operator will work for a match operator too.

**Parallel machine model** In this paper, we focus on the *shared nothing architecture* (i.e. each processor has exclusive access to its main memory and disk unit; all inter-processor communication is done via message passing on the interconnection network). Indeed, this type of architecture is usually considered as the favorite architecture for highly scalable and extensible parallel database applications [18]. We also suppose having the following architecture features :

- linear models for the communication time, for the processor time and for the disk access time.
- asynchronous communications (this enables to have the processing and the communications overlapping).

# 3 Optimization of a parallel match operator

Taking into account the previous work, our goals are :

1. To encapsulate an intra-operation parallelism in the parallel match operator
2. To garantee its optimal execution according to contextual parameters (like the number of processors available for the operation and the initial data partition between them).

In order to encapsulate a intra-operation optimization we present a match operator optimization module. During the query optimization the query parallelizer calls the match optimizer in order to determine an optimal parallel execution strategy for an binary relational operation. The match optimizer is then provided with the following contextual informations[3] :

1. the number of processors assigned to this operation, noted $p$
2. the number of tuples of the relation $R$ (resp. $S$) on each processor $- n_1 \ldots n_p$ (resp. $m_1 \ldots m_p$)
3. a boolean variable indicating if the relation $R$ is distributed on the processors by a hash function on the match attribute $- distr_R$
4. a boolean variable indicating if the relation $S$ is distributed on the processors by the same hash function as that used for $R - distr_S$
5. two boolean variables indicating if the relation $R$ (resp. $S$) is sorted on the match attribute on each processor $- sort_R$ (or $sort_S$)

According to these parameters, the match optimizer chooses for the given operation the best adapted algorithm (section 4). It sends to the query parallelizer an identifier of this algorithm, the estimated execution time and the new state of the contextual parameters.

**Remark** : The information used by the match optimizer are either available in the dictionary of the DBMS (e.g. relation cardinality) or estimated by the parallelizer himself (e.g. number of processors assigned to the operation).

---

[3] $R$ and $S$ denote the two relations involved in the operation, with $n$ and $m$ number of tuples respectively

# 4 A theoretical comparative study of the match algorithms

The results of our theoretical comparative study of the match algorithms in a shared nothing environnement are summarized in tables 1 and 2. We specifie the algorithm chosen by our match optimizer according to the values of the contextual parameters provided to him (see section 2.1). In other words, it is shown in which cases each class of algorithms (Nested Loops, Sort-Merge and Hash-Join) works the best. Mixed algorithms and improvements of standard techniques are also considered. Each case of these tables is commented with a proof or a paper reference.

## 4.1 Uniform initial data partition

Firstly we study the cases with a uniform initial data partition across all processors assigned to this operation ($n_i = \frac{n}{p}$, $m_i = \frac{m}{p}$, for $i = 1..p$), see table 1.

| Case | Distribution by hash func. | | Tuples sorted | | Chosen algorithm |
|------|-------|-------|-------|-------|------------------|
|      | $distr_R$ | $distr_S$ | $sort_R$ | $sort_S$ | |
| 1 |   |   | 0 | 0 | Hash |
| 2 | 1 | 1 | 1 | 1 | Local Sort-Merge on each processor |
| 3 |   |   | 1 | 0 | Nested Loops or Hash |
| 4 |   |   | 0 | 0 | Hash |
| 5 | 0 | 0 | 1 | 1 | Sort-Merge or Hash |
| 6 |   |   | 1 | 0 | Sort-Merge or Hash |
| 7 |   |   | 0 | 0 | Hash |
| 8 | 1 | 0 | 1 | 1 | If Sort-Merge is applied in case 5 then Sort-Merge else distribute $S$, do as in case 3 |
| 9 |   |   | 1 | 0 | If Sort-Merge is applied in case 6, then Sort-Merge else distribute $S$, do as in case 3 |
| 10 |   |   | 0 | 1 | Behave as in case 6 |

Table 1. Choice of an match algorithm according to contextual parameters

**Comments on the table 1 :**

In the first three cases, this uniform partition of tuples across is realized using the same hash function on the match attribute of each relation. Thus, a local matching, performed in parallel on each processor, produces the entire result of the matching of $R$ and $S$.

**Case 1** On the processors where none of the relations is sorted on its match attribute, a Hash method is applied. Its time complexity is $O(\frac{m+n}{p})$.

**Case 2** On the processors where both relations are already sorted, we apply the second step of the Sort-Merge algorithm, which consists in locally merging two sorted lists of tuples. On each processor the tuples of the result relation will be sorted on the match attribute. The time complexity of this method is $O(\frac{m+n}{p})$.

**Case 3** The relations $R$ and $S$ are distributed by a common hash function on the match attribute. Moreover, on each processor, the tuples of $R$ are locally sorted on the match attribute. We propose to locally apply the Nested Loops method (using the fact that one relation is sorted) on each processor, only if $m$, $n$ and $p$ verify one of the following conditions:

1. $m > n$ and $n < 4p$
2. $m > n$, $4p < n < 16p$ and $m < \frac{2n}{\log \frac{n}{4p}}$
3. $n > m$ and $n < 16p$
4. $n > m$, $n > 16p$ and $m < \frac{2n}{\log \frac{n}{4p}}$

Otherwise, the Hash algorithm is applied – see the exhaustive proof in appendix A.

**Note** : Our proof shows that Nested Loops outperforms the Hash algorithm when a big number of processors is available and/or relations are of very different sizes. These results fit well with the conclusions of [9].

In the next three cases (4,5,6), no relation is distributed by any hash function on the processors. Therefore, local matchings on each processor will not provide the entire result.

**Case 4** We use a Hash algorithm, which is known to be the best in the general case [3, 16], as this one.

**Case 5** This case requires to choose between Sort-Merge applied globally on the set of processors (this can be advantageous because the tuples of each relation are sorted on each processor) and a Hybrid Hash algorithm, the most performant in general. This problem was studied by Graefe in [10], where the author shows that Hash is more efficient, except when the result relation is required to be sorted on the match attribute.

**Case 6** A local Nested Loops, as in case 3, cannot be used. Just as in case 5, Graefe claims that Hybrid Hash is most efficient, except when the result relation is required sorted and its sorting is more expensive that the sort of relation $S$.

**Case 7** This case does not differ much from case 4. A Hash-based technique is to be applied. During the partition phase, the relation $S$ is distributed on the processors by the same hash function on the match attribute as $R$ is.

**Case 8** As in case 5, if the result relation is required sorted and its sorting is more expensive that the sort of relation $S$, a Sort-Merge algorithm is chosen. Otherwise:
- Relation $S$ is distributed on the processors using the same hash function as $R$.
- Then we behave as in case 3.

**Cases 9,10** The solutions of these cases follow naturally from the previous cases (see the table).

## 4.2 Non-uniform initial data partition

We will begin by a particular, but frequent type of non-uniform initial data partition: the tuples of each relation are partitioned uniformely across $p_1$ processors and there are $p_2$ processors with no loaded data, see table 2.

| Case | Distribution by hash func. | | Tuples sorted | | Chosen algorithm |
|------|--------|--------|--------|--------|------------------|
| | $distr_R$ | $distr_S$ | $sort_R$ | $sort_S$ | |
| 11 | | | 0 | 0 | Hash on $p_1$ or on $p_1 + p_2$ processors |
| 12 | 1 | 1 | 1 | 1 | Sort-Merge |
| 13 | | | 1 | 0 | If in case 11 $p_1 + p_2$ proc.are used then do idem else do as in case 3 |
| 14 | | | 0 | 0 | Hash |
| 15 | 0 | 0 | 1 | 1 | If Hash applied in case 5, then Hash else Sort-Merge |
| 16 | | | 1 | 0 | If Hash applied in case 6, then Hash else Sort-Merge |
| 17 | | | 0 | 0 | see case 7 |
| 18 | 1 | 0 | 1 | 1 | see case 8 |
| 19 | | | 1 | 0 | see case 9 |
| 20 | | | 0 | 1 | see case 10 |

**Table 2.** Choice of an match algorithm according to contextual parameters

**Comments on the table 2 :**
In the next three cases (11,12,13) each relation is distributed across $p_1$ processors

by the common hash function on their match attribute, besides we have $p_2$ non-loaded processors.

**Case 11** There is a choice between :
- considering that the partition phase of the Hash algorithm is accomplished and continuing the execution of this algorithm on $p_1$ processors
- realizing the partition phase by the redistribution of each relation by the hash function on their match attribute across $p_1 + p_2$ processors, then continuing the execution of the Hash algorithm on $p_1 + p_2$ processors

The redistribution makes better in most cases : when the number $p_2$ of non-loaded processors is high, or/and when the smaller relation does not fit entirely in the main memory of $p_1$ processors, or/and when communication is cheap. The precise calculation can be done, as before.

**Case 12** The tuples of each relation are sorted on each of the $p_1$ processors then we apply a local merging of the corresponding tuples from the two relations (second phase of Sort-Merge). The Hash algorithm, whose partition phase redistributes the relations across $p_1 + p_2$ processors, would be less performant. Because only redistribution by the hash function has the same cost as merging.

**Cas 13** The solution to this case follows naturally from cases 11 and 3.

In the cases 14,15,16 no relation is distributed across processors by a hash function.

**Case 14** This case does not differ much from case 4; we choose a Hash algorithm and during its partition phase each relation is distributed by a common hash function across all availables processors.

**Cas 15** We use case 5 as a reference :
1. If the result relation is not demanded to be sorted by the match attribute, Hybrid Hash is applied (as in case 5), and its partition phase consists in distributing both relations across $p_1 + p_2$ processors.
2. If the result relation must be sorted, we have to compare two approches : on the one hand it would be an optimal stage of Sort-Merge, thus it cannot derive the benefits from using the additional (non data-loaded) processors. On other hand, Hybrid Hash can use the additional processors in order to increase the degree of parallelism. However, after computing the result relation, the latter must be sorted, and this sort will be particulary expensive because of the big number of processors at work. Thus, the Sort-Merge algorithm is applied in this sub-case.

**Case 16** Here we lead a similar reasoning as above, with case 6 as a reference.

Eventually, the **cases 17-20** have to be considered. They share a common essence with the cases 7-10 respectively. However, some precisions must be brought :

- If the Hash algorithm is applied, then during its partition phase, both relations are distributed by a common hash function across all available processors $(p_1 + p_2)$.

- If Sort-Merge is applied, the non data loaded processors are not used, for reasons indicated in case 15.

Now we sum up these results in two general statements for *all* the possibles cases with a non-uniform initial data partition between processors:

- if both relations are distributed on the same processors by the same hash function on the match attribute and if their tuples are sorted on this attribute on each processor, then a local Sort-Merge is applied.
- otherwise, it is better to redistribute the relations in order to avoid the desastrous effects of a high data skew [19] and behave then conforming table 1.

In the table comments, we omitted to indicate the type of the Hash-based algorithm chosen (i.e. Simple, Grace or Hybrid Hash). Indeed, according to the comparative analysis described in [16] : Hybrid Hash is the most efficient.

## 5  Discussion

Parallel query optimization and intra-operation parallelism has been an active area of database research. In this section, we discuss the related work and outline two main advantages of our approach.

**Parallel match operator** A match operator was presented in [11], it is implemented with two sequential algorithms Sort-Merge and Hybrid Hash. In Volcano, the parallelization of the match operator is based on an external operator, called *exchange*, whose job is to distribute the data and trigger the execution, not to evaluate an optimal execution algorithm in the context of the query. In database machine Gamma [8] a join operation is also executed by a sequentual algorithm on each processor and is preceded by a hash partition of relations.

In contrast with these works, we presented in this paper a *parallel* match operator, for its optimization all advantages of parallel algorithms are used, and it is not necessary to make any condition on the preceded partition phase. Moreover, the contextual parameters of query execution are taked into account.

**Comparative study** For the parallel match operator optimization we are based on the parallel algorithms developed for a join operation: Nested Loops, Sort-Merge, Hash-Join. As far as we know, these three algorithms have never been compared all together for shared-nothing architectures. DeWitt and Gerber [7] studied the efficiency of various parallel Hash-Join algorithms, while Schneider and DeWitt compared Hash-Join algorithms with a local Sort-Merge technique preceded by a hash-distribution [16]. Valduriez and Gardarin [17] compared the three classes of algorithms described above but on a SABRE machine which is based on a very specific architecture (cache memory, filters). However, Hash-Join techniques are commonly considered as the best methods in the general case, whereas Sort-Merge methods perform better in the presence of data-skew

[19], or if the result is required to be sorted and the cost of the sorting of the result relation is high [10]. At last, De Witt et al. [9] claim that the Indexed Nested Loops technique outperforms Hash-Join methods when the relations are of very different size.

In that framework, our paper proposed an exhaustive comparative study of those three classes of algorithms, in a shared-nothing environment, taking into account the contextual parameters. All possible cases are examined. The third case of the table 1 is especially interesting, it is proved that Nested Loops dominates Hash Join in more cases than what was known before.

# 6 Conclusion

This paper has presented a new concept for relational parallel query optimization. The intra-operation parallelism is encapsulated into a single parallel match operator. A comparative study of the three main match algorithms is proposed for shared-nothing architecture in order to optimize a parallel match operator. This study give a strong reason why all three algorithms Nested Loops, Sort-Merge and Hybrid Hash should be available in a query-processing system.

Futhermore, our match optimizer is well-suited for collaboration with different types of query parallelizers.

Future work includes two main research axis. We are currently implementing our match optimizer on a iPSC860 parallel machine. Furthermore, we would like to look at integrating the tools and concepts we have developed in a project of parallel documentary databases.

# References

1. C.K.Barn, S.Padmanabhan, Join and data redistribution algorithmus for hypercubes, *IEEE Transactions on Knowledge and Data Engineering*, No 5(1), 1993
2. N.Biscondi, Parallel databases: a parallel operator of matching, *Technical Report*, INSA de Lyon, France, 1995
3. D.Bitton, H.Boral, D.DeWitt, K.Wilkinson, Parallel Algorithms for The Execution of Relational Database Operations, *ACM Transactions on Database Systems*, No 3,1983
4. K.Bratbergsengen, Relational Algebra Operations, *Lecture Notes in Computer Science*, No 503, 1990
5. L.Brunie, A.Flory, H.Kosch, New static scheduling and elastic load balancing methods for parallel query processing, *Proc. of the BIWIT Conference, IEEE Computer Society Press*, San Sebastian, Spain, 1995
6. L.Brunie, H.Kosch, A communications-oriented methodology for load balancing in parallel relational query processing, *Advances in Parallel Computing*, ParCo Conferences, Gent, Belgium, 1995
7. D.DeWitt, R.Gerber, Multiprocessor hash-based join algorithms, *Proc. of the 12th VLDB*, Stockholm, Sweden, 1985
8. D.DeWitt, R.Gerber, G.Graefe, M.Heytens, K.Kumar and M.Muralikrishna, GAMMA a high performance dataflow database machine, *Proceedings of the International Conference on Very Large Databases*, Kyoto, Japan, August 1986

9. D.DeWitt, J.Naughton, J.Burger, Nested Loops revisited, *Proceedings on Parallel and Distr.Inf.Sys*, San Diego, California, January 1993

10. G.Graefe, Query Evaluation Techniques for Large Databases, *ACM Computing Surveys*, No 25(2), 1993

11. G.Graefe, Volcano, An extensible and parallel query evaluation system, *IEEE trans. on Knowledge and Data Eng.*, No 6(1), 1994

12. G.Graefe, A.Linville, L.Shapiro, Sort versus Hash Revisited, *IEEE Transactions on Knowledge and Data Engineering*, vol.6, No 6, 1994

13. W.Hong, Parallel Query Processing Using Shared Memory Multiprocessors and Disk Arrays, PhD Thesis, University of California, Berkeley, 1992

14. D.Knuth, The Art of Computer Programming, Vol.3: Sorting and seaching, *Addition-Wesley Publishing Company*, 1973

15. P.Mishra, M.Eich, Join Processing in Relational Databases, *ACM Computing Surveys*, vol 24, No 1, 1992

16. D.Schneider, D.DeWitt, A Performance Evaluation of Four Parallel Join Algorithms in a Shared-Nothing Multiprocessor Environment, *ACM SIGMOD*, Portland, Oregon, USA, June 1989

17. P.Valduriez, G.Gardarin, Join and semi-join algorithms for a multiprocessor database machine, *ACM Transactions on database systems*, No 9(1), 1984

18. P.Valduriez, Parallel Database Systems: Open Problems and New Issues, *Distributed and Parallel Databases*, No 1, 1993

19. P.S.Yu, J.Wolf, D.Dias, J.Turek, An effecive algorithm for parallelizing hash joins in the presence of data skew, *7th International Conference on Data Engineering*, Kobe, Japan, 1991

# A    Proof for case 3

The most performant solution must be chosen between next ones :

- The local Nested Loops algorithm (using the fact that relation $R$ is sorted) on each processor.
- Local Sort of the $S$ tuples on the match attribute on each processor followed by local Merge.
- Local Hash on each processor (build a hash table with tuples of the smaller relation and probe on this table the tuples of second relation).

The following notation is needed to evaluate the proposed algorithms:

$\tau_{I/O}$ - time of an elementary input/output operation, e.g. read/write time of a tuple from disk/main memory to main memory/disk.

$\tau_{CPU}$ - time of an elementary processor operation, e.g. comparing two tuples, building a result tuple,...

$n, m$ - number of tuples in relations $R$ and $S$ respectively.

$p$ - number of processors assigned to the operation

The standart hypotheses of linear models of processor time and disk access time are used, supposing both relations can hold together in main memory.

1. According to the given hypotheses, the execution time of Nested Loops is composed of follow terms :

1.1 $(\frac{m}{p}f_{DM}^S)\tau_{I/O}$ – reading $\frac{m}{p}$ tuples of $S$ from disk to main memory. $f_{DM}^S$ is the probability that a tuple of $S$ is on the disk and not in the memory.

1.2 $(\min(\frac{m}{p}\log\frac{n}{p},\frac{n}{p})f_{DM}^R)\tau_{I/O}$ – reading $\frac{n}{p}$ tuples of $R$ from disk to main memory, the first term of min uses the fact that the tuples are sorted.

1.3 $(\frac{m}{p}\log\frac{n}{p})\tau_{CPU}$ – comparing tuples (logarithmic because $R$ is sorted).

1.4 $(\frac{mn}{p^2}\cdot Sel)\tau_{CPU}$ – building the result tuples. $Sel$ is the operation selectivity.

1.5 $(\frac{mn}{p^2}\cdot Sel)\tau_{I/O}$ – writing the result relation to the disk.

2. The execution time of the Sort-Merge algorithm is composed of :

2.1 $(\frac{m}{p}f_{DM}^S)\tau_{I/O}$ – reading $\frac{m}{p}$ tuples of $S$ from disk to main memory.

2.2 $(\frac{n}{p}f_{DM}^R)\tau_{I/O}$ – reading $\frac{n}{p}$ tuples of $R$ from disk to main memory.

2.3 $(\frac{m}{p}\log\frac{m}{p})\tau_{CPU}$ – sorting tuples of $S$.

2.4 $(\frac{m+n}{p})\tau_{CPU}$ – seaching for corresponding tuples in two sorted lists.

2.5 $(\frac{mn}{p^2}\cdot Sel)\tau_{CPU}$ – building result tuples.

2.6 $(\frac{mn}{p^2}\cdot Sel)\tau_{I/O}$ – writing the result relation to the disk.

3. For the Hash algorithm :

3.1 $(\frac{m}{p}f_{DM}^S)\tau_{I/O}$ – reading $\frac{m}{p}$ tuples of $S$ from disk to main memory.

3.2 $(\frac{n}{p}f_{DM}^R)\tau_{I/O}$ – reading $\frac{m}{p}$ tuples of $R$ from disk to main memory.

3.3 $(\min(\frac{m}{p},\frac{n}{p}))\cdot 2\tau_{CPU}$ – building the hash table with the tuples of the smaller relation.

3.4 $(\max(\frac{m}{p},\frac{n}{p}))\tau_{CPU}$ – hashing the tuples of the other relation.

3.5 $(\max(\frac{m}{p},\frac{n}{p})\cdot C_H)\tau_{CPU}$ – comparing each tuple with the corresponding line of the hash table, $C_H$ is a variable which depends on the hash table construction technique (here posed $C_H = 1$, see [16] for the details).

3.6 $(\frac{mn}{p^2}\cdot Sel)\tau_{CPU}$ – building result tuples.

3.7 $(\frac{mn}{p^2}\cdot Sel)\tau_{I/O}$ – writing the result relation to the disk.

Comparative study :
To choose between the Nested Loops and Sort-Merge algorithms, it suffices to compare the quantities :

$$(\frac{m}{p}\log\frac{n}{p})\tau_{CPU} + (\min(\frac{m}{p}\log\frac{n}{p},\frac{n}{p})f_{DM}^R)\tau_{I/O}$$

and

$$(\frac{m}{p}\log\frac{m}{p})\tau_{CPU} + (\frac{m+n}{p})\tau_{CPU} + (\frac{n}{p}f_{DM}^R)\tau_{I/O}$$

As $\min(\frac{m}{p}\log\frac{n}{p},\frac{n}{p}) \leq \frac{n}{p}$ we have :

$$\frac{T_{NL}-T_{SM}}{\tau_{CPU}} \leq \frac{m}{p}\log\frac{n}{p} - \frac{m}{p}\log\frac{m}{p} - \frac{m+n}{p} = \frac{m}{p}(\log\frac{n}{m} - \frac{n}{m} - 1) < 0,$$

because always : $\log \frac{n}{m} < 1 + \frac{n}{m}$.

Thus, Nested Loops is more performant that Sort-Merge, now we compare it with Hash-Join, the concerned expressions are :

$$(\frac{m}{p} \log \frac{n}{p})\tau_{CPU} + (\min(\frac{m}{p} \log \frac{n}{p}, \frac{n}{p})f_{DM}^R)\tau_{I/O}$$

and

$$(\min(\frac{m}{p}, \frac{n}{p})) \cdot 2\tau_{CPU} + 2(\max(\frac{m}{p}, \frac{n}{p}))\tau_{CPU} + (\frac{n}{p}f_{DM}^R)\tau_{I/O}$$

Two cases must be distinguished :

1. Case $m > n$

$$T_{NL} - T_H = (\frac{m}{p} \log \frac{n}{p})\tau_{CPU} + (\min(\frac{m}{p} \log \frac{n}{p}, \frac{n}{p})f_{DM}^R)\tau_{I/O} -$$
$$\frac{2m + 2n}{p}\tau_{CPU} - (\frac{n}{p}f_{DM}^R)\tau_{I/O}$$

It can be majorated, because $\min(\frac{m}{p} \log \frac{n}{p}, \frac{n}{p}) \le \frac{n}{p}$ :

$$\frac{T_{NL} - T_H}{\tau_{CPU}} \le \frac{m}{p} \log \frac{n}{p} - \frac{2m + 2n}{p} = \frac{1}{p}(m \log \frac{n}{4p} - 2n) \qquad (1)$$

- if $\log \frac{n}{4p} < 0$ i.e. $n < 4p$, then $T_{NL} - T_H < 0$     $\rightarrow$ Nested Loops
- if $\log \frac{n}{4p} > 2$ i.e. $n > 16p$, then $T_{NL} - T_H > 0$     $\rightarrow$ Hash (It is a case of egality in (1), because it is easy to verify that $\min(\frac{m}{p} \log \frac{n}{p}, \frac{n}{p}) = \frac{n}{p}$)
- for $4p < n < 16p$ : if $m > \frac{2n}{\log \frac{n}{4p}}$, then $T_{NL} - T_H < 0$     $\rightarrow$ Hash (it is also the case of egality in (1)), else $\rightarrow$ Nested Loops

2. Case $m \le n$

$$T_{NL} - T_H = (\frac{m}{p} \log \frac{n}{p})\tau_{CPU} + (\min(\frac{m}{p} \log \frac{n}{p}, \frac{n}{p})f_{DM}^R)\tau_{I/O} -$$
$$\frac{2m + 2n}{p}\tau_{CPU} - (\frac{n}{p}f_{DM}^R)\tau_{I/O}$$

We can again majorate :

$$\frac{T_{NL} - T_H}{\tau_{CPU}} \le \frac{m}{p} \log \frac{n}{p} - \frac{2m + 2n}{p} = \frac{1}{p}(m \log \frac{n}{4p} - 2n) \qquad (2)$$

- if $\log \frac{n}{4p} < 0$ i.e. $n < 4p$, then $T_{NL} - T_H < 0$     $\rightarrow$ Nested Loops
- if $0 < \log \frac{n}{4p} < 2$ i.e. $4p < n < 16p$, then Nested Loops too
- for $n > 16p$ : if $m < \frac{2n}{\log \frac{n}{4p}}$, then $T_{NL} - T_H < 0$     $\rightarrow$ Hash (it is a case of egality in (2)), else $\rightarrow$ Nested Loops

Our proof is now complete.

# Synthetic Workload Generation for Parallel Processing Systems

Hannes Pfneiszl, Gabriele Kotsis

Universität Wien
Lenaugasse 2/8, A-1080 Wien, Österreich
[pfneiszl|gabi]@ani.univie.ac.at

**Abstract.** In the performance evaluation for parallel systems, modeling and generating the workload (i.e. the (set of) programs) is one of the most important and crucial tasks. While benchmarks are frequently used to characterize the real workload in measurement studies, they often fail to adequately describe the real workload, that the analyst has in mind. What is needed is a support for generating synthetic workloads which are on the one hand able to characterize the real workload at the desired level of detail and which are on the other hand easy to construct.

In this paper we describe a tool which has been designed and implemented with respect to these demands. The basic idea is to provide a set of communication patterns (e.g. one-to-one, one-to-all) and computation patterns ("tasks"), which are the building blocks of the synthetic program. By "putting" these blocks together, the analyst can create the desired algorithmic structure. This skeleton is the input to an analysis and simulation tool (N-MAP) [Fers 95a]. Within this environment, various quantitative parameters describing the duration of computations and communications can be specified. The "execution" of the skeleton is then simulated based on the provided parameter values.

## 1 Introduction

### 1.1 Motivation

The term performance evaluation is used in computer science and computer engineering to refer to the set of concepts, methodologies, and tools that are needed to assess the performance of computer systems, hardware and software components of these systems as well as computer programs. Measurement and evaluation of uni-processor computer systems performance is a difficult but well established discipline since many years. More difficult and hardly understood is this for parallel processing systems due to the complexity of the internal structure of such a computer system and because of the difficulty of describing and predicting the workload for parallel systems. The basic motivation for the discipline in all of its numerous aspects is the need, both intellectually and practically crucial, to apply the quantitative viewpoint of science and engineering to computer systems and computer programs.

Till now, there is no serious workload-independent system performance index for (parallel) computer systems. MIPS (million instructions per second) or

MFLOPS[1] (million floating-point operations per second) are measures of either peak CPU power or mean CPU power, where a particular instruction mix is assumed in the latter case. Other indices that might seem to be workload-independent are in reality measured under well-known and standard benchmarks, and valid only for workloads that are well represented by those benchmarks. Therefore an adequate workload characterization is required in every predicative performance evaluation study.

Owing to the diversity of architectural approaches of a multiprocessor, the development of models that can provide a true measure of the "actual" performance of these machines under workloads of interest can be an extremely complex, if not impossible, problem. Since a multitude of architectural and application parameters jointly determine system performance and the modification of some factors affects others, it is not feasible to construct an elegant yet tractable analytical model that encompasses all performance effects. Nondeterminism present in parallel program execution on parallel processing systems introduces an additional degree of complexity. The inherent dynamic run-time behavior of parallel programs is impossible to capture accurately in analytical models.

In the face of the above difficulties, empirical results seem to be an attractive alternative for deriving performance measures. This has led to the use of programs with a prespecified workload to characterize and evaluate parallel computer performance, i.e. the benchmarking of parallel processing systems.

## 1.2 Benchmarking Parallel Processing Systems

Benchmarking of high-performance computer systems[2] has rightly become an active area of investigation [Mess 90], not to mention controversy. Implicit in every well-known scientific benchmark is the suggestion that the benchmark somehow captures the essence of many important scientific computations and applications. Just what are the important scientific computations and in what sense is their essence represented by a benchmark are questions that are typically at the center of any benchmark controversy. Generally, investigating the performance of a system through benchmarks has three major objectives:

1. provide input for improving the design of future advanced computer architectures
2. permit manufacturers to state the capabilities of their systems in a comparable fashion
3. assess the suitability of a given architecture for a class of applications.

Nearly all other objectives, e.g. benchmarks assist designers in optimizing hardware and software, benchmarks give a support when deciding to purchase a

---

[1] For massively parallel processing systems or supercomputers MFLOPS are an insufficient unit for peak performance rates. In this case, the measuring units are GigaFLOPS (billion floating-point operations per second) or even TeraFLOPS (trillion floating-point operations per second).

[2] See for example [Pfne 96] for a survey.

new system, benchmarks will teach programming styles that take advantage of architectural features, etc., are covered by those objectives.

Using standard benchmarks (e.g. LINPACK [Dong 95], NAS kernels [Bail 86]) to evaluate machine performance is a widely used practice. Considerable effort has been expended to develop benchmark suites (e.g. the Genesis suite [Geto 93]), that are considered to reflect real workloads. Although benchmarking is an excellent approach for performance evaluation, there are also a number of limitations of using it as an approach to "performance characterization":

- Each benchmark is itself a mixture of characteristics, and does not relate to a specific aspect of machine performance.
- They provide no insight as to which components of a given program workload have the potential of being the bottlenecks and to what extent.
- It is difficult to be confident in the ability of "a few lines of code" to be representative of tens of thousands of lines of codes, particularly if the algorithm implemented is not even used in the workload of the evaluated system.

From the standpoint of the person engaged in the performance evaluation activity, the use of a standard benchmark program suffers from one significant limitation – the lack of control over the workload characteristics of the benchmark. Selecting any standard benchmark as the basis for the performance evaluation automatically establishes an associated program workload that is built into the benchmark structure. Hence, it is not possible to experiment with changing individual parameters in the workload that affect performance so as to determine optimal settings for such parameters for a given architecture/application combination. Such selective characterization of performance along controlled performance dimensions is an integral part of the design and implementation of better algorithms and applications.

What is needed is a *synthetic workload generation* to omit the difficulties in connection with the predetermined workloads in benchmarks. These generated synthetic workloads have the advantage that they can be made parametric and hence flexible in representing workload characteristics.

## 1.3  Synthetic Workload Generation

In the past few years, synthetic workloads have been used in the evaluation of parallel systems. Some approaches were oriented towards the analysis of particular types of applications (e.g. [Fuji 90]), others were proposed in order to investigate components of a computer system (e.g. in [Bodn 91] distributed file systems are studied, or in [LaRo 92] memory management is analyzed).

Some results have been reported in [Cand 92] on using synthetic workloads for studying the performance of concurrent programs (using simulation). This approach is rather static, in that the user has no ability to experiment with different parameters to modify the synthetic workload. An attempt towards a user-oriented synthetic workload generation is presented in [Kao 92] and [Roge 93] for the analysis of distributed systems.

In this work, we propose synthetic workload generation for parallel systems as a general method which expediently produces a synthetic workload specified by the user rather than performing a single generalized experiment with static and/or predetermined workloads. It provides the building blocks for constructing a workload which closely models the application of particular interest to the investigator and the workload can be used to conduct a series of experiments tailored especially for a specific application. To a large extent, benchmark programs restrict this influence a user can have on the execution parameters of a benchmark. This of course is useful to make sure that the results are kept comparable, but the user is bound to a program which probably does not have the same workload as the application he is especially interested in. Giving the user a possibility to describe the behavior of a certain application it should be possible to generate a synthetic workload similar to the described program. To do so two approaches are conceivable:

- A first and rather static approach is to create a single program that is able to change its behavior according to the parameters.
- Another, more flexible approach, which is proposed in this work is to develop a program that makes use of these parameters, too, but also generates different synthetic programs. This means creating a synthetic workload generation program instead of developing a benchmark program itself.

The major advantage of the proposed approach is the fact that special features or complete applications (as shown by the example in Section 3) can be simulated without complete implementation. For example, different kinds of communication patterns can be generated by manipulating parameters for message size and task duration. A user does not have to implement his application program completely to investigate its behavior, rather the behavior of the application can be simulated by only determining the algorithmic (task) structure of the application program. Synthetic programs with selected sets of parameters can be generated and their execution can be simulated on (a model of) parallel systems. By varying the parameters systematically, those factors can be discovered which most affect the performance.

Generally, the idealized goal for synthetic workload generation is to automatically generate a synthetic workload which mimics the system performance and system behavior of an observed real workload under tunable parameter changes. But using a set of parameters to describe an application is a trade-off between the two contrary goals of easy usability and model correctness. A large number of parameters makes it easier to create a workload with a behavior closer to the application these parameters are derived from but also makes the synthetic workload program more difficult to handle. Too few parameters will have opposite effects.

# 2   The Synthetic Workload Generation Facility

The synthetic workload generation facility introduced in this work supports the specification, generation, and execution of synthetic workloads on (a model of) parallel systems. It provides the necessary support to efficiently produce synthetic workloads which are customized for a particular evaluation study. In detail, the synthetic workload generation facility consists of two parts (Figure 1):

1. the synthetic workload generation program SWG [Pfne 96] which generates a user-specified synthetic workload and
2. the N-MAP tool [Fers 95a] developed at the Institute of Applied Computer Science and Information Systems to simulate and execute the generated synthetic workloads.

There have been two primary objectives in the design of the synthetic workload generation facility. The first is to be capable of accurately representing actual workloads. By accurately modeling the structure of the workload, many of the behavioral characteristics can be captured. Representativeness is enhanced by the selection and modification of parameters in the workload. Parameters are defined for both the synthetic tasks and communication packets. These parameters are selected to reflect the properties which are specific to parallel software. The second goal in the design of the synthetic workload generation facility has been the ease of use. All components of the suite should be easy to use while retaining their flexibility and power. Ease of use is enhanced by the simple structure of the synthetic workload generation program and the features provided by N-MAP.

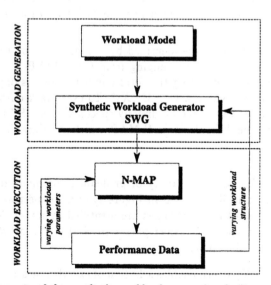

Fig. 1. Constituency of the synthetic workload generation facility

## 2.1 The Workload Model

Generally, a workload model is intended to describe (parallel) workloads in sufficient detail to be used as the basis for generating synthetic workloads. To be an accurate representation of a workload, the model must capture all relevant structural and behavioral details of the workload, since the structure and behavior of the workload affect the values of the performance indices that are measured during experiments. Changes in the workload cause changes in the values of the performance indices. Therefore a workload model has to provide a formalism that allows the user to express the connections between the workload, its characteristics, and the measured performance indices.

According to these facts, the workload model employed consists of a high level description of the structure of the workload. The N-MAP language provides language constructs for very intuitive notions in parallel programs: *tasks, processes* and *communication packets*. In a very abstract sense, a *task* refers to a contiguous, sequential block of program code. The functionality of a task in a parallel program is referred as its *behavior*. The quantification of its real or expected execution time is expressed with the *requirements* of a task in units of time. Communication objects, i.e. the actual data to be transferred among (virtual) processors, are referred to as *packets*. Analogous to tasks, packets are characterized by their *behavior* and quantified by their *requirements*. At least, an ordered set of tasks defines a *process*, seen as a stream of computational or communication task calls.

These language constructs are the elements of the basic building blocks of the workload model used by SWG. The blocks (in the following referred to as patterns) can be put together arbitrarily according to the workload structure and timing information can be assigned to the elements of the patterns according to the workload requirements. To see, how the provided patterns fit into the proposed workload model, a brief description of each pattern is given.

**Computation Tasks** Tasks are identified by a name given by the users, processors are identified by numbers ranging from 0 to MAXP-1, where MAXP is an N-MAP parameter, denoting the total number of processors. A task can be assigned to $k$ processors, $1 \leq k \leq MAXP$. To every task durations can be assigned, deterministic values can be directly specified within SWG, more complex expressions can be defined within N-MAP, which identifies the tasks by the user-defined names.

**Communication Patterns** A variety of predefined communication patterns are available (schematically depicted in Figure 2) and are discussed below. For every pattern, the data to be exchanged are identified by a user defined name. The "communication volume" (called packet in N-MAP) is defined in a way analogous to the task durations.

**Pattern i:K** The $i{:}K$ pattern enables selection of exactly one sending processor $i$ and a set of receiving processors $K$ ($1 \leq |K| \leq MAXP$). The processor

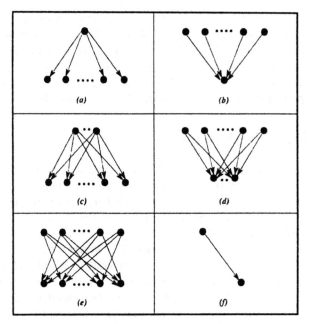

**Fig. 2.** General communication patterns

$i$ cannot be part of the set of receiving processors $K$ and vice versa. This pattern, called *single node broadcast*, is depicted in Figure 2(a). For ease of use, the case $|K| = MAXP$ (one-to-all) as well as the case $|K| = 1$ (point-to-point, depicted in Figure 2(f)), are defined as additional patterns.

**Pattern K:i** The pattern $K : i$ enables the selection of a set of sending processors $K$ $(1 < |K| \leq MAXP)$, each of them performing a send to one receiving processor $i$, where $i \notin K$ (see Figure 2(b)). Again, the case $|K| = MAXP$ is defined as a special case, called *single node gather*.

**Pattern K:L** The pattern $K : L$ enables the selection of a set of sending processors $K$ which make a broadcast to a set of receiving processors $L$, where $|K|, |L| > 1$ and $K \cap L = \emptyset$. It can also be called a *single node broadcast* from every processor $\in K$ to every processor $\in L$.

**Pattern K:R** The pattern $K : R$ enables the selection of a set of sending processors $K$ $(1 \leq |K| < MAXP)$ which perform a broadcast to all the remaining processors in $R$ $(R = N \setminus K$ and $K \cap R = \emptyset)$. Each processor $\in K$ performs *a single node broadcast* to every processor $\in R$.

The schematic representation is identical for these two patterns and is given in Figure 2(c).

**Pattern N:K** The pattern $N : K$ enables the selection of a set of receiving processors $K$, each of them receiving a message from all other processors $N$. This pattern is a gathering performed by a set of nodes, $K$. The schematic representation is given in Figure 2(d).

**Pattern K:K** The pattern $K : K$ enables the selection of a set of processors $K$, where this set is contemporary the set of the receiving processors and $|K| \leq 2 \leq MAXP$. This corresponds to a *total exchange* or *multinode broadcast* within a set of $K$ processors and is schematically depicted in Figure 2(e). The special case of $|K| = MAXP$ is called a *global exchange* where each processor performs a *single node broadcast* and *single node accumulation*.

# 3 Scenario, Walk through

At the current state of implementation SWG is controlled by the user through an interrogatory textual interface. Each possible building block is identified by a number, when entering this identification number, the program will ask for all the necessary input parameters. The sequence of the blocks is defined by the sequence in which the numbers are entered.

The output of SWG consists of two files. The `<name>.tss` (*task structure specification*) file contains the generated program code by SWG and is the input for N-MAP. The file `<name>.graph` file contains a verbal description of what has been done by the user. It contains the information about the patterns that have been generated, about the processors that have been used, and about the tasks and packets that have been declared. It also contains a simple graphical representation of the generated workload structure.

To explain some of the abilities of SWG a simple introductory example will be used. With the communication patterns provided by SWG a *butterfly* communication (see e.g. [Quin 87]) will be generated using 8 processors. This pattern allows a complete exchange of messages among $p$ processors in $\log p$ communication steps. Although an *all-to-all* communication pattern is provided as a default pattern by SWG, the *butterfly* communication pattern may be sometimes more efficient on a particular architecture (e.g. hypercube) in comparison to the *all-to-all* communication pattern *K:K*.

The command for starting the program is

```
swg <NUMBER OF PROCESSORS>   [SUN]
```

where `<NUMBER OF PROCESSORS>` is a parameter, defining the maximum number of processing elements and the parameter SUN is an optional parameter which must be added if the program is used on SunSparc/SunOS 4.1.x. If the program ist started with the parameter `help` brief information concerning usage of the program (including a brief description of the available patterns) is given.

Let us assume, that we have started the program with `swg 8` (on an SGI), e.g. we using 8 processors which are numbered from 0 - 7. This is necessary since N-MAP and the visualization tools also use this kind of enumeration. When started, SWG prompts you to enter a name for the program:

```
Enter a name for the program ( = process name):
```

The program name also determines the process name which is used in the generated synthetic workload program. To create the above stated example the name **butterfly** is entered. After entering the name a simple validity check of the name is made. SWG also uses the same directory structures as N-MAP to provide complete support of file manipulation features in N-MAP. The program tests if a program with the entered name already exists. If the name is already used, the user can choose between selecting a (different) new name or creating a new version of the existing program identified by a version number (e.g. 1.0). The complete directory structure used by SWG and N-MAP (depicted in [Fers 95b]) is then generated and the program continues displaying the following information on the screen:

```
#################################################################
#                                                               #
#      The following patterns can be chosen (e for end).        #
#                                                               #
#         b[?].   K processors execute (a) task(s)              #
#                                                               #
#      1[t?].   pattern i:K        4[t?].   pattern K:R         #
#      2[t?].   pattern K:i        5[t?].   pattern N:K         #
#      3[t?].   pattern K:L        6[t?].   pattern K:K         #
#                                                               #
# [Adding 't' enables task selection, adding '?' enables help.] #
#                                                               #
#################################################################
Your selection:
```

Each of these patterns can be easily selected entering the character stated before the name of the pattern. Note, that pattern b is a computation task, and patterns 1 to 6 represent communication patterns. Since it is typical in parallel programs that a phases of computation are followed by phases of communication, the option **t** is provided. In that case, the user may enter specific computation tasks to be executed by the processing elements involved in the communication (see below). The other optional parameter **?** provides a brief description and some help on how to use the pattern.

The range of the selectable processors for each pattern is $0 \leq$ processor $\leq$ MAXP-1. MAXP is the parameter entered with the program call. Besides, it is possible to repeat each pattern more than one time and there are no limitations in putting together different patterns. Tasks and packets are identified by name, e.g. two tasks/packets with the same name are assumed to be identical. This identity will also be used in the simulation (e.g. timings associated to a task/packet will apply to all tasks/packets with the same name). To enhance the recognizability of each task and packet when applying the visualization tool, tasks/packets with identical names are displayed in identical colors. Concerning the option **t** generally can be said that tasks can be entered before and/or after a broadcast of the sending processor and before and/or after the reception of the broadcast by the receiving processors. If the **t** option is selected for the pattern $K{:}K$, tasks can either be specified before the broadcast or after the broadcast (i.e. after every PE has received all messages).

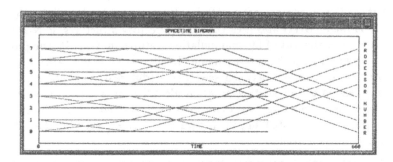

**Fig. 3.** ParaGraph: *Spacetime* display of the butterfly communication structure with different packet size at each stage

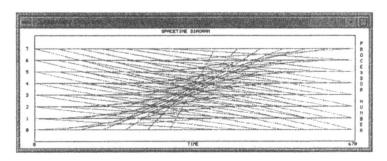

**Fig. 4.** ParaGraph: *Spacetime* display of the pattern *K:K* communication structure

Using the patterns defined in Section 2.1, we can start to generate the program code for the example **butterfly**. Generally, the *butterfly* communication pattern can be perfectly embedded in the hypercube topology but can even be used (more or less effective) on other topologies. To construct the pattern exactly $2^k$ ($k \geq 1$) processing elements must be available. In this case, the butterfly is said to consist of $k$ stages. In each stage, the pattern $i:K$ is used. Note, that in the data transfer, each processor, upon receiving a message, has to add in its own data and forward the enlarged message to the following processors. In our example, the number of processing elements is eight, so the number of stages is three, and the $i:K$ pattern will be used three times, defining a different packet at each stage which will have a different size.

If the user finishes the program SWG, a text editor is called to view the verbal description file **butterfly.graph** and the program N-MAP is started. When SWG starts N-MAP, N-MAP contains automatically the last generated synthetic workload program by SWG. In our case, the program **butterfly** is loaded. All settings concerning scenarios and cases have been made by SWG with default values so that the user does not have to make any necessary parameter settings.

Without making any changes, the user can press the *Simulate* button in N-MAP to start parsing/translating, compiling, and simulating the synthetic program. When simulation is finished, the execution trace can be visualized using different kinds of ParaGraph displays (e.g. spacetime displays as in Figure 3 and 4).

The main difference of the two patterns is the fact, that the butterfly structure uses different packets at each stage, whereas the $K$:$K$ pattern uses the same packet continuously. To vary the workload for the *butterfly* program and to experiment with different packet sizes, only a few settings have to be changed in N-MAP.

Many case studies concerning this rather easy synthetic workload program using different workloads could be stated at this time. But since each user is particularly interested in his individual workload parameter settings they are not of general concern and are omitted. A more complex example using SWG can be found in [Pfne 96].

## 4 Conclusions

In this paper, we have presented a new technique for synthetic workload generation for parallel systems. The basic idea is to provide a set of computation and communication patterns from which the structure of the synthetic workload can be composed. These patterns can either be used to mimic a typical application (e.g. the butterfly communication structure presented in this paper), or to represent a stress case for the system. Once the structure of the workload has been described, the parameters associated to the duration of computation and communication tasks can be specified. These parameters may either be chosen to represent realistic estimates or to represent extremal values.

A tool has been developed (Synthetic Workload Generator) to support the specification of the workload structure. In the current implementation, the tool has a textual interface, where the user is prompted to enter the desired patterns. To further improve the usability of the tool, a graphical interface is under design. In this graphical environment, the user could put together the building blocks using direct manipulation.

Although SWG has turned out being appropriate for a few examples (see [Pfne 96], an effort to model the workload of a complex real parallel application has not been attempted until now. Improvements concerning the user-interface (see above), the scalability and code-reusability are possible prospects for future work.

## References

[Bail 86]  D. H. Bailey and J. T. Barton. "The NAS Kernel Benchmark Program". Tech. Rep., Numerical Aerodynamic Simulation (NAS) Systems Division, NASA Ames Research Center, June 1986.

[Bodn 91]  R. R. Bodnarchuk and R. B. Bunt. "A Synthetic Workload Model for a Distributed System File Server". *Performance Evaluation Review, Special Issue, 1991 ACM SIGMETRICS*, Vol. 19, No. 1, pp. 50–59, May 1991.

[Cand 92] R. Candlin, P. Fisk, L. Phillips, and N. Skilling. "Studying the Performance of Concurrent Programs by Simulation Experiments on Synthetic Programs". *Performance Evaluation Review, Special Issue, 1992 ACM SIGMETRICS*, Vol. 20, No. 1, pp. 239–241, June 1992. Poster Session of Extended Abstracts.

[Dong 95] J. J. Dongarra. "Performance of Various Computers Using Standard Linear Equations Software". Tech. Rep. CS-89-85, University of Tennessee and Oak Ridge National Laboratory, November 1995.

[Fers 95a] A. Ferscha and J. Johnson. "Evaluation of Accuracy/Cost-Tradeoffs in the N-MAP Environment". Tech. Rep. D3H-4 (GZ 308.926), University of Vienna, PACT Consortium, June 1995.

[Fers 95b] A. Ferscha and J. Johnson. "Implementation of Workload Characterization Tools: The N-MAP Environment". Tech. Rep. D3H-3 (GZ 308.926), University of Vienna, PACT Consortium, June 1995.

[Fuji 90] R. M. Fujimoto. "Performance of Time Warp under Synthetic Workloads". In: D. Nicol, Ed., *Distributed Simulation. Proceedings of the SCS Multiconference on Distributed Simulation*, pp. 23–28, Society for Computer Simulation, San Diego, California, 1990. Simulation Series, Volume 22, Number 1.

[Geto 93] V. S. Getov, A. J. G. Hey, R. W. Hockney, and I. C. Wolton. "The GENESIS Benchmark Suite: Current State and Results". In: *Performance Evaluation of Parallel Systems, PEPS'93, November 29-30, 1993, Warwick, UK*, pp. 182–190, University of Warwick, 1993.

[Kao 92] W.-I. Kao and R. K. Iyer. "A User-Oriented Synthetic Workload Generator". In: *Proceedings of the 12th International Conference on Distributed Computing Systems*, pp. 270–277, IEEE Computer Society Press, Los Alamitos, California, 1992.

[LaRo 92] R. P. LaRowe, C. S. Ellis, and M. A. Holiday. "Evaluation of NUMA Memory Management Through Modeling and Measurements". *IEEE Transactions on Parallel and Distributed Systems*, Vol. 3, No. 6, pp. 686–701, Nov. 1992.

[Mess 90] P. Messina, C. Bailie, P. Hipes, J. Rogers, A. Alagar, A. Kamrath, R. Leary, W. Pfeiffer, R. Williams, and D. Walker. "Benchmarking advanced architecture computers". *Concurrency: Practice and Experience*, Vol. 2, No. 3, pp. 195–255, Sep. 1990.

[Pfne 96] H. Pfneiszl. *Synthetic Workload Generation for Parallel Processing Systems*. Master's thesis, University of Vienna, Institute of Applied Computer Science, January 1996.

[Quin 87] M. J. Quinn. *Designing efficient algorithms for parallel computers*. McGraw-Hill International Publishers, New York, 1987.

[Roge 93] S. A. Rogers. "A Synthetic Workload Generator for Evaluating Distributed Fault-tolerant Environments". Tech. Rep. ESL-AFT-040-93, MCC, 1993.

# Parallel Program Visualization with MUCH

D. Kranzlmüller, R. Koppler, S. Grabner,
Ch. Holzner, J. Volkert

GUP Linz
Johannes Kepler University Linz
Altenbergerstraße 69, A-4040 Linz, Austria, Europe
kranzlmueller@gup.uni-linz.ac.at
phone: ++43 732 2468 9499
fax: ++43 732 2468 9496

## Abstract

The use of visualization in parallel program development is manifold. It is applied from data and control flow over debugging, performance analysis and performance prediction until data distribution on distributed memory architectures. Most of these visualizations do not care about the physical topology of the underlying hardware although this can be of importance in the fields of performance analysis or error debugging.

We have developed a class library called MUCH (MUltiprocessor Class Hierarchy), which helps a user to model different multiprocessor architectures. These so derived multiprocessors can be used for visualization of multiprocessor topologies with different number of nodes and for the presentation of various aspects in different areas of parallelism in cooperation with other tools. In this paper we describe the structure of MUCH as well as its implementation in C++. We further present a few examples of cooperation with tools in the areas of performance analysis, trace driven simulation for error debugging, and data distribution for distributed memory machines.

**Keywords:** parallel program analysis, software visualization, class hierarchies

## 1 Introduction

The development of parallel programs is a task which can be very tedious and difficult. Reasons are that in comparison with monoprocessing both hardware and software are more complex, and the structure and behavior of parallel programs are strongly influenced by the underlying hardware. Two examples are

- Different interconnection networks may cause different implementations, since the partitioning into subtasks and the mapping of the subtasks onto the system has to match the hardware structure.
- The ratio of communication and computing power may affect the program design (e.g. to avoid as many messages as possible).

Furthermore there are phenomena which are only known in context with parallel processing like nondeterminism due to race conditions and contention problems.

In any case the developer of parallel programs needs more insight into the hardware than usual and he has to know how software matches the features of the machine architecture. In this context a hardware visualization tool is useful.

Such a tool should incorporate two features. One necessary feature is the level of detail. It depends on what is under investigation. For instance, if people search for a deadlock due to wrong communication, the use of a graph where nodes and edges correspond to processes respectively logical communication channels will be sufficient. But if a bottleneck within the network is caused by unfavorable communication structure, more details of the networks as e.g. network nodes with buffers will be necessary. Therefore the visualization tool has to support a *hierarchy* of different levels of abstractions. It should be possible to select the level of detail of the hardware model and the accuracy of the visualized program behavior.

A second feature should be *flexibility*. Firstly, the tool should provide a set of predefined hardware components to be used in various multiprocessors. Secondly, as new parallel machines emerge on the market every now and then, it must be able to easily include new hardware features in the model. A solution is to keep the tool capable of being extended. This implies the need for an interface to user-defined methods (e.g. like in ParaGraph [HeFi 93]), preferably with object-oriented methods like inheritance, dynamic binding. and polymorphism.

A lot of different graphical methods have been developed to accompany the user in each step of the software lifecycle. They can be categorized in support for visual programming and program visualization [Hyrs 95]. Many different tools, several taxonomies, classifications and surveys of computer graphics systems for assistance in program development have been proposed [KrSt 93], [ZhMa 94]. Nevertheless it seems that a solution which meets the requirements *hierarchy* and *flexibility* does not exist.

In this paper we describe the **MU**ltiprocessor **C**lass **H**ierarchy **MUCH** which presents an approach to combine the visualization of software and hardware and fulfills the requirements stated above. The target system is a parallel machine or a program running on a computer with more than one processor.

The result is a class library that allows modelling of multiprocessors with C++. Furthermore the behavior and operation of these machines can be visualized. Instead of a fixed tool with an interface, the whole system is open for the user.

The application of MUCH occurs in different fields of parallel program development. Currently we apply it to evaluate the program performance based on the underlying hardware architecture with static visualization, dynamic animation and simulation methods, and for graphical data distribution, where the quality of data-to-processor mapping determines the efficiency of program runs.

Several other areas of using a class library like MUCH are imaginable. The most important idea is to give the user a clear insight and understanding of the underlying hardware. Therefore this library might be very important for teaching and education of students, who have to learn the operation of a multiprocessor to produce efficient and reliable software in the future.

This paper is organized as follows. First we present an overview of the basic structure of MUCH. Section 3 describes how to model multiprocessors with the class library. Afterwards a few examples of using MUCH in real-world applications are presented. It is followed by a conclusion and an outlook on the future of MUCH.

## 2 Basic Structure of MUCH

### 2.1 The Class Hierarchy

The multiprocessor class hierarchy MUCH is implemented in C++. It uses the application framework ET++ [Gamm 92] as a basis for all visualization matters. The development of MUCH is based on design patterns [Gamm 95] to provide a high degree of reusability.

One of the key parts of MUCH is the abstract class MuchTopology, which contains data structures and methods for modelling the topology of a multiprocessor. To model a parallel system, the user derives a new topology from this abstract class. A topology (corresponding to MUCH) consists of the following three parts:

- a set of nodes,
- an interconnection network,
- and methods for manipulating the state of the multiprocessor.

The network between the nodes describes the connection between the processors. Each of the nodes itself consists of components to describe e.g. CPU nodes or I/O processors. The contents of a node are a processor, a routing unit, and memory.

Based on this description a simple hierarchy of MUCH can be derived as follows. There are the base classes MuchTopology, MuchNode and MuchNetwork. The class MuchNode can be split up into the classes MuchCPU, MuchRoutingUnit and MuchMemory.

Further refinement leads to more specialized classes. For example, MuchNetwork can be refined to MuchNetworkStatic and MuchNetworkDynamic, indicating the existence of static and dynamic networks. Another example is MuchTopology, which can be refined to a general hypercube topology and furthermore to the nCUBE topology.

This refinement process leads to the current implementation of MUCH, which consists of more than 140 classes. Due to the size of the hierarchy, a screenshot with the full graph is not included in this paper.

With this basic set of classes the user can already define a generic multiprocessor. However, some multiprocessors are already included in the hierarchy of MUCH. At present this is the distributed-memory computer nCUBE2 and the virtual shared-memory machine CONVEX Exemplar SPP 1200. Both models are described in more detail in section 3.

### 2.2 Modularity

Another concept integrated in MUCH is the Model-View-Controller (MVC) architecture. It is used to preserve additional modularity of the class hierarchy [Gamm 92].

The *model* administrates the data structures of the components. The *view* contains algorithms for displaying the model. The *controller* manages input events.

The main idea of this architecture is, that all the components could be reused independently and several models can be visualized with different views (e.g. a hypercube as multidimensional cube or as two dimensional graph).

A sideeffect of implementing the MVC architecture is, that the model can be used without any visualization. This is useful in connection with simulation, when visualization becomes a time-critical factor.

As a result MUCH contains two hierarchies, one for the visualization and one for the operation of the multiprocessor. In ET++ programs the controller part is included in the view classes.

### 2.3 The Modelling Process

The modelling process with MUCH is based on these hierarchies. First the user selects a topology for the multiprocessor to be visualized. The full model is then generated by adding the other components of the hierarchy. The following two cases have to be considered:

  a) The component is already integrated as element (class) in MUCH
  b) The component does not exist within the hierarchy.

In case a) the user simply adds the existing element to the topology (black-box reuse). In case b) either an existing class can be inherited and customized to present the new component (white-box reuse), or a totally new component can be defined. When applying b) the new elements can be included in the class hierarchy for future use. This increases the class hierarchy and provides additional components for other users during later modelling processes.

## 3   The functionality of MUCH

### 3.1  Building the nCUBE2 Model

Now the functionality of MUCH is described with a few examples. First we want to visualize the communication between two nodes of the distributed memory multiprocessor nCUBE2.

The operation is divided into two parts, an *initialization part*, which specifies the multiprocessor structure and an *action part* which defines the operations on the multiprocessor. The initialization can be done as follows:

```
MuchTopology *topology = new MuchTopology_nCUBE2(3);
```

This forces the initialization of all data structures necessary for modelling a nCUBE2 with hypercube dimension 3 (=8 nodes). The class MuchTopology_nCUBE2 is part of the library.

As dictated by the MVC architecture the initialization of the data structures for the model is only one part. The initialization of the visualization has to be carried out independently. The view statements are similar to the model statements and are therefore not included in this paper. As an example the corresponding view initialization of the statement above looks as follows:

```
MuchVTopology *vtopology = new MuchVTopology_nCUBE2(3);
```

After view initialization a window is opened and a graphical representation of a nCUBE2 is displayed as in figure 1[1].

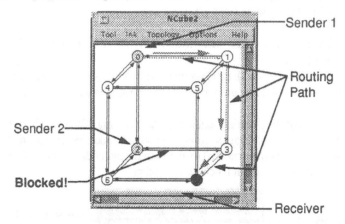

**Fig. 1.** Modelling a nCUBE2 with 8 nodes (deterministic routing)

When initialization has been completed, the user describes the action part of his model by means of methods of the topology object. For example, to model and visualize the communication between node 0 and node 7 one has to use the following statement:

```
topology->SelectPath(0,7);
```

The result represents the communication between the sender (processor 0) and the receiver (processor 7) across some intermediate nodes (processor 1 and processor 3) as shown in figure 1. The path is determined by the *e-cube* routing scheme (leftmost selection) [NiMc 93]. As the nCUBE2 uses wormhole routing for message transmission, the path has to be kept open until the whole message is transferred.

If another communication between node 2 and node 7 is issued with

```
topology->SelectPath(2,7);
```

this second communication is marked as being blocked by the first communication. After the communication is finished, the path between the sender and the receiver has

---

[1] Annotated arrows are used to indicate the colors of the original screenshot.

to be cleared. This can be done with the following method:

```
topology->DeselectPath(0,7);
topology->DeselectPath(2,7);
```

## 3.2 Extending the Functionality of the nCUBE2 Model

The functionality for the nCUBE2 is already fully included in MUCH. To add new architectures or new features to existing hardware models, one has to use inheritance in the following way. Suppose someone wants to add adaptive routing to the nCUBE2.
  With MUCH the following steps are necessary:

- Derive a new class `MuchAdaptiveRouting` from abstract class `MuchRouting`.
- Override the virtual base class function `NextChannel`, which searches for the output link to be used when routing messages through the network.

An example of an adaptive routing scheme (*p-Cube* routing [GlNi 92]) is visualized in figure 2. The nCUBE object is again configured with 8 nodes. When starting the transmission of two messages (from node 0 to node 7 and from node 1 to node 7), both messages can be transferred without blocking each other.

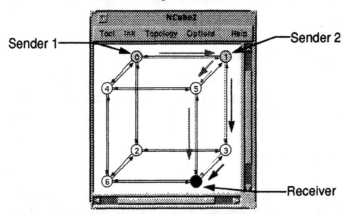

**Fig. 2.** Modelling a nCUBE2 with adaptive routing

## 3.3 Extending the Class Hierarchy - Modelling the CONVEX SPP

As stated above MUCH is extensible. We will demonstrate this with a second multi-processor model, that is included in MUCH. It is a model of a CONVEX Exemplar SPP 1200, which is a massively parallel machine with distributed shared memory. A concrete example of the machine consisting of 24 HP PA-RISC 7200 processors is installed at the computing center of the University Linz. With the knowledge of its architecture and of operation the modelling process with MUCH can be initiated.

The main problem of modelling the CONVEX SPP was the fact, that its architecture can be described on several layers. In the first place there is a top level view, consisting of connected hypernodes. Even without any knowledge of the hypernode structure, this first layer can serve as a basis for MUCH, similar to the nCUBE2 model. An example of a CONVEX SPP with 2 hypernodes (each containing 8 processor) is visualized in figure 3.

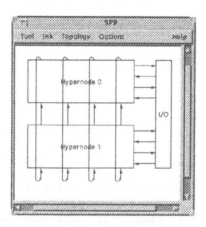

**Fig. 3.** CONVEX SPP hypernode model

As a first refinement the internals of the hypernodes can be modelled. There are several possibilities to describe this layer. One possibility is to describe each hypernode as consisting of four functional blocks and the load/store crossbar. This first refinement to the node layer model is visualized in figure 4, again for 2 hypernodes.

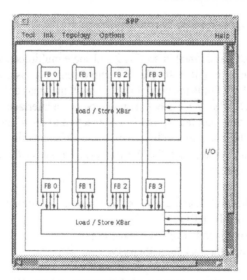

**Fig. 4.** CONVEX SPP node layer model

155

The next step is defined by the fact that each functional block of the CONVEX SPP consists of two HP PA-RISC 7200 processors. This leads to the third layer, the processor layer. Further refinement can be achieved, if the processors, their connections to the crossbar and the memory is modelled in more detail. The result is the fourth layer, which is visualized in figure 5. This figure shows only 2 functional blocks (4 proces-

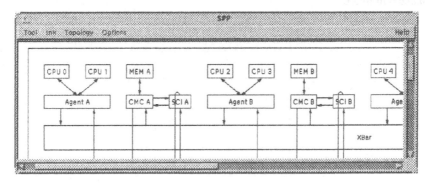

**Fig. 5.** CONVEX SPP detail model

sors) of a hypernode, because a display with all nodes would consume too much space.

Based on these layers the user can perform similar operations on the CONVEX SPP, as on the nCUBE2. The fact that the CONVEX SPP consists of several layers was the greatest difference to the nCUBE2 model. It forced to allow that a hypernode consists of several functional blocks, each consisting of several processors. As a result a redesign of the class hierarchy had to be carried out. But now several layers of a multiprocessor architecture can be modelled.

### 3.4 MUCH Visualizer

With the class hierarchy as defined in section 2 and some multiprocessor models, construction of applications is rather simple. We implemented a visualization tool call *MUCH Visualizer*, which fulfils the need for a tool in all the areas defined in section 1. The structure of *MUCH Visualizer* is based on two parts, an interface part and an operational part. The interface part must provide a connection to other applications, which might want to use the class hierarchy. Due to the different kind of applications, whether they are time-critical or not, the interface part consists of three different ports. Connections can be established via

- Inter-Application Communication (IAC) ports, a communication mechanism provided by ET++,
- Generic Data Interchange (GDI) protocol,
- sockets (using the socket++ library).

While IAC is implemented very easily with ET++ [Wein 91], GDI is a more generic format which is used in the graphical data distribution tool GDDT [Kopp 96]. Sockets have to be used, if the visualized data is time-critical, which is the case for simulations and animations.

The operational part of *MUCH Visualizer* includes classes from MUCH. Whenever a connection is established via the interface part, the operational part translates incoming commands to method calls to MUCH objects.

## 4 Examples

### 4.1 Performance Visualization

The following sections contain some examples, which demonstrate the use of MUCH in the development cycle of parallel programs. The first example is the visualization of performance bugs through blocking paths. For this kind of analysis MUCH works in combination with the visualization tool ATEMPT, which is part of a parallel debugger [Grab 95].

ATEMPT draws global communication of a parallel program as an event graph (see figure 6). While the event graph only provides the amount of blocking at the

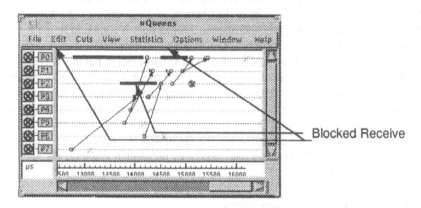

**Fig. 6.** Visualization of blocking communication with ATEMPT

responsible events, MUCH provides the actual blocking based on the underlying hardware architecture. The solution is a connection between ATEMPT (figure 6) and MUCH (figure 1) via the ET++ IAC mechanism.

### 4.2 Simulation and Animation

A second example is the trace-driven simulator PARASIT [Kran 95]. Trace-driven simulation is a well-known technique to debug parallel programs [NeMi 92]. The simulator follows a parallel program run based on tracefiles.

When starting the simulation with PARASIT, the user gets an abstract visualization with rectangles for each node and colors indicating the activities of the nodes. Figure 7 contains a screen shot of PARASIT. The socket-interface of MUCH Visualizer provides a possibility to combine PARASIT with MUCH. The result is a simulation (or an animation) which is performed on a graphical representation of a multiprocessor. Of course MUCH could serve for any simulator that incorporates the socket interface (e.g. [Dali 96]).

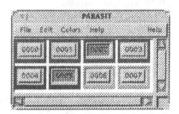

**Fig. 7.** Trace driven simulation with PARASIT

### 4.3 Graphical Data Distribution

The third example is graphical data distribution with GDDT [Kopp 96]. This tool allows the user to design and evaluate distributions of large objects onto distributed-memory multiprocessors by graphical means. An example is shown in figure 8. The left window contains a logical representation of the multiprocessor.

With MUCH the visualization of the processor window can be put into a more concrete form with the actual representation of the multiprocessor. While GDDT includes a logical representation, MUCH provides the actual representation on the machine. Each colored square in the logical processor window corresponds to a physical processor with the same color in the MUCH window.

Furthermore, if data are redistributed, the distribution process can be visualized dynamically with MUCH. The user discovers, how redistribution affects the network of the multiprocessor.

## 5 Conclusion and Future Work

All examples of section 4 lead to the conclusion, that visualization with MUCH can be useful to improve the user's understanding for the underlying hardware architecture. This understanding is also necessary in many areas of student teaching and parallel computing education. With MUCH the task of demonstrating the activities of a multi-processor architecture during operation is possible.

The difference between the MUCH library and similar tools, like Paragraph [HeFi 93], which includes also the representation of a hypercube topology, is the object-ori-ented approach. It was used to fulfill the requirements for a hierarchy with different levels of abstraction and flexibility in terms of extensibility and reusability. Through inheritance and overloading the user can extend existing classes easily. New features and other levels of detail as well as new hardware models can be added within the given frame of the class hierarchy.

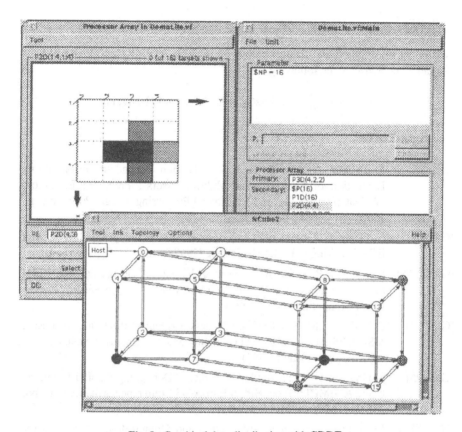

**Fig. 8.** Graphical data distribution with GDDT

The main difficulty in adding new multiprocessor models is the visualization. For example, it is difficult to model a hypercube multiprocessor with a lot of nodes (see figure 9 for an idea of the current solution). Nevertheless many ideas are provided by books on multiprocessor architecture, which include graphical representations for the description of hardware architectures (e.g. [Haye 88] and [Hwan 93]).

A central goal of MUCH is the general purpose. As shown with MUCH Visualizer only the interface has to be adapted. Then it is possible to use MUCH in context with many other tools, e.g. simulators with only textual representation could make use of the graphical display of MUCH. This is one goal for the near future. Another goal is the integration of many other different hardware architectures into MUCH, which might force to redesign parts of the hierarchy. As it is stated in [Gamm 95], it is "difficult if not impossible to get a reusable and flexible design the first time".

## Acknowledgment

The students Richard Schall and Johann Messner were strongly involved in the development and implementation of ATEMPT and GDDT.

## Remark

Additional information and demo-versions of MUCH, ATEMPT and PARASIT are available via WWW at the following URL:

http://www.gup.uni-linz.ac.at:8001/research/debugging

## 6 References

[Dali 96]  S. Dalibor, A.Hein, W. Hohl, "Application Dependent Performability Evaluation of Fault-Tolerant Multiprocessors", Proc. 4th Euromicro Workshop on Parallel and Distributed Processing, Braga, Portugal (Jan. 1996).

[Gamm 92]  E. Gamma, "Objektorientierte Software-Entwicklung am Beispiel von ET++", Springer, Berlin Heidelberg (1992).

[Gamm 95]  E. Gamma, R. Helm, R. Johnson, J. Vlissides, "Design Patterns - Elements of Reusable Object-Oriented Software", Addison-Wesley, Professional Computing Series (1995).

[GlNi 92]  C.J. Glass, L.M. Ni, "The Turn Model for Adaptive Routing", Tech. Rep. MSU-CPS-ACS-44, Dept. of Computer Science, Michigan State University, Michigan (March 1992).

[Grab 95]  S. Grabner, D. Kranzlmüller, J. Volkert, "Debugging Parallel Programs Using ATEMPT", Proc. HPCN Europe 95 Conference, Milano, Italy, pp. 235-240 (May 1995).

[Haye 88]  J.P. Hayes, "Computer Architecture and Organization", McGraw-Hill International Editions, Singapore (1988).

[HeFi 93]  M. T. Heath, J. E. Finger, "ParaGraph: A Tool for Visualizing Performance of Parallel Programs", Technical Report Oak Ridge National Laboratories (1993).

[Hwan 93]  K. Hwang, "Advanced Computer Architecture - Parallelism, Scalability, Programmability", McGraw-Hill Internatl. Editions, Computer Science Series (1993).

[Hyrs 95]  A. Hyrskykari, "Development of Program Visualization Systems", Technical Report A-1995-3, University of Tampere, Department of Computer Science, Finland (Apr. 1995).

[Kopp 96]  Koppler R., Grabner S., Volkert J.: "Graphical Support for Data Distribution in SPMD Parallelization Environments", Proc. IEEE 2nd Int'l Conference on Algorithms and Architectures for Parallel Processing, Singapore, (June 1996).

[KrSt 93]  E. Kraemer, J.T. Sasko, "The Visualization of Parallel Systems: An Overview", Journal of Parallel and Distributed Computing, Vol. 18, No. 2, pp. 105-117, (June 1993).

[Kran 95]   D. Kranzlmüller, S. Grabner, J. Volkert, "PARASIT - Parallel Simulation Tool", ACPC/TR 95-2, ACPC Technical Report Series, Austria (June 1995).

[NeMi 92]   R.H.B. Netzer, B.P. Miller, "Optimal Tracing and Replay for Debugging Message-Passing Parallel Program", Proc. Supercomputing 92, Minneapolis, pp. 502-511 (Nov. 1992).

[NiMc 93]   L.M. Ni, P.K. McKinley, "A survey of wormhole routing techniques in direct networks", IEEE Computer, Vol. 26, No. 2, pp. 62-76 (Feb. 1993).

[Wein 91]   A. Weinand, "Objektorientierter Entwurf und Implemen-tierung portabler Fensterumgebungen am Beispiel des Application-Frameworks ET++", Dissertation, University Zürich (1991).

[ZhMa 94]   K. Zhang, W. Ma, "Graphical Assistance in Parallel Program Development", Proc. VL'94 - 10th IEEE International Symposium on Visual Languages, St. Louis, USA, pp. 168-170 (Oct. 1994).

# Statement-Sets
## (Parallelism Enabled by Independence)

**Svend Erik Knudsen**

Informatikdienste, ETH Zentrum, CH-8092 Zürich, Switzerland
e-mail: knudsen@sd.id.ethz.ch

## Abstract

The possibility to specify a collection of statements (without any preferred execution order) is clamed to be important for the programming of parallel computers.

**Keywords:** programming model, parallel programming, independence, impossible program, Oberon, statement-set.

## 1    Introduction

In recent years, computer architects responded to the demand for higher performing computer systems designs based on better technology and more parallelism. Multiprocessors (symmetric multiprocessors (SMP), e.g.) have been build, sold, and successfully used for more than 25 years, now. Nowadays, even a desktop workstation might be a SMP. Such systems mainly execute individual programs by using one processor at any given time. The wall clock time needed for the execution of a program depends therefore more on a system's effective processor performance than anything else. The main benefit of SMP-systems has been in the increased throughput. Glass-house managers or system administrators might estimate this, but not necessarily the users.

It is still difficult to apply a substantial amount of parallelism to the execution of a single program. Data parallel problems are the main targets for current automatic parallelizing compilers[1, 2, 3]. Independence among probably irregular program parts is fundamental to enable their simultaneous execution. It is, however, generally impossible to automatically decide the independence among arbitrarily chosen program parts. This paper proposes to signal a collection of independent program parts by a syntactic notion. Such notions might help a system to execute such marked parts simultaneously.

Section 2 classifies the tasks we want to be faster (or cheaper) executed. Section 3 suggests independence as the attribute that allows simultaneous execution of program parts. Section 4 presents the concept of statement-sets as a syntactic notion to specify mutually independence among program parts. Sections 5 and 6 propose two new kinds of statements for Oberon to mark statement-sets and illustrate their usage by examples. Section 7 lists some performance figures of the prototype implementation. Section 8 surveys the implementation. The following section summarises our initial experience, and section 10 concludes the paper.

## 2 Transformational versus Reactive Programming

To concentrate on the essential point, we consider only transformations (i.e. transformational or functional program parts). Typically, high performance computer systems perform some given (and well understood) transformations most of the time. Such functions are most likely programmed in a sequential and imperative language like FORTRAN or C.

In the following considerations, we ignore programs with explicitly programmed parallelism. Such programs are often reactive and might including message passing or other forms of explicit process communication or synchronisation. We consider transformational and reactive programming as complementary programming models best used to fulfil conceptually orthogonal requirements.

Thus, we ignore the current legacy of thinking of reactive programming as being the natural programming model for programming transformations for a "parallel system". Furthermore, we do intentionally not search for a single programming model that covers the programming of both transformational and reactive problems.

## 3 On Sequential versus Arbitrary Execution

Current processors' architecture makes use of parallelism at many levels (e.g. gate level, pipelining, multiple functional units, processor level, instruction level, and operating system level). Parallel execution of a single program is only possible, if the program can be split into parts, and if some of these parts are mutually independent. An example might illustrate this theory [4]:

```
ma := MaxArray(a);
mb := MaxArray(b);
m  := Max(ma, mb)
```

Function MaxArray yields the value of the greatest element in an array, and function Max gives the greatest value of its two scalar arguments. The two first statements are independent and can, therefore, be executed in any order, even simultaneously. However, the third statement depends on values resulting from the execution of the first two statements. The execution of the last statement may not start until the two previous statements have been executed. It is implicitly assumed that the function MaxArray does not cause side-effects.

ALGOL-like programming languages [5] use the semicolon for the syntactic separation of statements. A semicolon does, however, also imply that the two separated statements have to be executed sequentially (one after another, in the written order). In the example above, this semantic of a semicolon is superfluous for the first semicolon, but not for the second one.

The following two statements summarise the pragmatic learning:

(1) Mutually independent program parts may be executed in arbitrary order.

(2) Mutually dependent program parts must be executed in sequential order.

Program parts are said to be mutually independent, if variables modified by one part are not accessed by any of the other parts.

For the remainder of this article, *independence* stands for *mutual independence*. Similarly, *independent* stands for *mutually independent*.

It seems impossible for a compiler to decide upon independence among arbitrarily selected parts of an arbitrary program. In some (often data-parallel and numeric) cases independence is certainly detectable. In other more complex and probably irregular but still typical cases, a compiler has only little or no chance to detect independence among program parts. (See Appendix.)

## 4    The Statement-Set Concept

The specification of a strictly sequential execution order is often an over specification, which might disable a compiler to apply simultaneous execution to independent program parts. For transformational problems, the explicit programming of parallelism (e.g. with threads or message passing) is also a kind of over specification, which typically causes an unnecessary slow execution on single-processor systems. Furthermore, we consider explicit "parallel programming" an unnecessary and error-prone programming style for the programming of transformational (i.e. functional) problems, conceptually even worse than the use of GOTO.

We call the notation to express *arbitrary* execution order of a collection of statements permitted a *statement-set*. Statement-sets can, in contrast to explicit "parallel programming", be considered pure directives indicating mutually independence among program parts.

## 5    Statement-Sets in Oberon

We made a prototype implementation of statement-sets for the programming language Oberon [6]. Oberon was chosen due to its few and clean constructs, and as there is much Oberon-knowledge at the ETH. The proposed extensions are, however, only *intended to illustrate our theses* about the importance of being able to specify independence among program parts. They should *not* be considered an agreed upon part of Oberon. Furthermore, the statement-set concept is *equally applicable and important* for programming languages like FORTRAN or C.

It is important for understanding of the following text to know the syntax of a *statement sequence* :

```
StatementSequence = Statement { ";" Statement } .
Statement = [ Designator ":=" Expr | .. ] .
```

A *statement sequence* is an ordered sequence of *statements* separated by semicolons.

In the prototype implementation, a statement-set expresses independence among statement sequences. Statement sequences are said to be independent, if a variable modified by one statement sequence is not referenced (used in expressions or assigned to) by any other of the statement sequences of the statement-set. The statement sequences of a statement-set may therefore be executed in any order, even simultaneously. The prototype implementation for Oberon supports two variants of statement-sets: the *set statement* and the *all statement*.

```
SetStatement = "{" StatementSequence {"," StatementSequence} "}"
```

The statement sequences separated by "," must be independent.

```
AllStatement = ALL ident ":=" Expr TO Expr [BY ConstExpr] DO
    StatementSequence END .
```

Every execution (instance, "iteration") of the statement sequence in an all statement must be independent. The control variable *ident* must be of an integer type (SHORTINT, INTEGER, or LONGINT), and its value may not be changed during the execution of the given statement sequence. The value of the control variable is not defined after the execution of the all statement.

The execution of the statement sequences of a statement-set (all statement and set statement) must not be terminated by a *return statement* or an *exit statement*. Otherwise, statement-sets can freely be used in programs; they may be nested, used in recursive procedures, e.g.

The following transformations on statement-sets are possible and reasonable for a target system with only one processor. A set statement is converted to a statement sequence by removing the brackets and replacing the commas by semicolons. An all statement is converted to a *for statement* by substituting ALL by FOR.

## 6   Some Examples

The examples illustrate the use of statement-sets. These declarations are used in all examples:

```
CONST n = 1000;

VAR matrix: ARRAY n,n OF REAL;
    a, b: ARRAY n OF REAL;
    m, ma, mb: REAL;
    i: LONGINT; j: INTEGER;
```

The example from section 3 reprogrammed with a statement-set.

```
{ ma := MaxArray(a), mb := MaxArray(b) };     (* set statement *)
m := Max(ma, mb)
```

This piece of a program searches the maximum value among all elements in *matrix*.

```
ALL i := 0 TO n-1 DO a[i] := MaxArray(matrix[i]) END;
m := MaxArray(a)
```

Procedure *QuickSort* sorts the elements in array *a* [5].

```
PROCEDURE QuickSort (VAR a: ARRAY OF REAL);

    PROCEDURE Sort (VAR a: ARRAY OF REAL; l, r: LONGINT);
      CONST stretch = 16;
      VAR i, j, ii, jj: LONGINT; h, key: REAL;

    BEGIN
      ii := l; jj := r; key := a[(ii + jj) DIV 2];
      REPEAT
        WHILE a[ii] < key DO INC(ii) END;
        WHILE key < a[jj] DO DEC(jj) END;
        IF ii <= jj THEN
          h := a[ii]; a[ii] := a[jj]; a[jj] := h; INC(ii); DEC(jj)
        END
      UNTIL ii > jj;
      i := ii; j := jj;

      IF (l<j) & (i<r) & (r-l>=stretch) THEN  (* independent *)
        {Sort(a,l,j), Sort(a,i,r)}            (* set statement *)
      ELSE                                    (* sort sequentially
*)
        IF l < j THEN Sort(a,l,j) END;
        IF i < r THEN Sort(a,i,r) END;
      END
    END Sort;

BEGIN
  IF LEN(a) > 1 THEN Sort(a, 0, LEN(a)-1) END
END QuickSort
```

# 7    Performance Figures

## 7.1  Run-Time System
The execution time figures of the current implementation are quite typical for the level of performance achievable for an implementation of statement-sets. Better performing implementations can however be imagined. The executions of the following pieces of programs illustrate the performance level of the implementation:

```
PROCEDURE ForN(n: LONGINT);
  VAR i: LONGINT
BEGIN FOR i := 1 TO n DO END END ForN;

1)  FOR i := 1 TO 1000000 DO END
2)  ForN(1000000)

3)  FOR i := 1 TO 1000000 DO ALL j := 0 TO 0 DO END END
4)  ALL i := 1 TO 1000000 DO END

5)  FOR i := 1 TO 1000000 DO { } END
6)  FOR i := 1 TO 100000 DO { , , , , , , , , } END

7)  ALL i := 1 TO 100000 DO ForN(10) END
8)  ALL i := 1 TO 10 DO ForN(100000) END
```

Execution times in seconds measured on a Sun SPARC 10 402 (with 2 CPUs running with 40 MHz clock and no secondary cache):

| program | sequential | 1 CPU | 2 CPUs |
|---|---|---|---|
| 1 | .080 | .081 | .081 |
| 2 | .061 | .061 | .061 |
| 3 | .203 | 2.64 | 5.31 |
| 4 | .081 | .768 | 1.56 |
| 5 | .080 | 2.43 | 4.74 |
| 6 | .008 | 1.87 | 3.08 |
| 7 | .090 | 1.76 | 1.83 |
| 8 | .060 | .060 | .030 |

The column *sequential* lists the execution times for the eight program pieces when the compiler generates sequential code.

The columns *1 CPU* and *2 CPUs* list the execution times when the compiler generates code for simultaneous execution and the code is executed by 1 or 2 processors respectively.

The performance figures above indicate that statement-sets can be applied for the programming of relatively small program fragments without causing excessive performance losses.

## 7.2  Use of statement-sets in routines
The following two problems are not necessarily typical for parallelization of applications. They are simply initial test cases for the modified compiler and its run-time system. Nevertheless, they demonstrate the feasibility of statement-sets, even for the programming of recursive routines.

### 7.2.1    Complex Fast Fourier Transformation
The in place in order complex Fast Fourier Transformation algorithm (cFFT) described [7] has been programmed in the "enhanced" Oberon. The columns *1 CPU* and *2 CPUs* list the measured *speedup* factors of the generated code for simultaneous execution executed by one respectively two CPUs. The column $n$ indicates the number of points for which the cFFT was executed.

| n | sequential | 1 CPU | 2 CPUs |
|---|---|---|---|
| 256 | 1. | 1.000 | 1.323 |
| 512 | 1. | 1.001 | 1.608 |
| 1024 | 1. | .949 | 1.584 |
| 2048 | 1. | .932 | 1.707 |
| 4096 | 1. | .951 | 1.633 |
| 8192 | 1. | .969 | 1.795 |
| 16384 | 1. | .975 | 1.729 |
| 32768 | 1. | 1.006 | 1.873 |
| 65536 | 1. | 1.011 | 1.808 |
| 131072 | 1. | .992 | 1.845 |
| 262144 | 1. | .994 | 1.772 |

### 7.2.2    Quicksort

1'000'000 randomly chosen 32-bit integers were sorted by Quicksort [8]. The used routine is an "improved" version of the Quicksort shown in section 6. In particular, the constant *stretch* is used in the same way to control the granularity (and thereby the number) of independent program parts.

| stretch | sequential | 1 CPU | 2 CPUs |
|---------|------------|-------|--------|
| 100     | 1.         | .971  | 1.72   |
| 1000    | 1.         | .991  | 1.82   |
| 10000   | 1.         | .997  | 1.85   |

### 7.2.3    Remarks

In both examples above, the same source code has been used for the generation of the sequential and the parallel code. The code variant is selected by a compiler option. Similarly, the same binary was used for the *1 CPU* and *2 CPU* cases. Here the run-time system (see next section) was configured by commands. In the case of the cFFT measurements, the same (self-scaling) codes were used for all values of $n$.

The non-linear speedups of the 1 CPU- to the 2 CPU-figures have mainly algorithmic and technical reasons:

Firstly, the initial activation of Sort in the body of Quicksort is executed sequentially. This single activation of Sort for splitting the 1'000'000 elements into two smaller (and independent) sorting-problems causes more than 5% of the whole work to be sequential. This single factor limits the *2 CPU* speedup to a factor less than 1.9. Similarly, the self-scaling Fast Fourier Transformation has also clean sequential program parts.

Secondly, the simultaneous execution of program parts with complex (and heavily changing) access-patterns by several CPUs typically increases the number of cache misses compared to the single CPU-case.

In both cases, the performance figures were obtained by executing the routines on a Sun SPARC 20  502 (with 2 CPUs running with 50 MHz clock and no secondary cache).

### 8    Prototype Implementation

We have implemented the two proposed statement-sets in the Oberon-2 compiler for Sun SPARC installed with the Solaris 2.3 operating system, a UNIX variant [9, 10]. The implementation was made easier by splitting the task into the following two parts: Firstly, the modifications in the compiler deal mainly with the scanning, parsing, and generation of sequential code. Secondly, a new run-time system module schedules the execution of independent procedures. Accordingly, the survey contains two parts: a description of the extensions to the compiler proper and a description of the supporting run-time system. Both the compiler and the run-time system are programmed in Oberon.

## 8.1 Modification in the Compiler

The extension of the compiler with the set statement and the all statement has been almost straight forward. This is mainly because no new complex constructs (like new data types) had to be introduced.

The statement sequence of the all statement is translated into a procedure with one value parameter with the same name and of the same type as the control variable itself. For each execution of the all statement, a routine of the supporting run-time system is called with five arguments: *SEK.All(staticLink, routine, low, high, step)*. The meaning and the use of the five arguments should be self-explanatory. *SEK.All* does not return until *routine* has been executed with all desired values of the control variable as argument.

Similarly to the all statement, all statement sequences of a set statement are translated into procedures. The addresses (and entry points) of these routines are entered into a table of procedures. Each set statement causes a routine of the run-time system to be activated: *SEK.Set(staticLink, procTab)*. *SEK.Set* terminates when all procedures referenced by *procTab* have been called.

The statement sequences in an all statement and a set statement might be of any type defined in Oberon with two restrictions: It is nor permitted to leave these statements by an exit or return statement. These restrictions are checked by the compiler.

In the current version of the compiler the compilation of statement-sets to the code mentioned above is enabled by a command line flag. The compiler generates sequential code, if the flag is not set. Section 5 describes simple transformations to do this.

## 8.2 Run-Time System

The execution of statement-sets is supported by a separately compiled Oberon module, currently called *SEK*. *SEK* schedules submitted routines on the available processors. Furthermore, the run-time system provides a command line interface to configure the system and to display collected statistics.

The code generator of the compiler submits execution-order independent procedures to the run-time system. The rule is that all routines submitted by any single call of *SEK.All* or *SEK.Set* are executed before the submitting routine terminates. The submitted procedures may be executed in arbitrary order (also simultaneously) because they are independent. The submitted routines might even be programmed with statement sets, i.e. they might call *SEK.All* or *SEK.Set*.

The run-time system maintains a queue of submitted procedures including the needed arguments for their execution (actual value of loop control variable in the all statement, e.g.). A submitted procedure is called a *job*. Such a job is described by a *job descriptor*. A job descriptor contains among other fields a reference to a *barrier lock*, an atomicly decrementable counter, which is decremented when the corresponding job has been executed. *SEK.All* and *SEK.Set* first calculate the number of jobs to execute under their control and initialise a locally declared barrier lock accordingly. Hereafter, all jobs are either submitted to the queue of jobs if possible or executed directly. After the submission of the jobs, the submitting routine (*SEK.All* or *SEK.Set*) is waiting in a loop until all submitted jobs has been executed. Jobs are activated in such waiting loops.

In the initialisation phase of the run-time system, a light weight process (Solaris: *LWP*) is by default created as *worker* for each processor minus one in the system. These workers try repeatedly to retrieve a job from the queue of submitted jobs and, if successful, to activate it.

The following program fragment gives an impression of the algorithms used in the run-time system to support the execution of statement-sets. The first running implementation consisted of about 150 lines of Oberon code.

```
...

TYPE
    BarrierLock = RECORD free: BOOLEAN; n: LONGINT END;
    Proc1 = PROCEDURE (LONGINT);

PROCEDURE ExecuteOne;
BEGIN
    (* Retrieve "job" from "queue" if possible.
       If successful: Execute "job";
       Decrement referenced barrier lock *)
END ExecuteOne;

PROCEDURE Set*(staticLink: LONGINT; VAR procTab: ARRAY OF PROC);
    VAR i: INTEGER; lock: BarrierLock;
BEGIN
    lock.free := TRUE; lock.n := LEN(procTab);
    FOR i := 0 TO LEN(procTab)-1 DO
        (* Enter "job" represented by procTab[i], staticLink and
           reference to lock into "queue", if possible.
           Otherwise Exec procTab[i] with staticLink;
           Decrement lock.n atomicly *)
    END;
    WHILE lock.n > 0 DO ExecuteOne END;
END Set;

PROCEDURE All*(staticLink: LONGINT; pi: Proc1;
               low, high, step: LONGINT);
BEGIN (* ... *) END All;


PROCEDURE Worker;
BEGIN
    LOOP ExecuteOne END
END Worker;
...
```

The current run-time system is about three times bigger than the initial version (< 500 lines). This is mainly due to some added features: Gathering and display of statistics, commands to set the number of light weight processes, and some code to suspend and resume light weight processes during otherwise idle periods.

The prototype still lacks come features for general usage: The integration with the Oberon system has not been completely made. The consequences for the feasibility test were however small. A more solid and better integrated implementation is essential for education or professional use.

## 9 Initial Experiences

### 9.1 Experiences concerning the modification of the compiler

In Section 8, we mentioned that the modification of the compiler were quite simple. This is mainly because the new statement types (i.e. all statement and set statement) can be transformed easily into constructs that are available in most imperative programming languages: declarations and activations of procedures.

### 9.2 Experiences concerning the run-time system

The separation of duties between the compiler, that mainly handles syntactic issues, and the supporting run-time system, that implements parallel execution and synchronisation, is recommendable. This has made the testing of the run-time system and its adaptation to other scheduling strategies easy. In particular, no modification of the compiler was necessary for any of our modifications of the run-time system.

### 9.3 Experiences concerning the use of statement-sets

Our experience so far certainly verify that statement-sets are useful.

The application of statement-sets requires "only" checking of the explicit usage of variables in the statement-set itself. Procedures called from a statement-set must either be free of side-effects or at least be mutually independent of operations in other statement sequences of the statement-set. The latter might be more difficult and sometimes even impossible to check. However, my experience is that these restrictions are felt quite logically and that they typically are easy to verify. Programming pure sequential programs do also require deeper and similar analysis of the usage of variables and of the side-effects of called routines. Freedom of side-effects of called routines is often implicitly assumed when writing sequential programs.

The locality of reasoning makes the application of statement-sets easy: The applicability of a subroutine does not depend whether if it has been implemented by use of statement-sets or not. Mainly the execution time is affected by this. The application of parallelism to the execution of a subroutine is therefore relatively simple.

The low overhead for the execution of a statement-set does help programming. Relative small program pieces, causing few hundreds of instructions to be executed, can easily be part of a statement-set.

The writing of numeric applications indicates a lack of generality of the for statement: In Oberon, the *step* must be a (compile time evaluated) constant. The programming of the Fast Fourier Transformation mentioned in Section 7 would have benefited from it by having been a general expression evaluated whenever the for statement is executed.

It seems almost necessary to be able to declare local variables for the statement sequences in statement-sets, e.g. for loop-control. ALGOL 60 and some of its successors allow such declarations. Some experiments have been made in that area. For clarity reason, these have not been mentioned here.

The command line flag causing the generation of sequential code for a statement-set helps the debugging and the measuring of overheads caused by the generation of non-sequential code.

Programs including the programming language extensions discussed above can interact with an operating system just like other typical sequential programs. The main caveat is that system calls in more than one statement sequence of a statement-set must (also) be mutually independent (i.e. at least MP-save). Even, reactive programs should not cause (conceptual) problems due to the added language constructs.

## 10  Conclusions

In recent years, it seemed necessary to let single applications be executed by several or many processors to either lower the time or the cost of its execution. Current compilers limit the automatic or simple application of parallelism to essentially data-parallel cases.

This paper suggests mutual independence of program parts to be an important attribute. Only independent program parts may be executed simultaneously. Statement-sets are suggested as programming language construct to express independence among program parts. The semicolon of ALGOL-like programming languages still have the duty to separate mutually dependent program parts: The result of the execution of mutually dependent program parts depends on the order of their execution.

The often perceived statement that parallelism is cumbersome to deal with, is hardly relevant for statement-sets. In this case, *programmers have to reason about dependence and independence among statements, program parts, operations, etc. -which they always have to do- and not about parallelism or asynchrony!*

We have shown that statement-sets are easy to implement in Oberon by a modification of an existing Oberon compiler. Actual programming experience indicate that the use of statement-sets is feasible, both if performance of compiled programs and ease of reasoning is considered.

Aspects like portability of programs, adaptability to different computer architecture's, easiness of debugging and conversion to sequential programs, and quality of generated code might be better than with tools currently used for "parallel" programming.

Statement-sets are worthwhile for more investigation. More theoretical and experimental work has to be done.

### Acknowledgements

This work (and this paper) would not have been done without the almost endless discussions with Alfred Schai. My Ph. D. supervisor Niklaus Wirth did both directly and indirectly keep me on the firm ground of clarity (simplicity). Josef Templ supported me by giving me many hints for the initial compiler modification and scheduler realisation. Later on, he even improved the modified compiler and its run-time support. The hint to and the FORTRAN code for the used Fast Fourier Transformation is due to Wesley Petersen. Herman Seiler did also spend many hours with discussions and did show the feasibility of statement-sets by implement statement-sets in his Modula-2 compiler. The two referees provided also important hints for the improvement of this paper.

## Appendix: Another Impossible Program

Two program parts are said to be independent if any variable modified by one of the program parts is not referenced (i.e. read or modified) by the other program part.

It can be proven that it is impossible to construct a program that decides, given an arbitrary program P with two parts as input, whether the parts are independent or not. The proof is similar to Strachey's method that shows the impossibility of constructing a program that decides, given an arbitrary program P as input, whether the program P will terminate execution or will run forever.

Thus, suppose it were possible to construct a Boolean function *Independent(p, p1, p2)*, where p identifies an arbitrary program with parts p1 and p2. *Independent* would return the value true, if *p1* and *p2* are independent, and false otherwise. To show that *Independent* cannot be constructed according to the specification, take module *Prog* as the special program *p* and its procedure *Part* both as part *p1* and part *p2*.

```
MODULE Prog;

    PROCEDURE Independent(p, p1, p2: Program): BOOLEAN;
    ...
    ... And side-effect-free.
    END Independent;


    VAR i: INTEGER;

    PROCEDURE Part;
    BEGIN
        IF Independent(Prog, Part, Part) THEN i := -i END
    END Part;

BEGIN
    i := 1
END Prog.
```

Now consider the value of *Independent(Prog, Part, Part)*.

Assuming this to be true leads to a contradiction, since according to the assumption this indicates that the procedure *Part* is independent of itself, which in this case it isn't.

On the other hand, assuming *Independent(Prog, Part, Part)* to be false also leads to a contradiction, since this indicates that *Part* is dependent on itself, which in this case it isn't.

Thus, either of the possible values of *Independent* lead to a contradiction. Consequently the function *Independent* cannot be constructed.

This proof is a variant of Strachey's impossible program-proof [11].

## References

1  Chapmann, et al., VIENNA FORTRAN Compilation System Version 1.0 User's Guide, Technical Raport, Institut for Software Technology and Parallel Systems, Univ. of Vienna, (Jan. 1993).
2  High Performance Fortran Forum, High Performance Fortran Language Specification, Version 1.0, Scientific Programmingf, 2(1 & 2 1993).
3  W. F. Tichy and C. G. Herter, Modula-2*: An Extension of Modula-2 for Highly Parallel, Portable Programs, Technical Report 4/90, Department of Computer Science, University of Karlsruhe, (Jan. 1990).
4  J.-P. Banâtre, D. Le Métayer. Programming by Multiset Transformation, Commununication of the ACM 36 (1993) 1, pp. 98-111.
5  P. Naur, Revised Report on the Algorithmic Language ALGOL 60, Commununication of the ACM 6 (1963) 1.
6  N. Wirth, The Programming Language Oberon, Department Informatik, ETH Zurich, Report 111 (Sep. 1989), pp. 11-28.
7  C. Temperton, Self-Sorting In-Place Fast Fourier Transformations, SIAM J. Sci. Stat. Comput. 12 (1991) 7, pp. 808-823.
8  C.A.R. Hoare, Quicksort, Computer Journal 5 (1962) 1, pp. 10-15.
9  J. Templ, SPARC-Oberon User's Guide and Implementation, Department Informatik, ETH Zurich, Report 133 (June 1990).
10  SPARC International, Inc. The SPAR Architecture Manual, Version 8, Prentice Hall, Englewood Cliffs, 1992.
11  Strachey, C. An impossible program, Computer Journal 7, (1965) 4, p. 313.

# Heuristics to Optimize the Speed-Up of Parallel Programs

AGUILAR Jose

Departamento de Computación. Facultad de Ingeniería
Universidad de los Andes. Av. Tulio Febres Cordero
Mérida - Estado Mérida. 5101. Venezuela
email: aguilar@ing.ula.ve        jose@math-info.univ-paris5.fr
Telf : (58.74) 440002      Fax: (58.74) 402979

**Abstract.** In this paper we propose methods to optimize the speed-up which can be obtained for a parallel program in a distributed system by modelling the assignment of the tasks of a parallel program as a graph partitioning problem. The tasks (set of instructions that must be executed sequentially) which compose the program are represented by weighted nodes, and the arcs of the graph represent the precedence order between tasks. Because this problem is in general NP-hard we propose and investigate several heuristic algorithms, and compare their performance. The approaches we present are: a neural network based algorithm (based on the random neural model of Gelenbe), an algorithm based on simulated annealing and a genetic algorithm based heuristic.

## 1. Introduction

In the context of parallel systems, the task assignment problem is an important issue. It is closely related to which is the manner of implementing task assignment so that the program's parallel execution is speeded up. Both directed and non-directed graphs may be used to represent parallel programs. A non-directed graph will only represent information exchange and concurrent execution between tasks, while a directed graph will deal with precedence relations concerning execution sequences of tasks, which may also be accompanied by information exchange. Both nodes and arcs of the graph model will in general be weighted, the former representing task execution times while the latter represent communication times or amounts of data being exchanged.

In this work we will retain a parallel program execution model based on an acyclic directed graph whose nodes represent the tasks and whose arcs represent the relations between tasks. The optimization of the parallel execution speed-up can be formulated in terms of a partitioning problem of the task graph, where each partition represents the tasks which have been assigned to a particular processor. The cost function used for partitioning characterizes the speed-up of the parallel program's execution on a set of identical parallel processors having local memory. An appropriate measure of speed-up should consider both computing times and communication times. Thus the problem we address is that of establishing a partition of the task graph representation of a parallel program, with certain objective functions to be optimized.

Many graphs partitioning problems are NP-hard, and in the present research we will consider a variety of heuristics which yield effective and nearly optimal solutions in for the cases of interest to this study. Clearly, we study approximate solution methods because exact solutions have excessive execution times when the program size is large. The approximate methods we discuss give suboptimal solutions in a reasonable (polynomial) execution time. In this research we consider several such heuristics: one of the heuristic will be based on the random neural model of Gelenbe [3, 4], one will use genetic algorithms [1, 5] and finally one will be based on the simulated annealing optimization heuristic [6, 9].

# 2. Problem Definition

In order to fix the framework of the work to be undertaken let us recall some of the basic considerations. We consider a distributed system architecture which consisting of a collection of $K$ homogeneous processors with distributed memory, i.e., with sufficient memory at each processor. The processors are fully interconnected connected with a reliable high-speed network.

A task graph is denoted by: $\Pi = ( N, A, \Omega, c)$, where $N = \{1, ... ,n\}$ is the set of $n$ tasks that compose the program, and $\Omega$, c denote the times related to task execution and to communication between tasks. Thus each task i that has a weight $\Omega(i)$ which defines its execution time, $i=1, ..., n$. $c_{ij}$ will denote the communication time needed to inform task j that task i has terminated its execution. $A = \{a_{ij}\}$ is the adjacency matrix representing the precedence order between the tasks. Since the graph is acyclic, we may number the tasks in a manner such that $a_{ij}=0$ if $i > j$ [7, 8].

The problem is that of assigning the $n$ tasks to $K$ processors. This means that we have to create a partition $(\Pi_1, ..., \Pi_K)$ of the set of n tasks in a way which optimizes performance. The problem is then characterized by the following objective: the total effective execution time of the parallel program must be minimized.

## 2.1. The Formal Problem

The sequential execution time of the program is $T_s = \Sigma^n_{i=1} \Omega(i)$, assuming that all tasks reside on the same processor and exchange information through common memory. The parallel execution time $T_p$, assuming an unlimited number of processors, is the largest sum of task execution times and communication times on a path in the graph. This can be written using the instant at which task i will terminate, which is

$$t_i = \Omega(i) \text{ if task i has no predecessors in the graph,}$$

$$t_i = \Omega(i) + \max_{j<i} \{ t_j + c_{ji} \} \text{ if } i \text{ has predecessors in the graph.}$$

Then it can be seen that $T_p = \max_{1 \le i \le n} \{ t_i \}$. Indeed, this is the time it will take if each task is executed on a different processor. Now, we assume that the tasks have been assigned to processors by the partition $\Pi = (\Pi_1, ..., \Pi_K)$. Clearly, once the program is partitioned and placed on K processors, the actual execution time will depend in a complex manner on the schedule that is used, since all tasks which have been assigned to the same processor will execute sequentially, and some tasks on different processors will also have to execute sequentially due to the precedence relations. The exact computation of this execution time is not trivial. However an optimistic estimate can be obtained. It is useful to notice that if the execution schedule is not organized correctly, the task assignment can lead to deadlocks. However, a deadlock-free schedule can be obtained for an acyclic task graph if the processor is always allocated to a task which has no non-executed predecessors. Thus in a distributed system, such decisions have to be taken with global information and not locally, since a task's predecessors will not necessarily reside on the same processor.

Assuming that tasks residing on the same processor communicate in zero time, the new communication times can be readily computed. It suffices to remove from communication times which deal with two tasks which are in the same block $\Pi_u$ of the partition. More specifically, the new intertask communication times will become

$$C(\Pi)_{ij} = c_{ij} \qquad \text{if } i \in \Pi_u , j \in \Pi_v \text{ and } u \neq v,$$
$$C(\Pi)_{ij} = 0 \qquad \text{if } i \in \Pi_u , j \in \Pi_v \text{ and } u = v.$$

To estimate the best possible execution time of the program with the partition $\Pi$ we first notice that the time $t(\Pi)_i$ when task i terminates now satisfies the following inequalities:

$$\Omega(i) \leq t(\Pi)_i \leq \Sigma_{j \in \Pi_u} \Omega(j), \qquad \text{if } i \in \Pi_u \text{ and has no predecessors outside } \Pi_u,$$

$$\Omega(i) + \max\nolimits_{j<i} \{ t(\Pi)_j + C(\Pi)_{ji} , j \text{ not in } \Pi_u \}$$
$$\leq t(\Pi)_i \leq \Sigma_{j \in \Pi_u} \Omega(j) + \max\nolimits_{j<i} \{ t(\Pi)_j + C(\Pi)_{ji} , j \text{ not in } \Pi_u \},$$
$$\text{if } i \in \Pi_u \text{ and has predecessors outside } \Pi_u .$$

Clearly, when it is assigned to the $K$ processors according to the partition $\Pi$, the program as a whole will terminate at some instant

$$T_p(\Pi) = \max\nolimits_{1 \leq i \leq n} \{ t(\Pi)_i \}$$

Ideally, we would like choose the assignment $\Pi$ which will minimize $T_p(\Pi)$. However this appears to be a very hard problem except under very simple assumptions. Notice also that though the assignment issue is very important, performance is also influenced by the order in which tasks are executed, since it is important to always choose to execute those tasks which will then enable the execution tasks at other processors [2].

## 3. The Solution Methods

From the above discussion, it appears reasonable to formulate some related optimization problems which are easier to address and whose solution would contribute to the optimum task assignment problem.

### 3.1 The Random Neural Model

The neural networks have been used over the last several years to obtain heuristic solutions to hard optimization problems. We will propose an approach using the random neural network model which has the property of being mathematically tractable and computationally efficient.

The random neural network model has been developed by Gelenbe [3, 4] to represent a dynamic behavior inspired by natural neural systems. This model has a remarkable property called "product form" which allows the computation of joint probability distributions of the neurons of the network. The basic descriptor of a neuron random network [3, 4] is the i-th neuron's probability of being excited $q(i)$, i=1, ... , n, which satisfy a set of non-linear equations:

$$q(i) = \{ \Sigma^n_{j=1} q(j)r(j)p^+(j,i) + L(i) \} / \{ \Sigma^n_{j=1} q(j)r(j)p^-(j,i) + l(i) \} \qquad (1)$$

Where:

- $L(i)$ is the rate at which *external excitation signals* arrive to the i-th neuron,
- $l(i)$ is the rate at which *external inhibition signals* arrive to the i-th neuron,
- $r(i)$ is the rate at which neuron i fires when it is excited,
- $p^+(i,j)$ and $p^-(i,j)$, respectively, are the probabilities that neuron i (when is excited) will send an *excitation* or an *inhibition signal* to neuron j.

We have $\Sigma^n_{j=1} p^+(i,j) + p^-(i,j) \leq 1$, for $1 \leq i \leq n$. Notice that the model is based on rates, much as natural neural systems operate. Thus, this is a "frequency modulated" model, which translates rates of signal emission into excitation probabilities via equation (1). For instance $q(j)r(j)p^+(j,i)$ denotes the rate at which neuron j excites neuron i. Equation (1) can also be translated into a special form of sigmoid which treats excitation (in the numerator) asymmetrically with respect to inhibition (in the denominator).

### The Random Neural Model for our Problem.

In this approach we will construct a random neural network of the type discussed above composed of nK + K neurons [9], where n is the number of tasks and K is the number of processors.

For each (task, processor) pair (i,u) we will have a neuron m(i,u) whose role is to "decide" whether task i should be assigned to processor u. We will denote by $q(m(i,u))$ the probability that m(i,u) is excited: thus if it is close to 1 we will be encouraged to assign i to u. In order to reduce communication times in the selected partition, will tend to *excite* any neuron m(j,u) if j is a successor or predecessor of i, and will tend to *inhibit* m(j,v) if j is successor or predecessor of i and u≠v. Similarly, m(i,u) will *inhibit* m(j,u), $\forall_{v=1, ..., K}$, if j is not a predecessor or successor of i. On the other hand, neurons m(i,u) and m(i,v), u≠v, will *inhibit* each other so as to indicate that the same task should not be assigned to different processors.

For each processor u we will have a neuron $\pi(u)$ whose role is to let us know whether u is heavily loaded with work or not. If u is very heavily loaded, it will attempt to reduce the load on processor u by *inhibiting* neurons m(i,u), and it will attempt to increase the load on processors $v \neq u$ by *exciting* neurons $\pi(v)$. In the same way, $m(i,u)$ will *excite* neuron $\pi(u)$ to increase the load on processor u. The parameters of the random network model expressing these intuitive criteria are chosen as follows:

- $L(m(i,u)) = 0$
- $L(\pi(u)) = n/K$, to express the desirable equal load sharing property,
- $l(m(i,u)) = 0$,
- $l(\pi(u)) = 0$,
- $r(m(i,u)) = nK$
- $r(\pi(u)) = n+K-1$
- $r(m(i,u))p^+(m(i,u),m(j,v)) = $    1 if $(a_{ij} = 1$ or $a_{ji} = 1)$ and u=v,
            0 otherwise.
- $r(m(i,u))\ p^-(m(i,u),m(j,v)) = $    1 if $u \neq v$ and $(a_{ij} = 1$ or $a_{ji} = 1$ or $i = j)$,
            or if $a_{ij} = 0$ and $a_{ji} = 0$,
            0 otherwise.
- $r(m(i,u))p^+(m(i,u), \pi(v)) = $    1 if u=v,
            0 otherwise.
- $r(\pi(u))p^-(\pi(u),m(i,u)) = $    1 if $q(\pi(u)) \sim 1$,
            0 otherwise
- $r(\pi(u))p^+(\pi(u),\pi(v)) = $    1 if $q(\pi(u)) \sim 1$,
            0 otherwise

The equation (1) for this case is:

$$q(m(i,u)) = \{ \sum_{(a_{ij} = 1 \text{ or } a_{ji} = )1} q(m(j,u))r(m(j,u))p^+(m(j,u),m(i,u)) \} /$$

$$\{r(m(i,u)) + \sum_{v \neq u}\sum_{(a_{ij}=1 \text{ or } a_{ji}=1 \text{ or } i=j)} q(m(j,v))r(m(j,v))p^-(m(j,v),m(i,u))$$

$$+ \sum_{v}\sum_{a_{ij}=0 \ \& \ a_{ji}=0} q(m(j,v)r(m(j,v))p^-(m(j,v),m(i,u))$$

$$+ q(\pi(u))r(\pi(u))p^-(\pi(u),m(i,u))\}$$

$$q(\pi(u)) = \{ L(\pi(u)) + \sum^n_{j=1} q(m(j,u))r(m(j,u))p^+(m(j,u),\pi(u)) +$$

$$\sum^K_{v=1} q(\pi(v))r(\pi(v))p^+(\pi(v),\pi(u)) \} / r(\pi(u))$$

## 3.2. Simulated Annealing

Simulated Annealing (SA) is a well known method [6] which uses the physical concepts of "temperature and energy" to represent and solve optimization problems using a Montecarlo simulation. The objective function of the optimization problem is treated as the "energy" of a dynamical system, while temperature is introduced to randomize the search for a solution. The state of the dynamical system being simulated is related to the state of the system being optimized. The idea of this method is to start with an initial solution, and then try to improve the solution through local changes. It is based on static mechanics, inspired in the analogy of a physical system behavior in the presence of a hot bath. The procedure is the following [6]: the system is submitted to high temperature and it is slowly cooled through a temperature level series. For each temperature level, we search for the system equilibrium state through an elementary transformation series, which will be accepted if they reduce the system energy $E_{new} < E_{old}$. As the temperature decreases, smaller energy increments are accepted, and the system eventually settles on a low energy configuration that is very close, if not identical, to the global minimum.

For this method, we have studied several parameters in [6, 9]: the initial temperature, the cooling rate and the threshold (Fac_accep) which define the probability that an uphill move of size $\Delta$ will be accepted. For the initial temperature, if it is very hot we have CPU time useless; or it is very cold we obtain bad results. In [6, 9] we have made a complete study and we have arrived to follow conclusions: The initial temperature value influences the execution time, which is larger for small initial temperature value. For graph of large size ($\geq$ 35 nodes), it is necessary to take a temperature $\approx 90°$ C to obtain good results.

The cooling rate defines the procedure to reduce the temperature: a reduction very rapid implies a bad local optimum. A reduction very slow is spendthrift in CPU time. Normally, we use a lineal reduction. Good results have been obtained when the reduction factor of the temperature is 0.93 between two steps. For low temperature values we consider that the system has reached a state near the minimum energy (ground state) which corresponds to an optimal solution, consequently we decrease slowly the temperature (0.965).

There are several functions to determine the probability of acceptance, normally named "heat bath" functions. We use $\exp(-\Delta /T)$, because there are mathematical motivations for using the exponential [9]. Other appealing possibility is the function $1-\Delta T$, which involves just one division and at least approximates the exponential. We study the value of probability (Fac_accep) to accept a movement. For this parameter, if the graph is large we obtain the best results for 0.9. For small graph is not important this parameter. This factor has a relation with the execution time. For small values the execution times are generally better because the system arrives more quickly to the equilibrium on each temperature level, but the results are bad.

### 3.3 Genetic Algorithm

This is an optimization algorithm based on the principles of evolution in biology. A genetic algorithm (GA) follows an "intelligent evolution" process for individuals based on the utilization of evolution operators such as mutation, inversion, selection and crossover [1, 5]. The idea is to find the best local optimum, starting from a set of initial solutions, by applying the evolution operators to successive solutions so as to generate a new and better local minimum. The procedure evolves until it remains trapped in a local minimum.

The GA applied in our problem follows the following next procedure [6, 9]: we define a space of research of n vectors where everyone represents an individual, and every individual represents a possible solution. Each vector has n elements and every element has a value among $1...K$, according to the group to which it belongs. Furthermore, we use the cost function defined on the first part to determine the cost of every individual. We begin with an initial population of individuals randomly defined and we choose the individuals with minimal cost for generating new individuals using the genetic operators. Since the population is constant, we substitute the worst individuals of initial solution by the best individuals generated. The procedure stops if we exceed a given number of generations without finding a better solution.

In this method two parameters are studied: the maximum number of generations (NUMGEN) and the probability (PM) of use the mutation operator after the crossover operator. The first parameter allows to optimize the speed-up of the algorithm to reach an optimal solution. We remark than the quality of the solutions improves more rapidly in the first generations that in the following. Thus, a satisfactory quality can be obtained rapidly without to wait that the algorithm converges. We define the maximum number of generations (NUMGEN) necessary to arrive to good results. If the graph is large, there is a relation between the generation number and the problem size. In this case, a large generation number will be necessary to have good results, which implies more execution time.

In this work, we used the crossover operator and then the mutation operator according to the PM probability. For the PM parameter, if the probability is large we obtain good results, specially for large graph. In this case, the crossover operator is inefficient because it is going to reproduce almost all time the same individual. A large PM implies an execution time large. In [11], Talbi and others define the probability to use each operator, which allow a dynamic variation of use of them in the population. Next works will study this approach.

## 4. Performance Evaluation

We have used the parameters that give the better performance in every method, according to the results of the work [6, 9]. We have used a SUN SPARCstation IPC with 16M of memory and a matrix as data structure. The random graphs used are defined for the average number of nodes ($n$) and the average degree of the successor nodes of a node ($d$). For each graph, the successors of a node are chosen randomly from a uniform distribution in the interval [1, d]. The execution time is in seconds. The parameters of the simulations are the following: the total number of subgraphs (K), the mean number of nodes per graph (n), the mean number of successors per node (d) and the balance factor (b). We generate 50 random graphs for the set of parameters where n = { 10, 20, 50}, K={2, 5} and d=2.

We study the following performance criteria: the execution time of the heuristics and the mean value of the solutions. Due to space limitations, the results presented in this section were chosen because they are representative of the phenomena studied.

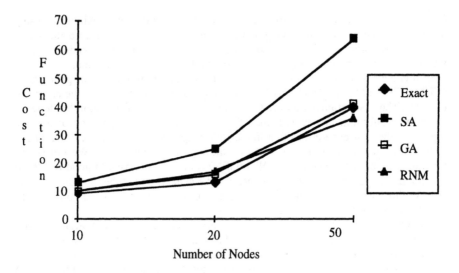

**Fig. 1. Results of the simulation for b = 1, K = 2 and d = 2**

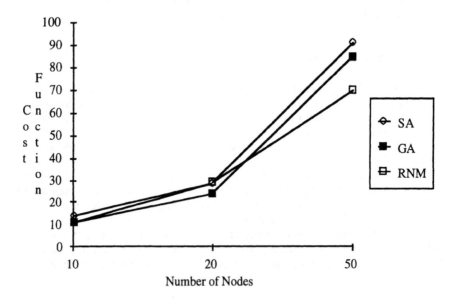

**Fig. 2. Results of the simulation for b = 1, K = 5 and d = 2**

The execution times are very large (Figures 1, 2, 3). The genetic algorithm and the simulated annealing, for graphs of 50 or more nodes, need a very large time to reach the suboptimal solutions. For graph of little size (of 20 or less nodes), the difference between the exact solution and the results of the other methods is not important, but the execution times are similar, what makes more interesting the exact solutions.

Otherwise, the approximate methods are more interesting, because they have a reasonable execution time.

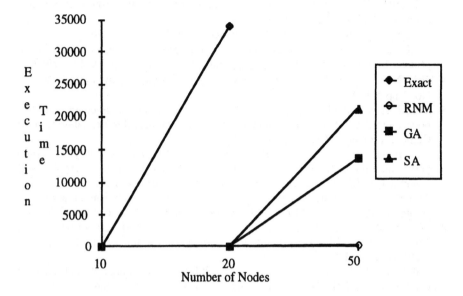

**Fig. 3. Execution time of the simulation for  b = 1, K = 2 and d = 2**

## 5. Conclusions

The experiments we have run show that the results obtained by each approximate method vary widely  depending on the size of the graphs considered. In our study, the Genetic Algorithm appears to give the best results, but with a substantially larger execution time. The Random Neural Model gives good results with short execution time.

The execution time for the Genetic Algorithm and Simulated Annealing are very large. For Genetic Algorithm, the reason is that generation calculations take relatively much more time. It is necessary to determine the better combination of genetics operators, to decrease the number of necessary generations to reach the suboptimal solution. For Simulated Annealing, since it is not possible determine coherent movements of nodes in every temperature level that decrease the energy, the solution is evaluated in a relatively longer time. The Genetic Algorithm and the Random Neural Model are easy to implement on a parallel machine, and this can considerably improve the speed obtained with these methods.

Future work will examine other combinatorial optimization methods for the solution of design problems in distributed systems (tasks migration, files allocation, ...), and will consider a combination of the Random Neural Model and Genetic Algorithms.

# References

1. GOLDBERG, D. "Genetic algorithms in search, optimization and machine learning", Addison-Wesley, 1989.
2. GELENBE, E. "Multiprocessor Performance". J. Wiley & Sons. 1989.
3. GELENBE, E, "Random neural networks with positive and negative signals and product form solution", <u>Neural Computation</u> Vol. 1, No. 4, pp 502-511, 1989.
4. GELENBE, E, "Stable random neural networks", <u>Neural Computation</u>, Vol. 2, No. 2 pp 239-247, 1990.
5. TALBI, E. and BESSIERE, P. "Un algorithme génétique massivement parallèle pour le problème de partitionement de graphes". Technical Report. Laboratoire de Génie Informatique. Grenoble-France. 1991.
6. AGUILAR, J. "Combinatorial Optimization Methods. A study of graph partitioning problem". Proceedings of the Panamerican Workshop on Applied and Computational Mathematics, PWACM, Caracas, Venezuela, 1993.
7. AGUILAR, J. "Modelling the explicit and implicit parallelism of a parallel program", Proc. XIV Intl Conf. of the Chilean Computer Science Society, 1994.
8. AGUILAR, J. "Heuristic algorithms for task assignment of parallel programs", Proc. Intl. Conf. Massively Parallel Processing Applications and Development, Delft, Holland, 1994.
9. AGUILAR, J. "L'allocation de tâches, l'équilibrage de la charge et l'optimisation combinatoire", PhD thesis. Rene Descartes University, Paris, France, 1995.

# Vectorization of Visualization Algorithms -
# A Practical Example

A. Spalt, S. Grabner, J. Volkert

Computer Graphics and Parallel Processing
University of Linz, Austria/Europe
[spalt|grabner|volkert]@gup.uni-linz.ac.at

**Abstract.** In scientific visualization, interactive image generation times are needed. Yet typical algorithms are computationally expensive, e.g. image generation algorithms for volume rendering, which is an important and widely used technique. Since vector computers are still among the most powerful machines available, we propose a vectorized variant of a volume rendering algorithm. Vectorization has a long research tradition. Many of the obstacles encountered in transforming loops of sequential programs into vector operations can be handled automatically by state of the art compilers. However, experiences in the course of our work revealed that there are still some shortcomings. It turned out that even for relatively simple optimization transformations it can be necessary to resort to assembler level programming. This is exemplified by a detailed analysis of the proposed algorithm. Results of the final implementation on a mini supercomputer conclude the presentation.

**Key Words:** Vectorization, Volume Rendering, Parallel Algorithms

## 1    Introduction

We developed a vectorized version of the widely used visualization algorithm of *direct volume rendering*. Supported by both theoretical results and vendors' statements, we assumed that the vectorization would be hardly more than setting some compiler flags. However, it turned out that there is still a gap between theory and practice! Only by assembler level programming was it possible to get some of the theoretically expected performance out of the vector machine available to the authors.

Vectorization is a well established optimization technique, which is integrated in state of the art compilers. Several analysis steps are necessary to determine whether a loop in a sequential program can be transformed into a vector operation like data dependency analysis, loop-carried dependencies and pointer tracking. Research in this area has come to a state where many of the obstacles encountered in the vectorization process can be handled automatically, i.e. by an optimizing compiler. If we look at commercially available compilers, many of the above topics can be found in the accompanying manuals. And a great optimism concerning the compilers' automatic program transformation capabilities can be observed. Our experience showed that this optimism is obviously not justified in all cases.

In the following, we first give a short introduction to volume rendering and previous work in this area. Then we describe the vectorized algorithm in more detail, followed by a section about algorithm analysis and some additional optimizations. The implementation and results sections reveal the inadequacies of automatic vectorization and show the performance gain achievable by manually tuning the algorithm at assembler level. A discussion section concludes the presentation.

## 2    Direct Volume Rendering - Method and Previous Work

Volume rendering has developed into an important and widely used technique in scientific visualization. It is applied in fields such as medicine [1], computational fluid dynamics [2], physics [3], and computational chemistry.

Volume rendering is an image generation technique. It starts from a sampled 3-dimensional function with scalar values, $F(i,j,k)$. These values are mapped onto the densities $\rho(i,j,k)$ of a cloudlike semi-transparent medium. The optical properties of the medium are: absorption, scattering and emission of light. If scattering is ignored, the well known color-opacity or RGBA model results [4]. The image generation formula is derived from the line integral which is evaluated along sight rays starting from the observer's eye point and running throughout the medium. The intensity at each pixel $(u,v)$ on the view plane is given as:

$$I^{\lambda}(u, v) = \sum_{i=0}^{T-1} \left( J^{\lambda}(u, v, i)\alpha(u, v, i) \prod_{j=i+1}^{T-1} (1 - \alpha(u, v, i)) \right), \quad \lambda \in \{R,G,B\} \quad \text{(Eq 1)}$$

where $J^{\lambda}(u,v,i)$  color component $\lambda$ at position $(u,v,i)$

$\alpha(u,v,i)$  opacity (closely related to $\rho$)

There are four types of algorithms which compute the above formula: ray casting [5], serial transformations [1], cell projection [2], and splatting [6]. For each of the above types of algorithms there is a hardware architecture which fits best. Conventional single processor machines or parallel machines with shared memory are best suited for the ray casting approach. The serial transformations variant has been especially designed for SIMD machines. Cell projection and splatting are quite similar. Both can take advantage of distributed memory MIMD type architectures. As will be shown in the sequel, the splatting method is very well vectorizable, too.

Although vector computers are still among the most powerful available machines, there are hardly any published attempts of developing a vectorized volume rendering algorithm. Many authors mention that additional vectorization of their proposed algorithms would lead to further performance improvements. Apparently, they did not find it interesting enough to realize their ideas. In the related field of SIMD architectures, extensive research is conducted [7, 8, 9]. Yet SIMD type computers are more flexible than vector machines. Therefore the algorithms proposed here cannot efficiently exploit the powerful but very specialized features of vector machines.

In [10] the authors use a CRAY Y-MP, among other tasks, for fast generation of low quality volume rendering images. They only vectorized a small part of the whole computation, namely the geometric transformation of the volume data according to actual viewing parameters. The whole task of image generation relied on the high *scalar* performance of their machine. A very similar approach is described in [11]. In this work the authors point out that the proposed vectorization is also of great relevance for RISC-like computer architectures because of their pipelined structure.

Previous work on the algorithm proposed in this paper is published in [12]. Results presented there stemmed from an initial implementation of the vectorized algorithm. No detailed analysis, as presented in the following sections, was performed then.

## 3　Vectorized Algorithm

The problem of vectorizing a sequential algorithm lies in the difficulty of organizing computations in such a way that source as well as target operands can be arranged as vectors. As such, they can be loaded, processed and stored according to a strict scheme. In the case of volume rendering, source operands (volume data) are 3-dimensional vectors and target operands (the generated images) are 2-dimensional vectors. If we consider accesses to individual elements during the progress of computation, there seems to be a dilemma. Either the computation proceeds one grid point after the other. Then accesses to pixels in the generated image become irregular. Or the computation follows the pattern of image pixels. In this case, the grid points are accessed irregularly.

However, there is a solution which makes a high vectorization ratio of the whole algorithm possible. An intermediate coordinate system is introduced on the view plane such that regular access to grid points causes regular access to pixels in this system. The whole image is generated in the oblique coordinate system. In a final step, a shear transformation is applied to produce the raster image in cartesian coordinates.

Some terminology is needed in this context. Volume data are defined on 3-dimensional (mostly) uniform grids. Let us assume a grid of extents $N_i \times N_j \times N_k$, where $N_i, N_j, N_k \in \mathbb{N}$, all other variables are $\in \mathbb{N}_0$. A *beam* is a set of grid points where two of the three indices are fixed. A jk-beam at position $(j_0, k_0)$ is for example defined as:

$$jk\text{-}beam(j_0, k_0) := \{(i, j, k) \mid 0 \leq i < N_i, j=j_0, k=k_0, 0 \leq j_0 < N_j, 0 \leq k_0 < N_k\}$$

ik- and ij-beams are defined analogously. A *slice* is a set of points where exactly one of the three indices is held constant. A *k-slice* at position $k_0$ is defined as:

$$k\text{-}slice(k_0) := \{(i, j, k) \mid 0 \leq i < N_i, 0 \leq j < N_j, k=k_0, 0 \leq k_0 < N_k\}$$

In analogy, there exist *i*- and *j-slices*. The geometrical interpretation of the point sets is clear: beams define lines which run parallel to one of the volume's coordinate axes. These are called *beam-lines*. Slices define *slice-planes* which are perpendicular to one of the axes.

In **Fig. 1.** an overview of the proposed algorithm is given. It starts with the following input parameters:

| | |
|---|---|
| $J^\lambda(N_i, N_j, N_k)$ | volume data, 3-dimensional matrix, values at grid points: R, G, B and $\alpha$ |
| *Foot* $(x, y)$ | 2-dimensional footprint function, describes influence of one grid point on view plane |
| *spread* | spread of footprint function <br> *Foot* $(x, y)$ is 0 for $\sqrt{x^2 + y^2} > spread$ |
| $T(4,4)$ | transformation matrix, relative to basic position of volume grid |
| $N_u, N_v$ | extents of generated image, in pixels |

The output of the algorithm is $Img^\lambda(N_u, N_v)$, an image of the volume data, according to the volume rendering model, (Eq 1).

## 4    Analysis and Optimization

In this section, a detailed analysis of the performance improvements achieved by the proposed vectorization strategy is given. For a good understanding it is necessary to present at least some of the program's basic parts in assembler code. We begin with a pseudo code description.

1. The volume data are subjected to viewing transformation $T$.

2. The volume grid is divided into slices. The slices' orientation is chosen such that slice planes are most parallel to the viewing plane, i.e. respective plane normals subtend the smallest possible angle.

3. The projection of the first slice determines the orientation of the axes and pixel extents of the oblique coordinate system OP.
The projection of the second slice determines the relative displacement $[d_o, d_p]$. Since parallel projection is used for image generation, $[d_o, d_p]$ remains constant for any pair of adjacent slices.
$C$ is translated (here in direction $\vec{p}$), such that the whole image of the volume data gets positive OP-coordinates.

4. The footprint function ($Foot$) is sampled according to the positions of pixel centers in the OP coordinate system ($Foot\_F$). In order to get a better approximation to the continuous footprint function, the sampling distance can be made a divisor of the actual pixel extents.

5. Slices are projected onto the viewing plane. The positions of projected grid points coincide with OP pixels or they are translated by multiples of $[d_o, d_p]$.

5.a For each new slice, a matrix ($Foot\_i$) is generated from $Foot\_F$. This matrix is valid for all grid points in the new slice.

5.b The contribution of each grid point to intensity values at pixel centers is determined by convolving the current slice with filter kernel $Foot\_i$ and combining the result with the image computed so far.

Result: Volume rendering image in the oblique coordinate system.

6. The image in oblique coordinates is resampled to cartesian coordinates, maybe clipping is necessary.

Result: Volume rendering image in cartesian coordinates.

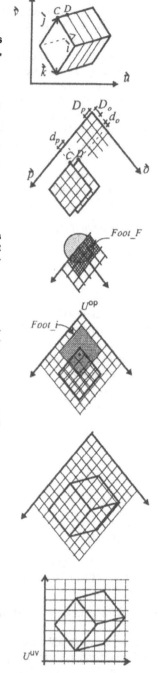

**Fig. 1.** Outline of the vectorized volume rendering algorithm

```
procedure VectorSplat (RGB_A J[N_i][N_j][N_k][4], 4x4Matrix T[4][4],
        float function Foot(x,y), float spread,
        int N_u, int N_v, RaGaBaa* Img[N_u][N_v][4])
transform volume J according to T;
determine slice orientation (6 cases);
case 1a: (i-Slices, starting with i-slice(0))
    determine coordinate system OP (generates start pixel [o0 p0] for i-slice(0));
    compute sampled footprint function Foot_F[F_F][G_F];
    allocate empty start image ImgOP[No][Np] in RGBA-format;
    allocate empty image of slice newImgOP[No][Np], RGB and α separately;
    for (i=0; i<=N_i-1; i++) {                                       // O(N)
        clear slice image newImgOP[No][Np];
        compute footprint approximation Foot_i[F_i][G_i];
        for (fp=0; fp<=G_i-1; fp++) {               // for all entries in Foot_i, O(1)
            pp= p0 + fp;
            for (fo=0; fo<=F_i-1; fo++) {                            // O(1)
                weight= Foot_i[fo][fp];
                If (weight == 0) continue;          // skip 0 values in Foot_i
                oo= o0 + fo;
                for (λ ∈ {R,G,B,A}) {                                // O(1)
                    for (j=0; j<=N_j-1; j++) {                       // O(N)
                        for (k=0; k<N_k-1; k++) {                    // vectorized
                            newImgOP[oo+j][pp+k][λ] += weight*J[i][j][k][λ];
} } } } }
        for (p=p0; p<=p0+Sp-1; p++) {                                // O(N)
            for (o=o0; o<=o0+So-1; o++)                              // vectorized
            help[o]= (1-ImgOP[o][p][a])*newImgOP[o][p][A];
            ImgOP[o][p][Ra] +=help[o]*newImgOP[o][p][R];       //  ImgOP (RaGaBaa)
            ImgOP[o][p][Ga] += help[o]*newImgOP[o][p][G];      //               over
            ImgOP[o][p][Ba] += help[o]*newImgOP[o][p][B];      // newImgOP (RGB_A)
            ImgOP[o][p][a] += help[o];
        } }
        compute new start pixel [o0 p0] for i-Slice(i);
    }                                                               // endfor (i)
case 1b: (i-Slices, starting with i-slice(N_i-1))
.....
case 3b: (k-Slices, starting with k-slice (N_k-1))
.....
compute Img[N_u][N_v][λ] from ImgOP[No][Np][λ];               // λ ∈ {R,G,B,A}
}
```

The pseudo code description shows the dramatic improvement: based on a sequential algorithm with $O(N^3)$ scalar operations, a vectorized variant with $O(N^2)$ scalar and vector operations was developed. The footprint matrix's extent does not depend on problem size $N$, so the corresponding loop is of $O(1)$. There are of course still some sequential parts in the algorithm. The impact of these parts depends on the ratio between scalar and vector performance of a target machine.

Readers with image processing knowledge will have noticed that the nested loops with induction variables $fo$ and $fp$ are nothing else but the well known convolution operation. The computation in the nested loops with variables $o$ and $p$ is also well known and often referred to as *alpha blending*. We want to analyze the convolution operation in more detail, because it will dominate the overall runtime of the program.

An analysis at assembly level reveals two "load vector" operations and one "store vector" operation per component $\lambda$, all contained in the innermost loop (this loop is not present at source code level). Some minor modifications relieve the heavy demands on memory bandwidth. The loops which concern the entries of the footprint matrix (induction variables $fp$ and $fo$) are interchanged to become the innermost ones, while the computation of components $\lambda \in \{R,G,B,A\}$ becomes the outermost loop. In a self-explaining assembly language (see [13]) the result, without strip mining, looks as follows (the assembler code fragment is taken out of actual code, but somewhat simplified to improve readability):

```
        . . .
        LD       R15, fff           ;offset of Foot_i[Foi][Fpi]
        LD       R12, nnn           ;address of newImgOP[oo][pp][lambda]
        LD       R22, No*4          ;stride for newImgOP
        LD       R5, vvv            ;address of J[i][0][0][lambda]
        LD       R25, Ni*Nj*4       ;stride for J
        LD       R30, Nk            ;vector lengths
        MOVI2S   VLR, R30           ;move into VectorLengthRegister
; loop j
L1:     MV       R2, R12            ;R2 is used as loop index
        LDI      R3, #0             ;R3: Index fo and fp
        LVWS     V1, (R5, R25)      ;LoadVectorWithStride R25
        . . .
; the loops for (fo...), for (fp...) were collapsed into one
L2:     LD       R4, Foot_i(R3)     ;load weight
        BEQZ     R4, L3             ;if (weight==0) goto L5
        LVWS     V0, (R2, R22)      ;newImgOP[oo+j][pp:pp+Nk-1][lambda]
        MULTSV   V2, R4, V1         ;weight*J[i][j][0 : Nk-1][lambda]
        ADDV     V3, V0, V2
        SVWS     (R2, R22)V3        ;StoreVectorWithStride
L3:     ADDI     R2, R2, #4
        ADDI     R3, R3, #4
        SLE      R30, R3, R15
        BNEZ     R30, L2
        . . .
        ADD      R5, R5, Ni         ;addr. of J[i][j][0][lambda]
        ADD      R12, R12, No       ;addr. of newImgOP[oo+j][pp][lambda]
        . . .
        BNEZ     R30, L1
        . . .
```

Based on this improved algorithm a detailed analysis of the innermost loop (L2) will be performed. To keep the analysis as general as possible, the idealized vector computer DLXV [13] will be employed as the basic model. The structure of a DLXV computer is displayed in **Fig. 2.**.

A DLXV contains 8 vector registers, each 64 double words (64 bits) long. Access to main memory is possible via a single load/store unit. Only one stream of data between main memory and vector registers is supported at a time. This constraint was typical for vector computers of the first generation, such as a CRAY-1. All functional units of the vector unit are pipelined, with the following start-up latencies:

| | |
|---|---|
| ADDV | 6 |
| DIVV | 20 |
| MULTV | 7 |
| LV, SV | 12 |

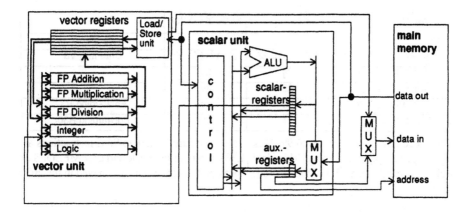

**Fig. 2.** Basic structure of the DLXV vector computer, c.f. [PaHe90], with own extensions.

The scalar unit is pipelined as well. Phases of machine instructions are pipelined in the same way as found in usual RISC processors. The above loop L2 will perform as follows on a DLXV (in clock cycles):

| Operation | Starts at clock # | Ends at clock # | Comment |
|---|---|---|---|
| L2:LD R4,Foot_i(R3) | 0 | 5 | scalar pipeline |
| BEQZ R4,L3 | 1 | 7 | Forwarding R4, 1 stall |
| LVWS V0,(R2,R22) | 3 | 3+12+64= 79 | |
| MULTSV V2,R4,V1 | 4 | 4+7+64= 75 | 3-level Forwarding R4 |
| ADDV V3,V0,V2 | (3+12)+1= 16 | 16+6+64= 86 | Chaining V0, V2 |
| SVWS (R2,R22)V3 | 79+1= 80 | 80+12+64= 156 | memory path used by LVWS |
| L3:ADDI R2,R2,#4 | 81 | 86 | |
| ADDI R3,R3,#4 | 82 | 87 | |
| SLE R30,R3,R15 | 83 | 88 | Forwarding R3 |
| BNEZ R30,L2 | 84 | 89 | Forwarding R30 |

The complete execution time of the above loop sums up to 156 clock cycles. In this time, 64*2 = 128 floating point operations (MULTSV, ADDV) are executed, i.e. 0.82 operations per cycle. By overlapping the first two instructions of each new iteration with vector operations of the previous one, another 3 cycles can be saved and 0.84 operations per cycle are achieved. On a machine with 50 MHz clock rate we would get 42 MFLOPS. The theoretical peak performance of this code would be achieved with 2 operations per clock executing in parallel, yielding 100 MFLOPS.

On an improved DLXV, more paths between main memory and vector registers exist. A meaningful assumption is that there are two data paths from and one to main memory, as e.g. in a CRAY Y-MP. In this case, the above diagram changes as follows:

| Operation | Starts at clock # | Ends at clock # | Comment |
|---|---|---|---|
| ... | ... | ... | as above |
| SVWS (R2,R22)V3 | (16+6)+1= 23 | 23+12+64= 99 | Chaining V3 |
| L3:ADDI R2,R2,#4 | 24 | 29 | |
| ADDI R3,R3,#4 | 25 | 30 | |
| SLE R30,R3,R15 | 26 | 31 | Forwarding R3 |
| BNEZ R30,L2 | 27 | 32 | Forwarding R30 |

The execution time decreases to 99 clock cycles, and furthermore to 96 if instructions are overlapped as explained above. This yields 1.33 operations per cycle and 66.7 MFLOPS on a 50 MHz machine. So 2/3 of the theoretical peak performance can be achieved in the inner loops.

# 5 Implementation

## 5.1 Hardware

The implementation of the proposed vectorized algorithm was carried out on a mini super-computer of the CONVEX Computer Corporation. Such mini supercomputers are substantially cheaper than "real" supercomputers - however, they are also much less powerful. The results presented below should be interpreted with this in mind.

We programmed on a CONVEX C3440, which is a 4 processor model of the C3400 series. The processors consist of a scalar unit with clock rate 50 MHz and a vector unit with two adders and two multipliers operating at 25 MHz. Each processor contains 8 scalar registers and 8 vector registers with 128 elements, all registers are 64 bits wide. Additionally, there are 8 address registers and some special communication and synchronization registers. 2 GB main memory is shared among the 4 processors. There are 64 memory banks which are 32 bits wide, they can be used as 32 banks of width 64 as well. The main constraint, at least as far as our application is concerned, is the fact that there is only one path between registers and main memory at a time. The peak performance of one vector processor is 100 MFLOPS with single precision. This performance is actually achievable, in vector loops without memory accesses and with both an addition and a multiplication.

## 5.2 Programming Environment

Computers of the C3400 series run a variant of the UNIX operating system. A number of development tools are available. We programmed in the C language and employed the compiler *cc*. It is capable of automatic vectorization and parallelization (shared memory) at the procedure or block level. Furthermore, we used the *Application Compiler APC* which provides some advanced features. Before the source code is actually compiled (with *cc*), the APC performs a number of program transformations and optimizations. Roughly, these are exploitations of static program analysis which is extended across block or procedure boundaries. Examples are automatic inlining of procedures, tracking of constant expressions, improved pointer tracking (especially important for C programs), and procedure cloning, i.e. generation of copies of procedures where some parameters are replaced by constant expressions. In addition, there is quite a number of procedure libraries available. Examples are SCIlib ([14], compatible with CRAY computers) and VECLIB [15]. To our surprise, neither of them contained a routine for the 2-dimensional convolution.

## 6 Results

The improvements which were derived in the analysis section bear a certain amount of generality, because the generic vector computer DLXV is not substantially different from actually available ones. Only the optimized version of the algorithm was implemented on the C3440.

There are two critical remarks concerning the Application Compiler APC. First, the improved pointer tracking feature across procedure boundaries seems to be still in an early stage of development. With dynamically allocated multi-dimensional arrays (i.e. all arrays in our program) the APC is unable of detecting vectorizable loops. Compiler directives had to be inserted which explicitly allowed vectorization (#pragma _CNX NO_RECURRENCE).

In a second issue the APC also failed. The compiler put *both* vector load statements (LVWS V1 and LVWS V0, see assembler code above) into the innermost loop L2. It did not recognize that the first load is loop invariant. Since loop L2 is only present at assembler level, no compiler directives at C level could help in this case.

In the following pseudo code, **SSplatSlice** is the routine, which does the main work (essentially a 2-dimensional convolution). Since the compiler did not generate efficient code for it, we had to apply optimizations at assembler level *by hand*. Only then we could achieve acceptable results. The assembler code presented in section 4 is part of the optimized version. In the following table, the algorithm is split up into phases with very different performance characteristics. For the end user, only the overall performance is of interest. Nevertheless, it is very instructive to look at each phase separately.

| **VectorSplat**($J,T,Foot,spread,N_u,N_v,Img$) | Sec. | Ratio (in%) | MFLOPS $N=127$ |
|---|---|---|---|
| transform volume $J$ according to $T$; determine slice orientation (6 cases); | 0.00 | 0.00 | n / a |
| case 1a: (i-Slices, starting with i-slice(0)) | - | - | - |
| determine coordinate system OP; .... (*see above*) | 0.03 | 0.32 | 5.32 |
| for ($i$=0; $i$<=$N_i$-1; $i$++) { | - | - | |
| clear slice image $newImgOP[No][Np]$; | 0.43 | 4.14 | 0 |
| compute footprint approximation $Foot\_i[F_i][G_i]$; | 0.38 | 3.66 | 8.45 |
| for ($\lambda \in \{R,G,B,A\}$) { SSplatSlice(&$J[i][N_j$-1][0][$\lambda$],..., &$Foot\_i[0][0]$,...,&$newImgOP[0][0][\lambda]$,...); } | 6.75 | 64.49 | 21.85 |
| for ($p$=$p0$; $p$<=$p0$+$Sp$-1; $p$++) { for ($o$=$o0$; $o$<=$o0$+$So$-1; $o$++) ... (*see above*) } } | 1.5 | 14.33 | 12.68 |
| compute new start pixel [$o0$ $p0$] for i-Slice($i$); | 0.03 | 0.32 | 0.00 |
| } /* for $i$ */ | - | - | - |
| cases 1b,... 3b: ..... | - | - | - |
| compute $Img[N_u][N_v][\lambda]$ from $ImgOP[No][Np][\lambda]$; | 1.23 | 11.78 | 4.65 |
| Total | 10.47 | 100 | 16.78 |

The performance of procedure **SSplatSlice**, roughly 22 MFLOPS, does not look very impressive. Theoretically, we should have achieved about 50% of the peak performance of 100 MFLOPS (see analysis section). Small test programs, again at assembler level, revealed the single path between memory and registers as the main problem. Inefficiencies when chaining vector loads with arithmethic operations, and strip mining overhead also had an impact on the resulting performance. However, we cannot give a detailed explanation, because in many memory access related issues, CONVEX literature [17] is not precise enough, and runtime measurements are also fraught with inaccuracies.

In the following chart the running time of the whole program with different optimization levels is plotted against problem size. Volume data are of size $N^3$ grid points. The label $O1$ identifies the scalar program, $O2$ the program after automatic vectorization.

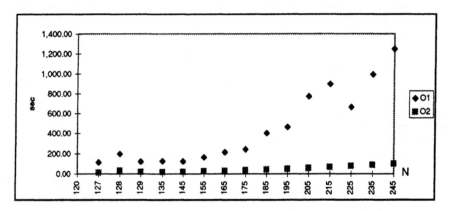

The next chart shows the improvement caused by manual optimization of procedure **SSplatSlice** ($O2Asm$) compared to automatic vectorization ($O2$).

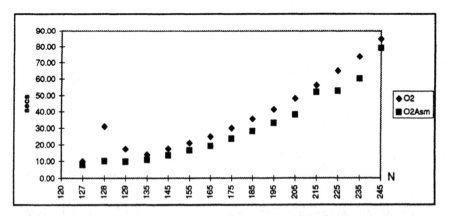

The performance gains are not as big as one would expect. The main reason for this is again the hardware limitation of just one path between memory and registers at a time. Remember there is one "load vector" and one "store vector" operation in the innermost loop. So much of the time is spent in waiting for the single path to become free. Strip mining overhead and inefficient chainig are further reasons of performance reductions.

# 7 Discussion

A volume rendering algorithm with $O(N^3)$ scalar operations could be transformed into an optimized version with $O(N^2)$ vector and scalar operations. Authors in previous papers, [10] and [11], also talk about the employment of vector computers for volume rendering. However, they only vectorized the first part of the algorithm, namely the viewing transformation of the volume data. The image generation itself was not vectorized.

Concerning image quality, generating the image in oblique coordinates allows the efficient computation of a highly oversampled footprint. This reduces aliasing artifacts.

Another advantage of the proposed algorithm is that the volume data have to be stored just once, without losses in computational efficiency. As long as no bank conflicts occur, a memory bandwidth of one element per clock cycle (ignoring start-up latency) is always possible. According to the architecture of vector machines, it does not matter how far away successive elements of vectors are in memory, i.e. how big the vector stride is.

The strict scheme of vector operations prohibits the exploitation of local data properties. One of the advantages of the splatting method is that grid points without contribution to the final image ($\alpha=0$) are just skipped by the (sequential) algorithm. This is no longer practical with vector statements.

Another drawback of the vectorized algorithm is that volume data have to be transformed to RGBA format before the computation starts. This means four single precision floating point values, i.e. 16 Bytes, per grid point. Raw volume data typically have one or four bytes per grid point. The transfer functions which map raw values to RGBA intensities and opacities causes a multiplication of the necessary amount of memory by factors of 4 to 16. However, applying the transfer functions during image generation is not meaningful on vector machines.

The transformation from oblique coordinates to cartesian coordinates causes a deterioration of image quality (aliasing). A straight forward improvement of image quality is achieved by supersampling in the OP coordinate system. Of course, this causes longer image generation times.

# 8 Conclusion and Further Work

With our work on vectorized volume rendering algorithms we wanted to give a contribution to the quest for real time volume rendering without custom hardware. Our experiences showed that there is still some research necessary in automatic vectorization.

Porting the vectorized algorithm to RISC architectures and getting similar performance gains seems possible. It is possible to execute vector operations with stride 1 on superscalar RISC machines with performances comparable to vector machines (see [16]). Here the cache supported by intelligent prefetch techniques takes over the function of the vector registers. Our next step will be to investigate this possibility. Furthermore, large parts of the proposed algorithm lend themselves to implementation on high end graphics hardware. Two functions which are most important in this context are alpha blending and texture mapping. In the near future we will have a machine with these capabilities available.

# 9   Acknowledgement

We would like to thank CRAY Research, Munich, especially Mr. Pichlmeier, for giving us the opportunity of testing an early version of the vectorized program on a CRAY Y-MP.

# 10   References

1.   Drebin R.A., L. Carpenter, P. Hanrahan: *Volume Rendering*, Computer Graphics, Vol. 22, No. 4, Aug. 1988, 65-74
2.   Upson C., M. Keeler: *V-BUFFER: Visible Volume Rendering*, Computer Graphics, Vol. 22, No. 4, Aug. 1988, 59-64
3.   Krueger W.: *Volume Rendering and Data Feature Enhancement*, ACM Computer Graphics, Vol. 24, No. 5, Nov. 1990, 21-26, 107-108
4.   Porter T., T. Duff: *Compositing Digital Images*, Computer Graphics, Vol. 18, No. 3, July 1984, 253-259
5.   Levoy M.: *Display of Surfaces from Volume Data*, IEEE CG&A, Vol. 8, No. 3, March 1988, 29-37
6.   Westover L.: *Interactive Volume Rendering*, Proceedings of the Chapel Hill Workshop on Volume Visualization, Chapel Hill, NC, ACM, May 1989, 9-16
7.   Vezina G., Fletcher P.A., Robertson R.K.: *Volume Rendering on the MasPar MP-1*, [18], 3-8
8.   Schröder P., G. Stoll: *Data Parallel Volume Rendering as Line Drawing*, [18], 25-32
9.   Wittenbrink C. M., Somani A. K.: *2D and 3D Optimal Parallel Image Warping*, Journal of Parallel and Distributed Computing, 25, 197-208, 1995
10.  Stredney D., R. Yagel, S.F. May, M. Torello: *Supercomputer Assisted Brain Visualization with an Extended Ray Tracer*, [18], 33-38
11.  R.K. Machiraju, R. Yagel: *Efficient Feed-Forward Volume Rendering Techniques for Vector and Parallel Processors*, Proceedings Supercomputing '93, ACM, 1993, pp. 699-708
12.  Spalt A.: *A Vectorized Algorithm for Volume Rendering*, Proceedings "COMPU-GRAPHICS '93", ACM Portugal, 1993, 154-163
13.  Patterson D.A., Hennessy, J.L.: *Computer Architecture: A Quantitative Approach*, Morgan Kaufman Publishers, 1990
14.  *CONVEX SCIlib User's Guide*, CONVEX Computer Corp., 1993
15.  *CONVEX VECLIB User's Guide*, CONVEX Computer Corp., 1993
16.  Weiss Sh.: *Optimizing a Superscalar Machine to Run Vector Code*, IEEE Parallel & Distributed Technology, Vol.1, No.2, May 1993, 73-83
17.  *CONVEX Theory of Operation (C3400 Series)*, CONVEX Computer Corp., 1993
18.  Proc. *1992 Workshop on Volume Visualization*, Boston, ACM, Oct. 1992

# Parallel Chaotic Iterative Algorithms for Image Reconstruction with Limited Projection Data

N.Gubareny , A.Katkov

Technical University of Częstochowa, Institute of Mathematics & Computer Science, 42-200 Częstochowa, Poland

**Abstract.** The parallel chaotic iterative algorithms for image reconstruction by method of asynchronous chaotic relaxation with delay using the Monte-Carlo method are proposed. These algorithms are some generalization of parallel chaotic iteration methods considered by Bru, Elsner and Neumann. The accuracy and the rate of convergence of these algorithms are evaluated through their computer simulation with application to physical researches by tomographic reconstruction from incomplete data. Numerical calculations for solving this problem for some modeling objects, comparing evaluations of errors and the rate of convergence of these algorithms are presented.

These algorithms may be realized effectively in speed independent computing network. This network consists of interacting speed independent processors, which are nonsynchronous devices, and duration of computational processes is defined by duration of transient processes in them. So computing time of each macroiteration for these algorithms in such network is considerably less than computing time for corresponding algorithms in synchronous computing structure.

## 1 Introduction

The most significant problems in important fields of applications are inverse problems. In particular it is very important class of inverse problems where a distribution function is reconstructed from its line integrals represented mathematically by the Radon transform. In recent years technique of computerized tomography found a wide application for solving such problems. In many applications where the projection data is sampled continuously in any direction it is currently more preferred analytical technique based on the inverse Radon transform. However in the most problems of physical researches (optical measurements, measurements of plasma emission intensity distributions, combustion problems, measurements of density distributions in fluid flows) the projection data is very limited as a rule and it is often impossible to obtain integral data from the object at all angles and/or the amount of data available at each angle is limited as well. In this case the projection operator can be represented algebraically and the problem of image reconstruction is reduced to solving system of linear algebraic equations which has several typical difficulties: it is inconsistent, underdetermined and has very large size. For solving such systems there often used different kinds of algebraic iterative algorithms the most well-known from which are ART and MART algorithms [4], [5]. They are generally simple, flexible and permit to use *a priori* knowledge of the object before its reconstruction that is very important in many applications. In the recent time with the development of special-purpose parallel computer technique the interest to them was increased with possibility of their parallelizing for shorting time to their convergence. The most full review of parallel computations in image reconstruction problems of computerized tomography is given by Y.Censor [6]. Another models of asynchronous parallel chaotic iteration methods were considered in work [7]. It is assumed that these models are fulfilled in network consisting of independent processors each of them executes its computations during although different but quite definite constant time.

In this paper we consider the algorithms for image reconstruction which may be realized in such speed independent computing network (SICN) consisting of speed independent processors (SIPs), work time of which is defined by duration of transient processes in them and therefore this time for each processor isn't constant but it is a random variable. The considered algorithms realized in such network are based on the asynchronous method of chaotic relaxation with delay [2] and the Monte-Carlo method. In dependence on number of SIPs, their fulfillment of definite operations and interaction with the central processor we obtain different chaotic iterative algorithms some of which are discussed in section 2, the architecture of corresponding computing networks is described in section 3. The computer simulation and experimental results of these algorithms with application for some modeling objects of physical measurements by tomographic reconstruction from incomplete data are represented in section 4.

## 2    Reconstruction chaotic iterative algorithms

Let an image function $f$ be defined in some domain $D \subset R^2$. It needs to restore function $f$ by given set of projection data, which is its integrals over straight lines:

$$p(\theta, l) = \int_{-\infty}^{+\infty} f(l\cos\theta - t\sin\theta, l\sin\theta + t\cos\theta)dt, \qquad (1)$$

where $\theta$ is a projection angle, $l$ is a coordinate along a projection line. As a rule in practice we have only discrete set of projection data for finite number of $\theta$ and $l$. For some problems of physical sciences the number of $\theta$ may be very small, for example 3 or 5. So we have such reconstruction problem: it is given set $p_{\theta_j}(l_i)$ for $j = 1, 2, ..., M$; $i = 1, 2, ..., N$; it needs to find an estimate $\tilde{f}$ of $f$.

One of the approach for solving this problem consists of discretizing the model and reducing it to solving the system of linear algebraic equations. For this purpose we construct the full discrete model of image object from its projections. First we divide reconstruction domain $D$ into $n$ small pixels and assume that image function $f$ has constant uniform value $x_j$ throughout the $j$th pixel for $j = 1, 2, ..., n$. Secondly we assume that sources and detectors are points and the rays between them are straight lines. Then we denote by $a_{ij}$ ($i = 1, 2, ..., m$; $j = 1, 2, ..., n$; $m = MN$) the intersection length of $i$th ray with $j$th pixel. Let

$p_i$ be the physical measurement and represent the line integral (1) along the $i$th ray. In this approximation it is replaced by a finite sum

$$p_i \simeq \sum_{j=1}^{n} a_{ij} x_j$$

and at the result we obtain the full discrete model of image reconstruction in matrix form:

$$\mathbf{p} = \mathbf{Ax}, \qquad (2)$$

where $\mathbf{p} = (p_i) \in R^m$ is the measurement vector, $\mathbf{x} = (x_j) \in R^n$ is the image vector and $\mathbf{A} = (a_{ij}) \in R^{m,n}$ is the projection matrix.

The general sketch of process of image reconstruction for discrete model is shown in Fig.1.

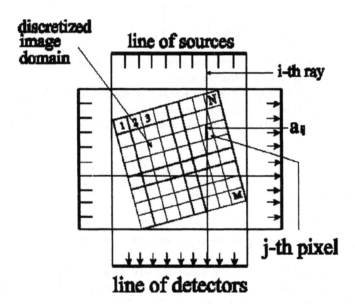

**Fig. 1.** Process of image reconstruction for discrete model

The basic idea of all ART methods is to run through all equations cyclically with modification of the present estimate $\mathbf{x}^{(k)}$ in such way that the present equation with index $i$ is fulfilled. It can be expressed as follows [4]:

$$\mathbf{x}^{(k+1)} = \mathbf{x}^{(k)} + \omega_k \frac{p_{i(k)} - (\mathbf{a}^{i(k)}, \mathbf{x}^{(k)})}{\|\mathbf{a}^{i(k)}\|^2} \mathbf{a}^{i(k)} \qquad (3)$$

with an arbitrary vector $\mathbf{x}^{(0)}$ and $\mathbf{a}^{i(k)} = (a_{i1}, a_{i2}, ..., a_{in})^T$, where $i(k) = k$ mod $m + 1$ and $0 < \omega_k < 2$ is a relaxation parameter.

Also it was developed the block-iterative version of such algorithm. Let set of projections $\{p_i\}$, $(i = 1, 2, ..., m)$ be decomposed into S subsets $\{\mathbf{p}_{[i]}\}$, where $\mathbf{p}_{[i]}$ consists of vectors $p_j \in H_i$ in accordance with decomposition

$$\{1, 2, \ldots, m\} = H_1 \cup H_2 \cup \ldots \cup H_S, \tag{4}$$

where

$$H_t = \{m_{t-1} + 1, m_{t-1} + 2, \ldots, m_t\},$$

$0 = m_0 < m_1 < ... < m_S = m$ (see [6]). Then matrix $\mathbf{A}$ and vector $\mathbf{p}$ may be decomposed into $S$ blocks so that:

$$\mathbf{A} = \begin{bmatrix} \mathbf{A}_1 \\ \mathbf{A}_2 \\ \vdots \\ \mathbf{A}_S \end{bmatrix}, \quad \mathbf{p} = \begin{bmatrix} \mathbf{P}_{[1]} \\ \mathbf{P}_{[2]} \\ \vdots \\ \mathbf{P}_{[S]} \end{bmatrix}$$

where $\mathbf{A}_i$ and $\mathbf{p}_{[i]}$ are the appropriate submatrices of $\mathbf{A}$ and subvectors of $\mathbf{p}$ respectively according to this decomposition.

The most well-known block-iterative Kaczmarz algorithm [10] for such decomposable matrix $\mathbf{A}$ and vector $\mathbf{p}$ has cyclic character as well and in special case, when diagonal relaxation matrix has a diagonal form, it may be reduced to such algorithm:

$$\mathbf{x}^{(k+1)} = \mathbf{x}^{(k)} + \omega_k \sum_{i \in H_{t(k)}} \frac{p_i - (\mathbf{a}^i, \mathbf{x}^{(k)})}{\|\mathbf{a}^i\|^2} \mathbf{a}^i, \tag{5}$$

where $t(k) = k \bmod S + 1$.

This algorithm includes algorithm (4) as extreme case when $|H_t| = 1$ for all $t = 1, 2, ..., S$.

Refusing the sequential cyclic fulfillment of every iteration (4),(5) in work [7] the authors proposed two different models of asynchronous parallel implementation of such kinds of algorithms on a parallel architecture which consists of $m$ independent processors (IPs) connected with a shared memory. In the first model each processor can executes an arbitrary number of local iterations before the next global approximation to the solution is formed. In the second model any processor can update the global approximation which resides in the central processor at any time. This model is a generalization of a sequential iterative scheme proposed by Ostrowski [9] and chaotic relaxation iterative scheme due to Chazan and Miranker [2]. We consider reconstruction chaotic iterative algorithms which belong to some modification of the second model on condition that they are fulfilled in SICN consisting of IPs and computing time of each processor is a random variable.

We use the basic notions of the theory of asynchronous iterative methods developed by Baudet [3]. The important significance in this theory has the notion of chaotic iteration which is originally due to Chazan and Miranker [2] who introduced it during the investigation of asynchronous iterative algorithms for solving systems of linear algebraic equations.

**Definition 1**

A sequence of nonempty subsets $I = \{I_k\}_{k=0}^{\infty}$ of set $\{1, 2, ..., S\}$ is *a sequence of chaotic sets* if

$$\limsup_{j \to \infty} I_j = \{1, 2, ..., S\} \tag{6}$$

(another words each of the integers $1, 2, ..., S$ appears in this sequence infinitely often). Such sequence is *admissible* due to Bru, Elsner and Neumann [7].

Assume that SICN consists of $S$ SIPs working locally independently. In this case the sequence of chaotic sets has simple interpretation: it sets the time diagram of work for each SIP during nonsynchronous work of SICN. Let the sequence of iterations $\{\mathbf{x}^{(k)}\}_{k=1}^{\infty}$ be calculated in SICN, then subset $I_k$ is the set of the numbers of those SIPs taking place really at the calculation of vector coordinates $\mathbf{x}^{(k)}$ on the $k$-th step of iteration.

The sequence of chaotic sets $I = \{I_k\}_{k=1}^{\infty}$ is characterized by such important property: for every $i \in N$ there exists such $T \in N$ that there are fulfilled the conditions:

$$\bigcup_{i=j+1}^{j+T} I_i = \{1, 2, ..., S\}$$

$$\bigcup_{i=j+1}^{j+T-1} I_i \neq \{1, 2, ..., S\}. \tag{7}$$

So this sequence is *regulated* due to [7]

**Definition 2**

The sequence $J = \{\sigma(k)\}_{k=1}^{\infty}$ of $S$-dimensional vectors $\sigma(k) = \{\sigma_1(k), \sigma_2(k), ..., \sigma_S(k)\}$ with integer coordinates satisfying for every $i = 1, 2, ..., S$ and $k \in N$ such properties:

$$0 \leq \sigma_i(k) \leq k;$$

$$\exists L \in N \quad \text{that} \quad k - \sigma_i(k) \leq L. \tag{8}$$

is called *a delay sequence* and $L$ is called *a delay number*.

The number $L$ defines the depth of used iterations and in fact reflects the possibilities of concrete computing system in which the algorithm is realized.

Consider two different modifications of chaotic iterative algorithms which are implementeded on SICN. At the first case we assume that we have $m = MN$ SIPs, in other words we have so many processors as the number of all equations in the system (3) or the full number of all rays in projection data in problem of image reconstruction. Introduce discrete time $\{t_k\}_{k=0}^{\infty}$, where $t_k = k\Delta t$, $\Delta t = const > 0$. We consider that at an initial time $t_0 = 0$ every $i$th processor has an initial value of image vector $\mathbf{x}^0$, coefficient vector $\mathbf{a}^i$ of matrix $A$, the value $p_i$ of projection vector $\mathbf{p}$, the weight $\alpha_i \in (0, 1)$ and set of relaxation parameters $\{\omega_k\}_{k=1}^{\infty}$. Let $\mathbf{x}^{(k)}$ be a value of image vector at time $t_k$. Now assume that change from state $\mathbf{x}^{(k)}$ to state $\mathbf{x}^{(k+1)}$ is implemented on SICN consisting of $m$ SIPs. In this case the work of every processor is fulfilled mutually independently and takes different intervals of time defined by codes of numbers, which the processors use for their computations at definite instant of time.

We will consider that every processor has speed of computation on the interval from $\Delta t$ to $L\Delta t$, where $L$ is a positive integer defining the delay of computing system and a number $1 \le i \le L$ for every processor is defined at random. Work of every processor depends on full group of pairwise incompatible events $A_1, A_2, ..., A_L$. In this case event $A_j$ indicates that $i$-th processor has to work during the time $j\Delta t$ $(j = 1, 2, ..., L)$ for computation of necessary value and then it returns to initial state.

Let $\eta^k = \{\eta_1^k, \eta_2^k, ..., \eta_m^k\}$ be a sequence of independent discrete random variables; $\eta_i^k$ be a discrete random variable concerning to work of $i$-th processor and $\eta_i^k = j$ if the event $A_j$ takes place for $i$-th processor at time $t_k$.

At each instant of time $t_k$ the work of SICN is defined by means of a sequence of independent discrete random variables

$$\xi^k = \{\xi_1^k, \xi_2^k, ..., \xi_m^k\}$$

where $\xi_i^1 = \eta_i^1$, and if $k > 1$ then

$$\xi_i^k = \begin{cases} \eta_i^k & \text{if } \xi_i^{k-1} = 1; \\ \xi_i^{k-1} - 1 & \text{if } \xi_i^{k-1} \neq 1. \end{cases} \tag{9}$$

for $i = 1, 2, ..., m$.

At any time $t_k$ the sequence $\xi^k$ shows a phase of work of each processor. In this case if $\xi_i^{k-1} = 1$ then new computations are fulfilled in those pixels which belong to $i$th ray on $k$-th step, i. e. only these values of pixels are restored; computing values are put into central memory and new information from central processor is put into $i$-th processor computing time of which equals to $\eta_i^k$. If $\xi_i^{k-1} \neq 1$ then processor continues its work and values in corresponding pixels aren't changed.

Computational process in each SIP is defined by the sequence of chaotic sets $I = \{I_k\}_{k=1}^\infty$ and delay sequence $J = \{\sigma(k)\}_{k=1}^\infty$, which are built by means of sequence $\{\xi^k\}_{k=1}^\infty$. Chaotic set $I_k$ is built by vector $\xi^k$ in such way:

$$I_k = \{j \in (1, 2, ..., m) \mid \xi_j^k = 1\} \tag{10}$$

So if $\xi_j^k = 1$ then $j \in I_k$ and if $\xi_j^k \neq 1$ then $j \notin I_k$. Therefore $I_k \subset \{1, 2, ..., m\}$.

From the building of vector $\xi^k$ and assumption that for every $i = 1, 2, ..., m$ and $k \in N$, $\eta_i^k \le L$ it follows that for every $k \in N$ it is true the equality:

$$\bigcup_{i=k}^{k+L} I_i = \{1, 2, ..., m\}. \tag{11}$$

This condition signifies that at any time interval with length $(L+1)\Delta t$ every coordinate of image vector is restored if only one time.

The delay sequence $J = \{\sigma(k)\}_{k=1}^\infty$ can be built in such way:

1. if $k = 1$ then $\sigma_i(k) = 0$;

2. if $k > 1$ then

$$\sigma_i(k) = \begin{cases} \sigma_i(k-1) & \text{if } i \notin I_k \\ k-1 & \text{if } i \in I_k \end{cases} \qquad (12)$$

where $i = 1, 2, ..., m$.

From this building it is obviously that $0 \leq \sigma_i(k) \leq k-1$ and $\sigma_i(k) \geq k-L$, i.e. inequality $k - \sigma_i(k) \leq L$ is true for every $k \in N$ and $i = 1, 2, ..., n$. So the sequence $\{\sigma(k)\}_{k=1}^{\infty}$ satisfies to conditions (8) and number $L$ defines the delay of system.

Change of value from $\mathbf{x}^{(k-1)}$ to $\mathbf{x}^{(k)}$ is calculated on SICN, consisting of $m$ SIPs, using sequence of chaotic sets and the delay sequence by such diagram. Let at the instant of time $t_k$ a number $i \in I_k$ then $i$-th processor ends its calculations by such formula:

$$\mathbf{y}^i = \mathbf{x}^{\sigma(k)} + \omega_k \frac{p_i - (\mathbf{a}^i, \mathbf{x}^{\sigma(k)})}{\|\mathbf{a}^i\|^2} \mathbf{a}^i \qquad (13)$$

where $\sigma(k) \in J$.

In this paper we assume that a few independent processors can end their work at the same time. In this case it must be intermediate processor which computes the convex combination of all $r(k)$ vectors obtained by processors ending their work at the same time:

$$\mathbf{y} = \beta_1 \mathbf{y}^1 + \beta_2 \mathbf{y}^2 + ... + \beta_{r(k)} \mathbf{y}^{r(k)} \qquad (14)$$

and then it calculates the convex combination of obtained vector $\mathbf{y}$ with the current vector $\mathbf{z}$ from the shared memory:

$$\mathbf{z}^* = \alpha_k \mathbf{y} + (1 - \alpha_k)\mathbf{z} \qquad (15)$$

and sends vector $\mathbf{z}^*$ as $k$-th iteration to the shared memory from which every processor loads up the current vector as its initial approximation.

Other $i$-th processors, for which $i \notin I_k$, continue their work and don't change corresponding values of pixels.

We will call this chaotic iterative algorithm as algorithm ASI.

Now we consider the block-iterative version of this algorithm. Let set of projections $\{p_i\}$, $i = 1, 2, ..., m$ be decomposed into S subsets $\{p_{[i]}\}$ according to decomposition (4). In this case we assume that we have only S SIPs that equals to the number of decomposed blocks of matrix $\mathbf{A}$ and vector $\mathbf{p}$. We apply the asynchronous relaxation method to the block-iterative Kaczmarz algorithm [10]. At the instant of time $t_k$ the $i$th processor, for which $i \in I_k$, ends such operation:

$$\mathbf{y} = \sum_{r \in H_i} \gamma_r \left[ \mathbf{x}^{\sigma(k)} + \omega_k \frac{p_r - (\mathbf{a}^r, \mathbf{x}^{\sigma(k)})}{\|\mathbf{a}^r\|^2} \mathbf{a}^r \right], \qquad (16)$$

where $\sigma(k) \in J$, $\{1, 2, ..., m\} = H_1 \cup H_2 \cup ... \cup H_S$ and $\sum_{r=1}^{S} \gamma_r = 1$

Then we fulfil the same operations (14),(15) as in algorithm ASI.

This algorithm we will call as ASBI.

Coming from sequence $I = \{I_k\}_{k=1}^{\infty}$ we will build the sequence of indexes $\{k_t\}_{t=1}^{\infty}$ which is satisfied the conditions:

1. $k_{t_1} < k_{t_2}$     if $t_1 < t_2$;

2. for every $t \geq 1$ there are true the conditions:

$$\bigcup_{i=k_t+1}^{k_{t+1}} I_i = \{1, 2, ..., m\};$$

$$\bigcup_{i=k_t+1}^{k_{t+1}-1} I_i \neq \{1, 2, ..., m\}. \tag{17}$$

Such sequence always exists according to condition (7), it is defined uniquely and called minimal sequence. With regard to condition (11) we have $k_{t+1} - k_t \leq L + 1$.

Consider the sequence of iterations $\{\mathbf{x}^{(r)}\}_{r=k_t+1}^{k_{t+1}}$ for which each component of vector $\mathbf{x}^{(k_t+1)}$ is restored if only one time in comparison with vector $\mathbf{x}^{(k_t)}$. Such sequence of vectors is called *macroiteration*, and number $t$ is called *the number of macroiterations*.

Similar as in work [8] it may be shown that these algorithms ASI and ASBI convergent to the minimum norm least squares solution if the system (2) has a solution and an initial vector $\mathbf{x}^0 \in \text{Ker}(\mathbf{A})$. When the system (2) is inconsistent then the minimum norm least squares solution can be found as shown in the work [11] as a part of some consistent system.

# 3   Realization of chaotic iterative algorithm on parallel computing structures

Chaotic iterative algorithms are naturally reflected on network consisting of SIPs each of which is intended for computing mathematical operations according to (13),(16). As follows from these algorithms the massive operations in them are addition, multiplication and division. Time intervals for computing the sequence of operations defined by algorithms (13),(16) are random values. Interactions of SIPs in parallel structure are defined by signal of ending calculations according to formulas (13),(16).

The main requirement of synchronous computations is to provide the right work of the slowest elements in synchronous structure. As a result always the higher speed of work of other elements isn't used. It is well known that designing of more or less complicated computing structure is connected with generating of a set of synchrosignals delaying of the other. Providing with stability of parameters of synchrosignals and their sufficient power is a problem namely because they must be connected with every functional element of complex computing structure. In this case the considerable part of crystal space and power dispersion of crystal is wasted for realization of conception of synchronous computations. In computers with non von Neumann architecture and especially in massively parallel computing structures it needs to refuse from principle of synchronous computing not owing to its uneffect but owing to problems connecting with its technical realization.

Definition of the exact end moment of transient process in logical circuits opens certain perspectives in the organization of parallel computational processes, the most interesting from which are parallel computational processes with elements of self-organization. Namely this circumstance is put into basis of work of SICN in which every processor generates signal of end of transient process. This signal may be used for loading new input operands and so it may provide more effective work of computing structure.

The theory of work of SICN was proposed long enough [1] and its development consists of both elaboration of general theory and elaboration of devices for logical analysis of change of input and output operands of checked circuit. Increasing complexity of circuit for logical analysis of checked object state may lead to the fact that the time necessary for forming confirmation signal may be approximately equal to the time for providing synchronization in synchronous circuits. There exists another way of solving this problem.

Investigations show that logical elements are source of enough powerful electromagnetic radiation which is generated mainly during their switching from one state to another. Level of electromagnetic radiation depends on manufacture technology of integral microcircuits and their types. As it has been turned out the highest level of generation of electromagnetic waves have circuits TTL (Transistor Transistor Logic), the lowest - HTL (High Threshold Logic). In general case the higher switching speed the higher level of electromagnetic radiation. For TTL-logic it approximately equals to 50 Mkv/Mgc. This electromagnetic radiation may be fixed and used for control of computational processes.

Self-organizing computational processes are more effective in global parallel nonsyschronous structure consisting of SIPs made in technology of speed independent circuit [1]. In this realization of parallel structure the interactions of SIPs are defined by end moment of transient process in each functional element. For this purpose the changes of Boolean derivatives for binary components of variables taking part in the mathematical operations are analyzed. The chaotic character of interactions of SIPs in computing structure is naturally represented by the chaotic nature of computational algorithms considered above.

## 4 Computer Simulation and Experimental Results

As modeling objects for computing experiments there were used functions consisting of $k$ Gaussian peaks:

$$f(x,y) = \sum_{i=1}^{k} c_i \{ -a_i^2 \left[ (x - x_{oi}) \cos \varphi_i - (y - y_{oi}) \sin \varphi_i \right]^2 -$$

$$-b_i^2\big[(x - x_{oi})\sin\varphi_i + (y - y_{oi})\cos\varphi_i\big]^2\} \tag{18}$$

which presents the most typical possible measurement situations in the physical sciences and in particular in optical investigation of plasma.

Though the modeling function (18) exists in all two-dimentional plane $\mathbf{R}^2$ as the image domain we choose the finite square $D = \{x, y \in R^2 | -1 \leq x,\, y \leq 1\}$ because outside this domain the function $f(x, y)$ approximately equals to 0. Therefore in our computer simulation we supposed that function $f(x, y)$ equals to 0 output this square. Input data was chosen by parallel rays for M different angles $\theta_1, \theta_2, ..., \theta_M$. The projections data were calculated by corresponding analytical formulas. The image domain was divided into $32 \times 32$ pixels. The experimental results in this paper are presented for modeling function (18) with such parameters: $k = 2$; $a_1 = a_2 = 9.5$; $b_1 = b_2 = 4.5$; $c_1 = c_2 = 5$; $\varphi_1 = \varphi_2 = 0$; $x_{o1} = x_{o2} = 0$; $y_{o1} = 0.5$; $y_{o2} = -0.5$. This modeling function was restored by algorithms ASI, ASBI described in section 2 and comparized with synchronous algorithm ART-2, and block-iterative Kaczmarz algorithm. To compare these algorithms there were chosen the different levels of delay and the number of projection data. The data sets include projections at three angles $(-60°, 60°, 180°)$ and the number of rays at every projection equals to 51. As *a priori* knowledge of the object it was used the sign of the object, its extent and its smoothness. For a visual comparison of the quality of the image reconstruction of modeling object by different algorithms the experimental results of the computer simulation are given in the view of reconstructed surfaces in Fig.2. The delay number for algorithms ASI and ASBI was equal to 20. The number of SIPs was equal to 153 for algorithm ASI and 3 for algorithm ASBI. The reconstructed surfaces shown in Fig.2 were obtained after 100 iteration by algorithm ART-2 and 100 macroiterations by algorithms ASI and ASBI.

For iterative relaxation algorithms it is very important the choise of initial data, relaxation parameters and stopping criteria. For this aim the convergence of these iterative algorithms was studied in dependence on different of these conditions. The convergence characteristic plots are given in view of graphs for such numerical characteristic as root-mean-square error:

$$\delta = \Big|\, \frac{\sum_{i=1}^n (f_i^T - f_i)^2}{\sum_{i=1}^n (f_i^T)^2} \,\Big|\, 100\%$$

where $f_i^T$ - value of given modelling function in the center of $i$-th pixel; $f_i$ - value of reconstructed function in $i$-th pixel. The dependence of root-mean-square error on number of iterations (macroiterations) for modelling function by these algorithms is shown in Fig.3 for $L = 20$, $n = 32 \times 32$, $M = 3$, $N = 51$, $\mathbf{x}^0 = 0$.

These computer experiments show that the best convergent characteristics has algorithm ASBI.

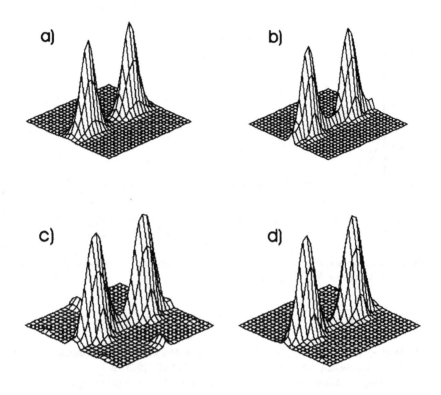

**Fig. 2.** The reconstruction surfaces of $f(x, y)$ by b) - algorithm ART-2, c) -algorithm ASI, d) - algorithm ASBI. Ideal function $f(x, y)$ is given in a).

## 5 Conclusion

The aim of this paper was elaboration, investigation and comparing the chaotic iterative algorithms for image reconstruction by means of asynchronous method of chaotic relaxation with delay that imitate the chaotic self-organizing processes in SICN. There were studied quality and convergence of these algorithms. It was shown that they gives good results by comparison with corresponding synchronous well-known iterative algebraic algorithms. The best result in terms of convergence properties has algorithm ASBI. It is shown that these methods have approximately such speed of convergence as corresponding synchronous methods. But taking into account that computing time of each macroiteration for algorithms ASI and ASBI is considerably less we can say that the equivalent speed of SICN, on which these algoorithms are implemented, is considerably higher.

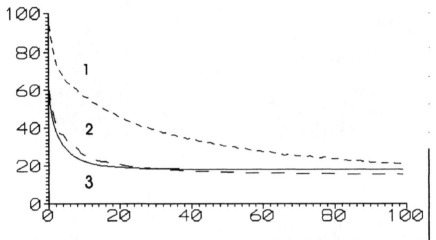

**Fig. 3.** Dependence of root-mean-square error on number of iterations by 1) -algorithm ASI, 2) - algorithm ASBI, 3) - algorithm ART-2

## References

1. Muller, D.E.: Infinite sequences and finite Machines. Proc. Fourth Ann. IEEE Symp. on Switch. Circuit Th. Log. Design **S-156** (1963) 9–16
2. Chazan, D., Miranker, W.: Chaotic relaxation. Linear Algebra Appl.2 (1969) 199–222
3. Baudet, G.M.: Asynchronous iterative methods for multiprocessors. J. Assoc. Comput. Mach. **25** (1978) 226–244
4. Herman, G.T.: Image Reconstruction from Projections. Academic New York (1980)
5. Herman, G.T., Lent, A., Rowland, S.: ART: Mathematics and application (a report on the mathematical foundations and on the applicability to real data of the Algebraic Reconstruction Techniques). Journ. of Theoretica Biology **43** (1973) 1–32
6. Censor, Y.: Parallel application of block-iterative methods in medical imaging and radiation therapy. Math. Programming **42** (1988) 307–325
7. Bru, R., Elsner, L., Neumann, M,: Models of Parallel Chaotic Iteration Methods. Linear Algebra Appl. **103** (1988) 175–192
8. Elsner, L., Koltracht, I., Neumann, M.: On the Convergence of Asynchronous Paracontractions with Application to Tomographic Reconstruction from Incomplete Data. Linear Algebra Appl. **130** (1990) 83–98
9. Ostrowski, A.M.: Iterative solution of linear system of functional equations,I. Math. Anal. Appl. **2** (1961) 351–369
10. Eggermont, P.P.B., Herman, G.T., Lent, A.: Iterative algorithms for large partitioned linear systems with applications to image reconstruction. Linear Algebra Appl. **40** (1981) 37–67
11. Miller, V., Neumann, N.: A note on comparison theorems for nonnegative iteration matrices. Numer. Math. 47 (1986) 427–434

# Digital's TruCluster Architecture

by Gerhard Hausberger, Digital Equipment Corporation

## Introduction

The TruCluster product from Digital Equipment provides a new way of interconnecting independent Unix systems to *Clusters*. These systems provide much better availability, scalability and cost effectiveness than other computing models. Single-node systems for example provide uniform accessibility to resources (CPUs, storage, networks, etc) and services (files, databases, applications) in a single-management domain. They are limited in scalability - although the system performance has increased dramatically over the past years. If such a single-node system fails, the result is a complete loss of its services to users and clients of the system.

Multinode computers include Symmetric multiprocessor systems (SMP) and massively parallel processors (MPP). They also inlcude network-based computing systems like workstation farms. SMP configurations have tightly coupled CPUs with common access to system resources. MPP systems were designed to support complex, high-performance parallel applications using systems with hundreds of processors. These expensive special-purpose machines and their SW-environment are not very easy to administrate.

Clusters have clear advantages over large-scale parallel systems and distributed heterogenous systems. Clusters can be expanded cost-effectively by adding standard systems to existing ones. Their CPU-performance and IO-subsystem-performance scales very well. They are inherently more tolerant of failures (both: system- and operator-errors) due to looser coupling of the individual systems - if one system goes down, the rest keeps running.

Traditional cluster-interconnects are based on networks and network protocols e.g Ethernet, FDDI, ATM. In the past couple of years the increase of the microprocessor perfomance was dramatically bigger than the enhancements on the networking side. Apart from the primary classification parameter of a network: *throughput* or *bandwidth* this is particularly true for *message latency* and protocoll related *CPU-overhead*.

## Memory Channel

Digital has developed a new network for cluster interconnects: Memory Channel (MC). The Memory Channel implements a cluster-wide virtual shared memory model. Unlike standard networks, MC's performance depends almost totally on semiconductor technology, thus should improve at a rate similar to that of microprocessors [1]. The develpoment focus for this new interconnect technology was on cluster, and on cluster communications traffic. The characterization of the Memory Channel shows three major performance areas:

- bandwidth (maximum sustained data rate):        100 Mbytes/sec.
- latency (elapsed time for communication):        < 5 µsec
- overhead (CPU time for communication operation):   < 0.5µsec

The bandwidth of the Memory Channel is high enough for large data transfers from node-to-node (e.g. data blocks, arrays, database cache blocks) and is approximately 10-times the bandwidth of traditional networks (e.g. FDDI). On the other hand, very low latency and CPU-overhead is important to keep cluster- and application-communication as effective as possible. The overall performance of a cluster configuration is greatly influenced by the capability of exchanging a large amount of *lock-information* and *status-messages*. These messages tend to be small (from >32 to hundreds of Bytes). Traditional networks are not very effective in transmitting these kind of information. Short messages have to be packed or assembled in larger blocks for transmission. On standard network protocols, there is a large amount of CPU overhead involved for transmitting network packets and for error processing. The Memory Channel with its cluster-wide virtual shared memory model has a very low latency (<5 µsec), and with its low error rate (practically zero - handeled by MC-Hardware) gives us the possibility of transmitting high amounts of short messages with low overhead.

## Memory Channel Implementation

The Memory Channel implements a form of distributed shared memory. Digital's MC-implementation is based on a previous design by Encore Computer Corporation [2]. The basic network primitive is a memory-mapped circuit that provides a write-only connection between a page of virtual-address space on a transmitting node and a page of physical memory on a receiving node [1]

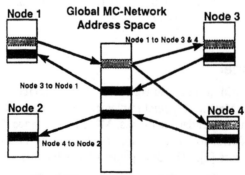

**Fig. 1 Memory Channel Connections**

Figure 1 shows some basic MC-communication connections. Node1 can reserve itself a certain amount of memory out of the MC-network global address space. Node3 and Node4 can map to this memory segment. When Node1 writes into this memory area the content is visible to Node3 and Node4. Communication from Node3 back to Node1 can occur in the same way that Node3 does a reservation on part of the MC-network address space and Node1 maps into this area. Several connections are possible: Unidirectional-, unidirectional connection with broadcast, and bidirectional (two unidirectional).

The Memory Channel has page-level connection granularity on 8Kbytes pages on Digital-Alpha systems. The Memory Channel adapter hardware is a single slot industry standard PCI bus option. This allows cost effective, standards based adapter cards, and a great variety of systems (e.g Alpha, Intel) the use of this new interconnect technology. Two systems can be connected directly via the MC-cable, more than two systems require a MC-hub. Systems with MC-interconnects can be configured with *no single point of failure*.

## TruCluster System

The TruCluster product is a collection of loosely coupled independent systems connected by the high-performance interconnect *Memory Channel*. Each node can be a uniprocessor or multiprocessor system running Digital Unix. Each cluster member has its own copy of the operating system and services and thus is isolated from software or hardware faults on other cluster members. For data-availability reasons two or more nodes have access to the same storage bus (SCSI).

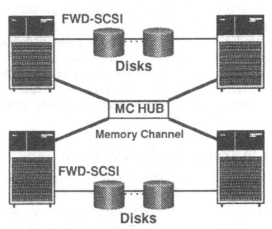

**Fig. 2 Four Node Cluster System**

In this example, there are four nodes connected via Memory Channel establishing a TruCluster configuration. Two nodes on each side have access to the same storage bus. This enables a failover of services in the cluster environment. In case of loss of a system, the other node on the storage bus is able to provide access to the data disks and initiate a restart of the services. This application failover is an element of the Digital DECsafe Available Server Environment [3]. The TruCluster product is designed to support the operation of highly available database systems through several of its key components. One of them is the *distributed remote disk* (DRD). It provides a transparent access of all cluster members to cluster storage regardless whether the nodes have access to the same storage bus or not. Another element, the *distributed lock manager* (DLM)[4] manages the administration of locking information on objects in a distributed database. Another component which is used by the DLM is the *connection manager*. It controls the admitting and removing of cluster members.

## Distributed Remote Disk

The distributed remote disk (DRD) subsystem was developed to support database applications by presenting a clusterwide view of disks accessed through the character or raw device interface [5]. Database systems like the Oracle Parallel Server (OPS) or Informix XPS (in the near future) use the DRD subsystem. The DRD subsystem provides a clusterwide namespace and access mechanism for both physical and logical volumes (LSM - logical storage manager). The DRD-devices are assigned to a single cluster member at a time. This node serves the DRD-device to the other cluster members. In case of a system failure or on I/O-load balancing reasons, this DRD-service may be passed on to other cluster members on the same storage bus, which is then responsible for serving this DRD-device to the remaining cluster members. The datatransfer between the serving node and the requesting nodes takes place on the Memory Channel. MC also supports direct memory access (DMA) between the I/O-adapter of the serving node and the main memory of the requesting node [5]. This enables a serving node to transfer the data out of a disk operation directly into the memory of the requesting node without any local CPU intervention.

## Applications in TruCluster Environment

The TruCluster environment is transparent to users and applications. The failover of applications in case of system failure or operator intervention (e.g. for system maintainanc reasons) is done in a similar way as in DECsafe Available Server. Software components on each node monitor the status of the resources (storage, networks, etc). In case one system fails the storage and the associated applications are moved (restarted) on the surviving systems.

Nevertheless, there are applications like the *Oracle Parallel Server* (OPS)[6] - a parallelized version of Oracles database system - which uses the TruCluster key components (distributed remote disk, distributed lock manager, Memory Channel). The Oracle Parallel Server is a database environment, distributed over the cluster members. With OPS there are different *Oracle instances* running on the cluster members. They may be assigned to work on *one physical database*. So users or clients may be connected to any cluster member and can have access to the same database.

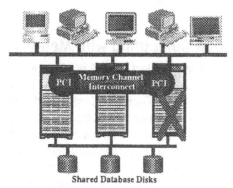

**Fig. 3 TruCluster with OPS**

The database resides on storage on the common storage bus (DRD). Each database instance has its own redo-log-files but they have a shared control-file and shared database files. If one systems fails, a recovery on the outstanding transactions will be done, and the remaining instances can continue transparently. An application on top of OPS may be restarted eventually. Oracle OPS uses the Memory Channel and distributed lock manager for exchanging datablocks and lock information.

Digitals TruCluster with its high-performance, low-latency Memory Channel interconnect, together with Oracles OPS made it possible to reach a new industry-leadership in performance and price-performance with database environment on open systems. Oracle archived 30,390 tpmC ($305/tpmC) on a 4-node Alpha-Server 8400 5/350 cluster (32 CPUs total).

The current available TPC-C results show that Oracle Parallel Server on other Unix cluster

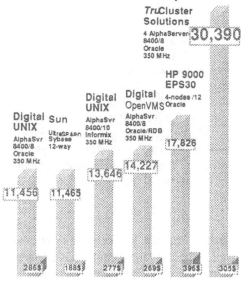

**Fig. 4 TPC-C Results, June 1996**

environments (HP 9000 EPS30) with traditional network interconnects (FDDI) is able to archieve slightly over the half of Oracle/Digitals TPC-C numbers. One reason for that is that Oracles OPS can take full advantage of the better bandwidth and latency characteristics of Digitals Memory Channel. Thus OPS can exchange more lock information and has better throughput on exchanging datablocks (block pinging) using the Memory Channel interconnect.

## High Performance Computing with Memory Channel

In addition to the TruCluster product Digital is offering the Memory Channel Driver for Digital Unix, as well as layered products on top of the Memory Channel driver like DECpvm - a Digital MC-optimized version of the Parallel Virtual Machine programming environment from Oak Ridge National Labs - and the High Performance Fortran's (HPF) automatically generated message passing using Digitals Parallel Software Environment (PSE).
Compared to a FDDI network the latency of a process-to-process connection via PVM using the Memory Channel decreased by a factor of 25 [1].

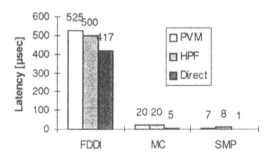

**Fig. 5 Latency by Connectiontype**

In Figure 5 we compare the process-to-process latency using standard interfaces like PVM and HPF, and a direct user written connection in different environments: A network connection using FDDI, over Memory Channel, and on a SMP-system from CPU-to-CPU. Thus the Memory Channel with its optimized software components is the next logical step to connect SMP-systems to larger entities. Currently a cluster of up to 8 nodes is supported using the Memory Channel driver (e.g 8x 12CPUs (AlphaServer 8400) total 96 CPUs).

## Conclusion and Future

The TruCluster product with the Memory Channel interconnect meets our expectation offering a high-performance, high-available commercial database environment, as well as expand the capabilities of SMP-systems by connecting them together in the high performance computing area. This has been proofed by industry-standard benchmarks like TPC-C.

Digital has plans to use the MC-interconnect technology for other operating systems (e.g. OpenVMS). The Memory Channel will be enhanced to allow even more throughput, greater distances, and more nodes. The next big step for the TruCluster software will be a distributed cluster file system for Digital Unix that will complement the distributed remote disk (DRD).

## References

[1]     Richard B. Gillet, Digital Equimpent Corporation, Memory Channel Network for PCI, IEEE Micro, 0772-1732/96/$5.00, 1996 IEEE

[2]     Encore 91 Series Technical Summary (fort Lauderdale, Fla.: Encore Computer corporation, 1991)

[3]     L. Cohen & J. Williams, "Technical Description of the DECsafe Available Server Environment" Digital Technical Journal, Vol 7, No. 4 (1995):89-100

[4]     W. Snaman, Jr. And D.Thiel, "The VAX/VMS Distributed Lock Manager", Digital Technical Journal, vol 1, no 5 (Sept 1987): 29-44

[5]     Wayne M. Cardoza, Fredrick S. Glover, and William E. Snaman, Jr, "Design of the TruCluster Multicomputer System for the Digital UNIX Environment" Digital Technical Journal, 1996

[6]     Oracle Parallel Server in the Digital Environment, Oracle, June 1994, Part A19242

**Ing. Gerhard Hausberger** is technology consultant for the Unix/Open Systems space at the Technology Center at Digital Equipment Österreich AG, Vienna.

# The ParaStation Project

Joachim M. Blum, Thomas M. Warschko, and Walter F. Tichy

University of Karlsruhe,Dept. of Informatics
Postfach 6980,76128 Karlsruhe,Germany
email:{blum,warschko,tichy}@ira.uka.de

**Abstract.** ParaStation is a high speed communication subsystem which
enables a cluster of workstations or PCs to offer performance comparable to a dedicated parallel machine. Each node is still usable as a regular workstation or PC. Speedups of 7.4 on a 8 node cluster have been
achieved even on communication intensive programs. The ParaStation
software supports a real multitasking environment and combines the advantages of workstation clusters and of parallel machines.

## 1   Introduction

The basic concept of the ParaStation approach is to build a scalable and efficient parallel processor from off-the-shelf workstations and PCs. In ParaStation
this is done with a second interconnection network dedicated to parallel computation together with well-known programming interfaces such as UNIX sockets
and PVM. By taking advantage of mass production, the resulting system is
considerably less expensive than traditional parallel machines.

The ParaStation system [8] is based on the retargeted MPP network of Tri-
ton/1 [6, 7]. The goal is to offer MPP-like communication performance while
supporting a standard, but efficient programming interface. The communication
hardware is a PCI-bus interface card which can be used in many platforms including Intel PCs, Digital Alphas, and Motorola PowerPCs. Other platforms,
such as HP, Sun, and SGI, will follow.

## 2   Existing Platforms

ParaStation already supports two different platforms. The initial realization was
based on Digital Alpha workstations running Digital Unix (OSF/1). Recently
we have ported the software to Intel Pentium PCs running Linux. Both systems
support multiple programming interfaces and show high performance on all layers. The port of Windows NT on Alphas and PCs is scheduled to be completed
during summer 96.

The ParaStation network provides a high data rate, low latency, scalable
topology, flow control at link level, minimized protocols, and reliable data transmission. It is dedicated to parallel applications and is not intended as a replace-
ment for a common LAN. This restriction allow the use of specialized network

features, optimized point-to-point protocols, and controlling the network at user-level without operating system interaction.

The ParaStation system library (see figure 1) consists of three building blocks: the hardware interface layer, the central system layer, and the standardized user interface (sockets).

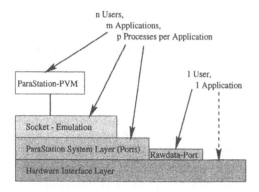

**Fig. 1.** ParaStation system library

The hardware layer provides the necessary abstraction of the underlaying hardware to maintain a transparent and system independent interface to the upper layers.

Since messages at this level are addressed to nodes rather than individual communication channels, message headers simply contain the address of the target node, the number of data words contained in the packet, and the data itself. When sending a message, data is copied directly from user-space memory to the interface board and the receiving function does the same vice versa, eliminating all intermediate buffering.

The ParaStation system layer establishes multiple communication channels between applications and supports a multiuser/multiprogramming environment. To meet our primary design goal of efficiency we have reassembled operating system functionality at user level.

To support individual communication channels (called *ports* in ParaStation), the system layer maintains a minimal software protocol which adds information about the sending and receiving port in each packet. This concept is sufficient to support multiple processes by using different port ids for different processes. Critical sections while sending and receiving messages are locked with semaphores, which are also implemented in user space by using processor-supported atomic operations.

As a result, the implementation of these concepts does not need system calls at all. Furthermore, we provide a zero-copy behavior (no buffering) whenever possible. This leads to high bandwidth and low latencies.

The socket layer provides an emulation of the standard UNIX socket interface (TCP and UDP connections), so applications using socket communication can be ported to the ParaStation system with little effort. For connections outside a ParaStation cluster, regular operating system calls are used. Send/recv calls, which can be satisfied within the ParaStation-cluster, do not need any interaction with the operating system.

ParaStation implementations of standard programming environments like PVM [1, 2], P4 [3], TCGMSG [5], or MPI (mpich) [4] use ParaStation sockets for high-speed communication. This approach allows us to easily port, maintain, and update these packages. We use the standard workstation software.

## 3 Performance

ParaStation achieves high communication performance on all existing platforms. Process to process latencies as low a 1.6 $\mu$s (Linux PCs) and 2.5 $\mu$s (Alphas) have been demonstrated. On the level of the well known Unix socket interface (TCP/IP functionality), latencies of 15 $\mu$s and 20 $\mu$s have been achieved, respectively. The bandwidth can be as high as 15 MBytes/s (10.5 MBytes on Alphas). On the socket level a throughput of 11.7 MBytes/s (PC) and 8.8 MBytes/s (Alpha) is possible.

Focusing on latency and throughput only is too narrow for a complete evaluation. It is necessary to show that a low-latency, high-throughput communication subsystem also achieves a reasonable application efficiency. Our approach is twofold. First, we took a *heat diffusion* benchmark to test application performance on our proprietary interface. This benchmark requires both high bandwidth and low latency. In each iteration the edges of the distributed partitions have to be exchanged and every 20 iterations all data is gathered by one node to display the result. A speedup of 7.4 is achieved on a 8-node cluster (DEC-Alpha).

Second, we installed the widely used and publicly available ScaLAPACK math library, which first uses the BLACS package and then PVM as communication subsystem. Thus, the complete protocol hierarchy as presented in the previous section is involved. The application benchmark for ParaStation (*xs-lu*) is an equation solver for dense systems. Remarkable is a speedup of 6.2 on an eight-node cluster (Alpha 21064A,275MHz) with a aggregate performance of one Gigaflop. Since ScaLAPACK is available for several platforms, this result is directly comparable to other systems.

## 4 Future Platforms

Due to the widesread availability of PCI-bus systems, ParaStation is not limited to DEC-Alpha and PC platforms. IBM PowerPC as platform is possible and Sun (Ultra-Sparc), SGI and HP have announced PCI-based systems.

Beside the support of various platforms we plan to improve the performance of the communication hardware. The next generation hardware will use fibre optic communication links to get a process to process bandwidth of 100 MBytes/s.

Fibre optic links also enable us to extend the distance between two distinct nodes to more than 1 km.

## 5 Conclusion

ParaStation proves that efficient parallel computing is possible on a cluster of workstations. A ParaStation network performs similar to parallel machines. Message passing standards such as PVM and MPI are available, simplifying porting of existing parallel programs. Each node is still usable as regular workstation and the parallel application can share processor resources whenever requested.

## References

1. A. Beguelin, J. Dongarra, Al Geist, W. Jiang, R. Manchek, and V. Sunderam. *PVM 3 User's Guide and Reference Manual*. ORNL/TM-12187, Oak Ridge National Laboratory, May 1993.
2. Joachim M.
   Blum, Thomas M. Warschko, and Walter F. Tichy. PSPVM:Implementing pvm on a high-speed Interconnect for Workstation Clusters. In *Proc. of 3rd Euro PVM Users' Group Meeting*, Munich, Germany, Oct.7-9, 1996.
3. Ralph Buttler and Ewing Lusk. *User's Guide to the p4 Parallel Programmimg System*. ANL-92/17, Argonne National Laboratory, October 1992.
4. William Gropp, Ewing Lusk, and Anthony Skjellum. *Using MPI*. MIT-Press, 1994.
5. R. J. Harrison. Portable tools and applications for parallel computers. *International Journal on Quantum Chem.*, 40:847–863, 1991.
6. Christian G. Herter, Thomas M. Warschko, Walter F. Tichy, and Michael Philippsen. Triton/1: A massively-parallel mixed-mode computer designed to support high level languages. In *7th International Parallel Processing Symposium, Proc. of 2nd Workshop on Heterogeneous Processing*, pages 65–70, Newport Beach, CA, April 13–16, 1993.
7. Michael Philippsen, Thomas M. Warschko, Walter F. Tichy, and Christian G. Herter. Project Triton: Towards improved programmability of parallel machines. In *26th Hawaii International Conference on System Sciences*, volume I, pages 192–201, Wailea, Maui, Hawaii, January 4–8, 1993.
8. Thomas M. Warschko, Joachim M. Blum, and Walter F. Tichy. The ParaStation Project: Using Workstations as Building Blocks for Parallel Computing. In *Proceedings of the International Conference on Parallel and Distributed Processing, Techniques and Applications (PDPTA'96)*, New Horizons, Sunnyvale, California, USA, August 9–11, 1996.

# PPARDB / PVM: A Portable PVM Based Parallel Database Management System

N. Papakostas, G. Papakonstantinou, P. Tsanakas

National Technical University of Athens
Digital Systems and Computers Laboratory
Department of Electrical and Computer Engineering
Zographou Campus, Zographou, GR-15780, Greece
Tel.: +30 1 772 1529, Fax: +30 1 772 1533
E-Mail: nass@dsclab.ece.ntua.gr

Databases have always been very important applications for any computing environment. Parallel databases share the advantages and disadvantages of parallel systems. The various parallel databases that have been developed, e.g. Bubba [BORA90], are not compatible with each other, require different programming approaches, sometimes run on specialised hardware and in general are not yet capable of boosting widespread adoption and use of parallel systems the same way serial databases undeniably did for Von Neuman computers.

Making parallel databases portable is a serious step towards the creation of parallel databases that will play a significant role in the general acceptance of parallel systems. To the best of our knowledge, portability issues of parallel databases have not yet been extensively investigated ([HU95], [FRIE90]). In our work we do not focus in the traditional parallel databases research issues such as performance and efficiency, data partitioning and availability, optimisation etc. Instead, we are looking for methodologies to make parallel databases portable and, therefore, available to a wider range of parallel systems, consequently making them available and appealing to a wider range of users and applications.

In this paper we present the porting of a parallel database management system that was originally developed for a Transputer network, PARDB [THEO92], to an heterogeneous workstation network. The obvious choice for a communications layer that would enable the use of such a network as a virtual parallel computer is PVM [GEI94], given PVM's maturity and widespread use for a variety of scientific programming tasks. PVM offers the primitives required for the operation of the database, i.e. for sending, receiving, broadcasting and multicasting a message, creating and handling processes and signals, process synchronisation etc. Also, the crowd computational model supported by PVM nicely fits the one master / multiple slaves relationship of the database processing elements. The resulting portable parallel database management system is named PPARDB / PVM, for Portable Parallel Database Management System / PVM based.

PPARDB / PVM is a Shared-Nothing relational parallel database management system that uses horizontal partitioning of the relation tuples and employs operator parallelism. It also has a layered architecture that greatly simplifies porting, since network, hardware and operating system dependencies can be consolidated in a single layer that is the one to be adapted for each new architecture, while the rest of the system remains unchanged. All machine or operating system dependencies have been removed and standard POSIX calls have been used.

Multithreading has not been used for PPARDB / PVM mainly since portable and standard thread management primitives are not yet widely available to most operating systems, especially UNIX-derived ones. Apart from that, threaded or "lightweight" process versions of PVM, like TPVM [FERR94] or LPVM [ZHOU95] are not yet portable and robust enough for the task in hand.

PVM has not undergone any design changes. In fact, there are not any required PVM changes and the system can run on top of standard PVM, for obvious compatibility and portability reasons. All required parallel database portability modifications have been done on the database management system itself and not on the communications layer. PVM is used only as a communications subsystem for message passing among the parallel database nodes.

The system is in its final debugging stage. It is implemented on top of a 10 Mbps Ethernet network consisting of 8 Sun SPARCstation and SGI Indy workstations running Solaris, SunOS and IRIX.

Our work on PPARDB / PVM has shown that parallel databases need not be specialised software systems running on specialised hardware. They can run on inexpensive and standard configurations, like a set of networked workstations. They can also be portable to various diverse architectures, making them more appealing, from an application availability point of view, to a wider user community.

## References

[BORA90]   Boral H. et al., "Prototyping Bubba, A highly parallel database system", IEEE Transactions on Knowledge and Data Engineering, Vol. 2 No. 1, March 1990.

[FERR94]   Ferrari A. and Sunderam V.S., "TPVM: Distributed concurrent computing with lightweight processes", Dept. of Mathematics and Computer Science, Emory University, 1994.

[FRIE90]   Frieder O., "On the design, implementation and evaluation of a portable parallel database system", Proceedings of the PARBASE-90 International Conference on Databases, Parallel Architectures and their Applications, Los Alamitos, USA, 1990.

[GEI94]    Geist A. et al., "PVM: Parallel Virtual Machine", MIT Press, Cambridge, USA, 1994.

[HU95]     Ron-Chung Hu and Stellwagen, R., "Navigation Server: A highly parallel DBMS on open systems", Proceedings of the 11th International Conference on Data Engineering, Taipei, Taiwan, March 1995.

[THEO92]   Theoharis T., Papakonstantinou G. and Tsanakas P., "The design of PARDB: a parallel relational database management system", Proceedings of 7th ISCIS Conference, Antalya, Turkey, November 1992.

[ZHOU95]   Zhou H. and Geist A., "LPVM: A step towards multithreaded PVM", Oak Ridge National Laboratory, Oak Ridge, USA, 1995.

# A New Language for Automatic Data Generation

Éva Szabó, István Forgács

Computer and Automation Institute, Hungarian Academy of Sciences

Chris Bates

National Transputer Support Centre, Sheffield

Innes Jelly

Computing Research Centre, Sheffield Hallam University, Sheffield

## 1 Introduction

Benchmarking a database machine is the process of evaluating its performance under experimental conditions but using a realistic workload. Ideally for each different application area a different benchmark should be used, requiring a different application-specific test database. If we want to have a realistic database schema containing realistic test data several conditions must be met: realistic data structure [1], semantic computability [1, 3], realistic probability [2], scalability. A new language called DGL, Data Generation Language, has been developed to allow easy and rapid generation of any relation al database.

## 2 Formal Description of the DGL

A DGL program consists of a declaration, one procedure for each database table, and a program which provides the control structure.

### 2.1 Declarations

The declaration section involves variable and constant declarations, set and structure descriptions for the database, semantic and probability descriptions, these terms will be explained below.

Whilst variable and constant declarations are similar to those of high level languages, DGL contains four unique language constructs which simplify database generation:
a.) structure description: an abstract data type which describes complex multi-level data structures. For example, larger towns are partitioned into districts, whilst smaller ones may not be. From the programmers point of view the language should have a construct which handles these situations uniformly.

```
STRUCTURE_DESC {variable = (variable {, variable}),}
END;
```

An example of this:

```
STRUCTURE_DESC town     = (district),
               county   = (village, district),
               district = (street),
END;
```

b.) data set declaration allows, as its name suggests, the enumeration of possible values for a variable. The form of the data set declaration is:

*DATA_SET variable[.variable] = ([type_id,] variable [= expr]{, variable [= exp]});*

With the aid of this construct, and the structure description, different nesting structures can be treated in the same way:

*DATA_SET town = (CHAR(20), Bp = "Budapest", Vac = "Vac", Diosd);*

*DATA_SET Bp.district = (one = 1010, two = 1020, .... twenty = 1204);*

c.) probability description: allows a realistic spread of data values. If this description is omitted, then the probability of each element of a data set or file occuring in the completed database will be uniform.

*PROBABILITY_DESC variable = ([variable]:num {,[variable]:num});*

where "variable" can be omitted when the order of variables is fixed:

*PROBABILITY_DESC towns = (Budapest:0.45,Szeged:0.23,Vac:0.17,Ozd:0.15);*
*PROBABILITY_DESC towns = (0.45, 0.23, 0.17, 0.15);*

We extend the DATA_SET declaration to incorporate a probability description so that very compact descriptions become possible:

*DATA_SET variable[.variable] = ([type_id,] variable [=expr][:num]{,variable[= exp][:num});*

d.) semantic description shows the relationship between data sets or variables. To be more effective this description may include a probability description.

*repeat ::= expression|variable {,expression|variable} → variable | ˆ set variable| const [: num] {,variable | ˆ set variable|const [: num] }*
*SEMANTIC_DESC variable → variable = (repeat {; repeat | constant});*

Examples of semantic descriptions:

*SEMANTIC_DESC c_acc → holders = ((c_acc MOD 17) → 2; (c_acc MOD 19) → 3, 1);*

may be interpreted as follows:

If c_acc MOD 17 = 0 then holders = 2
ElseIf c_acc Mod 19 = 0 then holders = 3
Else holders = 1

### 2.2 Procedures and the Program Section

Each procedure is responsible for the generation of a single table. The first part of each procedure gives the definition of the table, with syntax similar to SQL syntax. The procedure body follows the table description and the BEGIN keyword. Since DGL is a structural language, nested procedures are permitted. The definition section of a procedure declaration contains just the table definition. All other declarations are placed in the main program.

Both the main program and the procedures have program sections. Within the main program this is mainly procedure calls. The program section of a procedure is the key element of a DGL program as it is here that the method for assigning values to individual fields is given.

Operators are the same as in Pascal and have the same precedence. Statements such as IF, IF-ELSE, CASE, FOR and WHILE are included in DGL. The syntax is again similar to that of Pascal.

DGL requires some in-built functions: GETMEMBER makes a random assignment to a variable, GETDATE generates a random date, RANDOM generate a random number, NEXTKEY generates a new primary key, WRITE puts records in the database.

## References

[1] C. Bates, I. Jelly, J. Kerridge: Modelling Test Data for Performance Evaluation of Large Parallel Database Machines - *Distributed and Parallel Database Journal,* Kluwer Academic Press, Jan 1996

[2] I. Jelly, J. Kerridge, C. Bates: 'The Sheffield Parallel Benchmark', User Guide, Joint Technical Report, National Transputer

[3] Kerridge, I. Jelly , C. Bates: Benchmarking Parallel SQL Database Machines, *Proceedings of the British National Conference of Databases* 1994

# Horizontal Fragmentation in Distributed Object Database Systems

Ladjel Bellatreche and Ana Simonet

Laboratoire TIMC-IMAG,
Faculté de Médecine de Grenoble
38706 La Tronche cedex - France
e-mail : Ladjel.Bellatreche@imag.fr, Ana.Simonet@imag.fr

**Abstract.** Object-Oriented Database Management Systems (*OODBMS*) are becoming popular and are being used in a large number of application domains, many of which are inherently distributed. Optimal application performance of a distributed object-oriented database system requires class fragmentation and the development of allocation schemes to place fragments at distributed sites in order to minimize data transfer. Our approach is top-down, and the entity of fragmentation is the class. Fragmentation algorithms have been proposed for the relational model, but the object model is relatively untouched. In this paper, we present an algorithm for horizontal fragmentation in a model consisting of complex attributes and simple methods. This type of fragmentation facilitates query decomposition, optimization, and parallel treatment for distributed *OODBMS*.

## 1 Introduction

Distributed Database Systems are a marriage between databases and networks. Our work consists in breaking a database into small fragments and allocating them on the different sites. There are two ways to perform fragmentation: Vertically and Horizontally.

Vertical fragmentation consists in partitioning a relation into subsets of attributes while horizontal fragmentation partitions a relation into subsets of tuples.

The horizontal fragmentation has been study in the relational model [2] and [3]. For example in systems like Gamma or Bubba, all relations are horizontally partitioned so as to achieve parallelism of join queries. In this poster, we show how the method used in relational databases for horizontal fragmentation can be extended to the object model.

## 2 Distributed Design

The design methodology of Distributed database Systems varies according to the system architecture. Two majors approaches are considered:

The **top-down** approach is used in *homogeneous* systems (We speak of an homogeneous systems when there is one global database schema to partition). It consists in taking the global database entities and their relationships, and combining it with access pattern information to produce a set of local databases.

The **bottom-up** approach is used in multidatabase systems (i.e., when the databases exist at a number of sites); we then speak of *heterogeneous* database systems. In our method we have taken the top-down approach: from a class and factors such as application access patterns (i.e., queries) and frequency of queries, fragmentation is performed and gives a set of fragments which will be allocated on the different sites.

## 3  Object Model

Object database systems have been gaining popularity since the late 80s. Several Object-Oriented Database Systems have become commercially available. Most of the work done in object database systems deals with heterogeneous systems. Contrary to the relational model, little work has been done on homogeneous systems, i.e., single database systems. An object is defined by sets of attributes and methods. We identify two types of attributes: a **Simple** attribute has a primitive type (for example, Name is a *string*) and a **Complex** attribute has a class as part of its type (Manufacturer is a *Company*) as shown in Fig. 1. The hierarchy which arises from the aggregation relationship between the classes and their attributes is known as composition hierarchy. Two type of methods are possible [1]: **Simple** methods, which call no other method, and **Complex** methods, which call other method(s) to calculate the value of an attribute. Simple methods are methods to access the value of an attribute, e.g., r_name. Objects having the same attributes and methods are grouped into a class. Classes are organized into an inheritance hierarchy by using the specialization property(ISA), in which a subclass inherits the attributes and methods defined in the superclass(es). A class with simple attributes and simple methods can be fragmented using the same technique defined in the relational model [2]. In this work, we consider a class with *complex* attributes and *simple Methods*.

## 4  Horizontal Fragmentation Algorithm

We recall that horizontal fragmentation consists in breaking a class model $C$ into a set of fragment classes where each fragment has a nonempty set of objects. Because we have adopted the top-down approach, we must have the following parameters: a set of sites S, a sample of Queries Q with respect to the 80/20 rule which considers that 20% of user queries account for 80% of the total data access in the distributed database system, and the access frequencies, where $f_{i,j}$ indicates the frequency with which the query $q_i$ is executed from the site $s_j$. We note that each query is a sequence of method invocations.

## 4.1 Basic Concepts

Before describing the horizontal fragmentation algorithm, some definitions are presented.

A class $C_1$ consists of a number of attributes, and the value of an attribute $A$ of an object belonging to a class $C_1$ can be an object or set of objects belonging to another class $C_2$ (this class is the domain of the attribute $A$ of class $C_1$). $C_2$ may in turn consist of a number of attributes whose domains are other classes. Let $C_1$ be a class with complex attributes which we call "owner class". The definition of an owner class forms a rooted directed graph (RDG) where the nodes are the classes, and there is an edge between a pair of classes $C_1$ and $C_2$ if $C_2$ is the domain of an attribute of $C_1$. The owner class is the root of the RDG. We note that the classes with simple attributes represent the leaves of the RDG and we call them the "member classes" of $C_1$. A path in the RDG from the Owner class $C_1$ and a member class $C_n$ is represented as $C_1.C_2...C_n$. We denote the length of the path by $n$. The leaves of a RDG can be fragmented using the same techniques defined in the relational model. The fragmentation of an owner class based on the fragmentation of a member class is known as derived horizontal fragmentation.

**Definition 1.** *An Implicit Object Join* ($\bowtie$) between two classes $C_i$ and $C_j$ in the class composition hierarchy is the set of instances in the class $C_i$ which are referenced by instances in the class $C_j$. This Join is based on the OID of the complex attribute in $C_i$ which references the class $C_j$.

## 4.2 Algorithm

Let $C$ be a class with complex attributes is to be fragmented, then we can found a path from the class $C$ and a member class $C'$ with length n (n $\geq$ 1) (i.e., $CC_1...C'$). We partition horizontally the member class $C'$ in $\alpha$ horizontal fragments named $\{F\_1, F\_2,...,F\_\alpha\}$ using the same techniques used in [2]. Now we partition an owner class according to the horizontal fragmentation of its member class as follows: the horizontal fragments of the class $C$ are defined as :

$$C\_i = C \bowtie C_1 \bowtie ... \bowtie F\_i \ (1 \leq i \leq \alpha) \tag{1}$$

*Example 1.* In Figure 1, we give the class composition hierarchy of a class *Vehicle*.

We assume that the class Vehicle will be fragmented. This class contains a complex attribute "Manufacturer". There is a path with length two from the class Vehicle to the class Division which contains simple attributes. The class Division is fragmented into two horizontal class fragments based on the predicate defined on the attribute Location. Let *Div1* be a class fragment with its Division located in Paris, and *Div2* be a class fragment with its Division located in Linz.

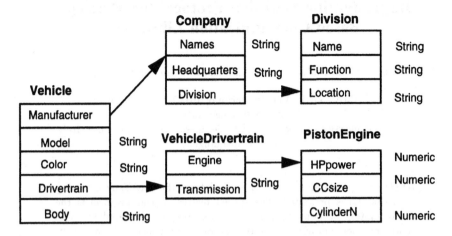

Fig. 1: The Class Composition Hierarchy of the class Vehicle

The class Vehicle can be horizontally fragmented into two horizontal fragment classes: *Vehicle1* corresponding to the vehicles manufactured by the company located in Paris, and *Vehicle2* corresponding to the vehicles manufactured by the company located in Linz. These two fragments are defined as follows:

$$Vehicle1 = \text{Vehicle} \bowtie \text{Company} \bowtie Div1$$
$$Vehicle2 = \text{Vehicle} \bowtie \text{Company} \bowtie Div2$$

## 5 Conclusion

We are now working on horizontal fragmentation schemes for more complex class models. This horizontal fragmentation algorithm facilitates work on the issues of parallelization. Various techniques are used to improve performance of object-oriented database query processing, especially those relating to a specific form of parallelization (inter and intra query parallelism). Since the fragments defined by our algorithm may be overlapping, we choose a solution that consists in updating all the object occurrences in all the fragments.

## References

[1] K. Karlapalem, S.B. Navathe, and M. M. A. Morsi, *Issues in Distributed Design of Object-Oriented Databases*, in Distributed Object Management Edited by M. T. Ozsu, U. Dayal, P. Valduriez, Morgan Kaufmann Publishers Inc., 1994.

[2] S.B. Navathe, M. Ra, R. Varadarajan, K. Karlapalem, and K. Sreewastav, *A Mixed Partitioning Methodology for Initial Distributed Database Design*, In Journal of Computer and Software Engineering, forthcoming Volume 3, Number 4, 1995.

[3] M. T. Ozsu and P. Valduriez, *Principles of Distributed Database Systems,* Prentice Hall, 1991.

# Implementing Snapshot Protocol for Message Based Communication Libraries

Andrea Clematis[1], Vittoria Gianuzzi and Giovanni Sacchetto[2]

[1] IMA - CNR, Via De Marini 6, 16149 Genova, Italy
clematis@ima.ge.cnr.it
[2] DISI, Universitá di Genova, Via Dodecaneso, 35 16146 Genova, Italy
gianuzzi@disi.unige.it

**Abstract.** A snapshot protocol derived from the Lay-Yang colouring algorithm [2] is presented. The special feature of this protocol is the use of system acknowledgement messages, already generated by most communication libraries, to detect snapshot termination. Formal definitions, demonstrations, message complexity (which is $O(n)$ where $n$ is the number of processes) as well as comparisons with other communication protocols are discussed in [1]. In the following we provide a short description of an implementation based on the PVM library.

The snapshot protocol is based on a cut algorithm which defines a consistent cut of a distributed computation. The cutting point of each process is a new event called *cut event*. A cut algorithm is composed by two parts: a local part, where the cut event is positioned in each process, and a global part, for protocol coordination. The local part of our algorithm is the same as described by Lai and Yang in [2], while the global part detects the termination of differently coloured protocol phases using message acknowledgement.

We assume the existence of a low level communication component (CC) within each process, which performs input-output operations on behalf of the user processes and implements the message acknowledgement protocol, and of a starter process aware of the fixed set of processes belonging to the system. Our cut algorithm must be implemented within the CC, so that to exploit the acknowledgement mechanism. It works in two rounds.

FIRST ROUND: let white be the current color of the computation (as initially). On request of the starter process, its CC broadcasts a *BeginCut* control message to the CC of every process in the system, including the starter itself. The CC of each process changes the local process color according to the Lai-Yang algorithm. A control message (called *R1Cut*) is sent back to the starter CC when the occurrence of the *cut event* has been notified to the user process and all the acknowledgements of the previously sent white messages, have been received.

SECOND ROUND: after the receipt of all *R1cut* messages, the starter CC broadcasts an *EndCut* control message to notify the processes that no in-transit messages are present in the network. In order to keep the cut intervals separated, and to avoid a possible deadlock when selective receive is allowed, the starter waits for the receipt of an *R2Cut* message from each process, indicating that all the messages in transit have been received by the receiver process, before performing another cut.

The cut event is considered by the CC as a message, and it is delivered to the user process upon a receive request. Then, a user process is aware of the positioning of the cut event as well of the kind of the received messages (in-transit or not).

In PVM (Parallel Virtual Machine) inter node communications are handled by daemons, using the UDP protocol plus an acknowledgement system to provide reliability. In turn each daemon is interfaced with user processes using the TCP protocol, thus providing reliable FIFO communications. To implement the cut protocol we need to modify the daemon which handles all intra-node communications. The FIFO communications which exist between the daemon and the local processes ensure the correctness of the whole protocol.

We have implemented an experimental version for a local area network, in which the *starter* process is the process (unique for the whole computation) which initially spawns all other processes and which lives forever.

Two functions have been implemented: INT INFO=PVM_STARTCUT() and INT BUFID=PVM_RECV(INT TID, INT MSGTAG, INT *TRANSMSG). The first one is called by the starter to activate the cut. The second one is an extension of the PVM receive function, with one more parameter and with additional return codes. *transmsg* returns 1 if the received message is in transit through the cut, 0 otherwise. *bufid* takes the negative values *PvmCutEvent* and *PvmTermCut* in order to notify the user of the positioning of the cut event and of the termination of the cut, so that the user can beaware that no more in-transit messages can be received. In such a case the message does not carry any application dependent data. Other parameter values are the same as in the original PVM.

The information about the cut is provided to the user process that may take advantage of it, depending on the specific application, e.g. a semi-automatic checkpoint system in which the user obtains a consistent recovery line and invokes a state saving routine. For that it concerns performance, the snapshot protocol introduces very little overheads. Information about the prototype can be found at www.disi.unige.it/person/GianuzziV

**Acknowledgements**: We thank G. Dodero for her useful suggestions.

# References

1. Gianuzzi V.: An optimal snapshot protocol for acknowledged message passing. Tech. Rep. DISI-TR-96-6. submitted for publication (1996).
2. Lai T.-H., Yang T.-H.: On distributed snapshots. Inform. Process. Lett. **25** (1987) 153–258.

# A/D Graphs – A Data Structure for Data Dependence Analysis in Programs with Pointers

Wolfram Amme, Eberhard Zehendner

Computer Science Department,
Friedrich-Schiller-University,
D-07740 Jena, Germany

We propose a new data structure for data dependence analysis in programs with pointers, the so-called A/D graphs. A/D graphs integrate the advantages of alias graphs [4] and storage graphs [3]. With A/D graphs we are able to determine all data dependences of a program statement from a single graph corresponding to the statement; this results in a considerable more economic storage usage for the analysis. Moreover, our method is fast and is based on a well-known general algorithm to solve data flow systems for which we can easily prove termination and correctness.

The nodes of an A/D graph represent the objects in storage at a specific program point. A pointer reference of one object to another is expressed by an edge in the graph. There are two kinds of nodes: simple and condensed. A simple node represents one object in storage. In contrast, a condensed node stands for an unknown number of objects. By introducing condensed nodes we achieve the finiteness of our graphs. From an A/D graph we can derive the combination of paths by which we can access the storage cells at one program point and the program statements which read respectively wrote the contents of an object last.

The following figure shows a program and a corresponding A/D graph that describes the store immediately before execution of statement 13. The nodes of this A/D graph record write accesses to memory cells. The program segment presented here generates a linked list with 10 elements and initializes these as a function of the index value. In the A/D graph two list elements are shown as

```
1: New(p);
2: i := 0;
3: q := p;
4: WHILE i < 10 DO
5:    IF i < 5 THEN
6:       q^.data := i
7:    ELSE
8:       q^.data := 2 * i
9:    New(q^.next);
10:   q := q^.next;
11:   i := i + 1
12: END;
13: x := p^.next^.data
```

distinct nodes; the further 8 list elements are represented by a single condensation node. From this A/D graph we infer a flow dependence of statement 13 on statements 1, 6, 8, and 9.

We have developed a single-pass data dependence analysis by solving a monotone data flow system for restricted imperative languages. The target programs are restricted to handle data structures with only one level of indirection, or linked lists. The data flow information set L is the set of all A/D graphs that can be used to describe the store for thus restricted programs.

In [2] we describe the union operator ∪ and the semantic functions of our montone data flow system. For interprocedural analysis we proved that (L, ∪) is a semi-lattice and that the semantic functions are monotone. When we restrict our programs to data structures with only one level of indirection these functions are even distributive for intraprocedural analysis.

The number of nodes in an A/D graph might grow exponentially with the number of variables. For this purpose we use in practice bounded A/D graphs. In bounded A/D graphs each node and each variable in the A/D graph points to a limited number of objects.

The practical meaning of these results is that we can use a general iterative algorithm from data flow analysis for data dependence analysis in programs with pointers. By doing so we can perform intraprocedural as well as interprocedural data dependence analysis with storage quadratic in the number of program statements.

The use of A/D graphs for data dependence analysis promises a significant improvement over known methods. Though we have constructed an experimental system to obtain preliminary data on the usefulness of our method, we still lack a sound comparison of the results to that of other systems. Currently—in our project ParaMod—we are working towards an integration of A/D graphs into the SUIF [1] system. As a further step we are attempting to extend the present research to programs with arbitrary, in particular recursive, structures. Our final aim is to be able to analyze any imperative program that does not use pointer arithmetic.

# References

1. S. Amarasinghe, J. Ander, C.W. Tseng: An overview of the SUIF compiler for scalable parallel machines. SIAM Conference on Parallel Processing for Scientific Computing, San Francisco, 1995.
2. W. Amme, E. Zehendner: A/D Graphs. A Data Structure for Data Dependence Analysis in Programs with Pointers. Proceedings of the 4th Workshop on Parallel Systems and Algorithms (PASA'96), Julich, 1996.
3. S. Horwitz, P. Pfeiffer, T. Reps: Dependence analysis for pointer variables. Proceedings of the ACM SIGPLAN Symposium on Compiler Construction, Portland, 1989, p. 28–40.
4. J.R. Larus, P.N. Hilfinger: Detecting conflicts between structure accesses. Proceedings of the ACM SIGPLAN' 88 Conference on programming Languages Design and Implementation, ACM SIGPLAN Notices, Vol. 21 (1988) 21–34.

# A Partition Method for Solving Block Pentadiagonal Linear System on Intel Hypercube iPSC/860

Ladislav Halada[1] and Mária Lucká[2]

[1] Slovak Technical University, Dep. of Mathematics,
Nám. slobody, 812 31 Bratislava, Slovak Republic,
*halada@dekan.sjf.stuba.sk*
[2] Institute for Control Theory and Robotics,
Slovak Academy of Sciences,
Dúbravská cesta 9, 842 37 Bratislava,
Slovak Republic, *utrrluck@savba.sk*

**Abstract.** We present a parallel partition algorithm for the solution of block pentadiagonal linear systems suitable for computation on computers with distributed memory. The method belongs to the direct methods and is based on the partition method derived in [1] for non-block banded matrices. The parallelization is achieved by dividing of the original block matrix into large blocks that can be processed almost independently. The time measurement results achieved by implementation of this method in the message passing Fortran on Intel hypercube iPSC/860 have shown a dependence of the effectivity of the implementation on the size of the large blocks.

## The Block Partition Method

Let us assume a block pentadiagonal linear system $AX = B$ of the size $N \times N$, with block elements $p \times p$. If $N = KM$, $K > 2$, then $A$ can be partitioned into $M \times M$ block tridiagonal form, where each diagonal block is a block pentadiagonal matrix of the size $K \times K$. This block pentadiagonal system can be solved on $M$ processors as follows:

1. Partitioning of $A$ into $M \times M$ block tridiagonal form and their distribution on $M$ processors.
2. Elimination of the block elements each of size $p \times p$ below the main diagonal except the two rightmost columns of each diagonal block. This process creates nonzero matrices in the two rightmost columns of each subdiagonal block.
3. Elimination of the block elements above the main diagonal in all diagonal and superdiagonal blocks except for those matrices in the two rightmost columns of the diagonal blocks. So non zero blocks of the size $p \times p$ are created in the two rightmost columns of each diagonal block and four non zero matrices in the superdiagonal blocks.

4. Elimination of the non zero matrices created in 2. First the matrices in the first diagonal and subdiagonal block must be eliminated on the first processor, then those of the second one, etc. Then, $A$ is an upper block triangular matrix. This process is synchronous with respect to the subdiagonal matrix in the last row of the diagonal block and the last two rows of the subdiagonal blocks.

5. Elimination of the non zero matrices created in 3. First the superdiagonal matrix on the $M$-th processor and $M - 1$-th superdiagonal block must be eliminated, then those of the $M - 1$-th and $M - 2$-th block, etc. Then, $A$ is the block diagonal matrix.

6. Solution of the block diagonal system of linear equations.

The numerical experiments were realized for block sizes $p$ varying from 3 up to 12 and the number of the blocks $N$ from 180 to 450 . The results of numerical experiments in double precision arithmetic with size $p = 4, 6, 8, 10$ and matrix size of $N \times p = 1800$ rows are presented in Table 1. The relationships

| $M$ | $p = 4, N = 450$ | $p = 6, N = 300$ | $p = 8, N = 225$ | $p = 10, N = 180$ |
|---|---|---|---|---|
| 1 | 0.373 | 0.573 | 0.801 | 1.114 |
| 3 | 0.246 | 0.383 | 0.564 | 0.798 |
| 7 | 0.125 | 0.196 | 0.288 | 0.567 |
| 15 | 0.101 | 0.153 | 0.244 | 0.461 |

Table 1:Time measurement results for $N \times p = 1800$

given above confirm the suitability of the given method for implementation on this type of parallel processor system, because the speedup is proportional to the number of processor used. However, the effectivity of the implementation is strongly dependent on the value of $\frac{K}{M}$. The experiments on the hypercube Intel iPSC/860 at the University of Vienna have shown, that this proportionality is valid only for $\frac{K}{M}$ greater than five. Construction of a parallel algorithm based on the computation of a reduced system [2, 3] and their comparison with the described method is the problem to be solved in the future.

# References

1. Meier, U.: A Parallel Partition Method for Solving Banded Systems of Linear Equations, Parallel Computing **2** (1985), 33–43
2. Mattor, N. et all: Algorithm for Solving Tridiagonal Matrix Problems in Parallel, Parallel Computing **21** (1995), 1769–1782
3. Johnson, L.: Solving Tridiagonal Systems on Ensemble Architectures, SIAM J.Sci.Stat. Comput., **8**, 354–392

# Parallel Image Processing by Using Homogeneous Computing Structures

Roman M. Palenichka and Andrij Yu. Lutsyk

Institute of Physics and Mechanics of the Ukrainian National Academy of Sciences, Lviv, Ukraine

E-mail: pal@vision.ipm.lviv.ua

The proposed investigation belongs to the intersection of four important fields of computer science: image processing and recognition, new perspective architectures, parallelization of computation and optimization of time-consuming operators for image processing. Requirements of real time for image processing force to build maximal fast algorithms which are equivalent to the maximal parallelization algorithms for many applications. To substantially speedup the implementation of time-consuming operators and save the hardware expenses of parallel systems, the principle of recursive computation of local operators is used. There are two major types of recursion used in low-level image processing: temporal recursion and spatial recursion [1]. They can be combined in one efficient implementation to further accelerate the processing or to save the hardware expenses. The use of temporal recursion allows to represent a local operator with a large window size as a sequence of operators using small windows (e.g., 3x3) which could be later implemented in a pipeline or concurrent manner.

The paper suggests a new approach to the developing of architectures of high-speed parallel systems for low-level image processing. Homogeneous computing structure (HCS) and homogeneous storing structure (HSS) are the basic elements of this approach [2]. The HCS represents a mesh-connected array of one-bit processors working in a multipipeline mode. The high speed of the system is provided by the structural and hierarchical organization of computing process which is based on the hardware implementation of all nodes of the data-flow graph for a given operator. The program is loaded into the HCS once before starting to solve a problem, and the data stream processing is carried out without the storage of intermediate results. The data streams applied to the information inputs of the processor elements are processed in a multipipeline manner in accordance with the program moving from one element to other in the mesh of the HCS. The parallelization of a given local operator (represented by the data-flow graph) is performed hierarchically on three different levels, starting from the level of local functions through the level of binary operations on two pixels (words) and finishing on the level of individual bits. Each lower level of the parallelization is embedded into the higher one yielding together the maximal possible parallelization in the framework of HCS approach. The time complexity of some algorithms for low-level image processing has been reduced to $O(1)$ per pixel as compared to the original time complexity $O(N)$ per pixel due to the pipelined-parallel implementation on the HCS, where $N=LxL$ is the window size for the local operator.

Examples of execution of some algorithms for image filtering and segmentation on the system are presented. Attention is paid to the non-linear and adaptive image filtering which is represented by time-consuming local operators when implementing it on a conventional (sequential) computer. They include systolic algorithms for non-linear image processing since the HCS offers a very convenient mean for implementation of the systolic algorithms.

## References

1. B. A. Bokhonko, R. M. Palenichka and P. Zinterhof. Recursive implementation of image rank-order filtering, Proc. Int. Workshop PARCELLA'94, pp. 277-287 (1994).
2. A. Lutsyk, Yu. Rytsar and T. Kuczynskyj. High-speed system for image processing based on homogeneous computing structures, Proc. Int. Workshop PARCELLA'94, pp. 297-305 (1994).

# Author Index

# Springer-Verlag
# and the Environment

We at Springer-Verlag firmly believe that an international science publisher has a special obligation to the environment, and our corporate policies consistently reflect this conviction.

We also expect our business partners – paper mills, printers, packaging manufacturers, etc. – to commit themselves to using environmentally friendly materials and production processes.

The paper in this book is made from low- or no-chlorine pulp and is acid free, in conformance with international standards for paper permanency.

# Lecture Notes in Computer Science

For information about Vols. 1–1059

please contact your bookseller or Springer-Verlag